STORM PROOFING

CHACR

CHACR MISSION STATEMENT

To conduct and sponsor research and analysis into the enduring nature and changing character of conflict on land and to be an active hub for scholarship and debate within the Army in order to support the development and sustainment of the Army's conceptual component of fighting power.

Storm Proofing

Preparing Armies for a Future War

Edited by
Andrew Sharpe, Andrew Stewart, Matthias Strohn

 Helion & Company

Helion & Company Limited
Unit 8 Amherst Business Centre
Budbrooke Road
Warwick
CV34 5WE
England
Tel. 01926 499619
Email: info@helion.co.uk
Website: www.helion.co.uk
X (formerly Twitter): @Helionbooks
Facebook: @HelionBooks
Visit our blog at helionbooks.wordpress.com

Published by Helion & Company 2025
Designed and typeset by Mach 3 Solutions (www.mach3solutions.co.uk)
Cover designed by Andrew Simms, CHACR

ISBN 978-1-804517-63-5

British Library Cataloguing-in-Publication Data.
A catalogue record for this book is available from the British Library.

For details of other military history titles published by Helion & Company Limited, contact the
above address, or visit our website: http://www.helion.co.uk

We always welcome receiving book proposals from prospective authors.

Contents

Contributors

Leo Blanken is an Associate Professor of Defense Analysis at the Naval Postgraduate School, where he co-founded the Applied Design for Innovation graduate curriculum. He is the author of *Rational Empires: Institutional Incentives and Imperial Expansion and* co-editor of *Assessing War: The Challenge of Measuring Success and Failure*. He collects and DJs rare soul records from the 1960s.

Colonel **Shaun Chandler** is a serving British Army infantry officer currently serving as Commander Soldier Academy (North) overseeing infantry basic and initial trade training. He is a PhD candidate on the University of Buckingham's Modern War Studies Programme under the supervision of Professor Matthias Strohn. His area of research is twenty-first century operational art.

Warren Chin is currently based at Rabdan Academy and Zayed Military University where he is the Programme Chair for Defence and Security. He has written extensively on the relationship between technology and the changing character of war and explored the implications of these changes for the future of conflict in his latest book, *Technology War and the State*.

Colonel **J. P. Clark**, U.S. Army (retired) was the lead author of the service operating concept, the U.S. Army in Multi-Domain Operations, 2028. His service includes duty as an exchange officer in the British Army Headquarters, the chief of the Strategy Division on the Army Staff, and as an instructor at both West Point and the U.S. Army War College.

Thomas Crosbie is an Associate Professor of military operations at the Royal Danish Defence College. He is the author of *The Political Army: How the U.S. Military Learned to Manage the Media and Public Opinion* (Columbia University Press, 2025), among other works, and editor of the Military Politics book series with Berghahn Books.

Justin Davis is the Head of Strategy at Saronic Technologies, where he leads the integration of product development and business capabilities concepts. Previously he served as a U.S. Navy SEAL for over twenty years, during which time he participated in thirteen combat and contingency deployments as well as staff tours focused on research and development. He co-founded the Applied Design for Innovation graduate curriculum at the Naval Postgraduate School.

Brigadier General **Armel Dirou** is a French cavalry and mountain troop General officer. His career has alternated between operational, educational, procurement, diplomatic and strategic analysis posts, both in France and overseas. With a doctorate from the Sorbonne university, he is also a graduate of the Royal College of Defence Studies, the Joint Staff College (FR) and the High Mountain Military School at Chamonix-Mont-Blanc.

Dr **Spencer Jones** is an award-winning historian and author. He is Senior Lecturer in Armed Forces and War Studies at the University of Wolverhampton and serves as the Regimental Historian for the Royal Regiment of Artillery. You can learn more about his work at www.drspencerjones.co.uk.

Colonel **Michael Lanzinger** is a German General Staff Officer with a degree in political science. He was deployed abroad twice to Afghanistan and once in Bosnia, commanded a *Panzergrenadierbataillon* and worked in operations and military policy for NATO, the Army and the Ministry of Defence in Berlin and London. He is currently the German LO to PJHQ and MOD.

Dr **Paul Latawski** is a Senior Lecturer in the Department of War Studies, Royal Military Academy Sandhurst. His official research work includes the evolution of urban warfare and the history of British Army doctrine. His area studies specialist research includes the history of the Polish Armed Forces in the West, Polish wartime resistance and contemporary Polish defence.

Michael S. Neiberg is Professor of History and Inaugural Chair of War Studies at the United States Army War College in Carlisle, Pennsylvania. His latest book is *When France Fell: The Vichy Crisis and the Fate of the Anglo-American Relationship* (Harvard University Press, 2021), which won the 2022 Society for Military History Book Prize.

Cecilia Panella is the Senior Strategy and Policy Analyst at Saronic Technologies. She previously served as a faculty member in the Defense Analysis Department at the Naval Postgraduate School, where she taught and published on issues surrounding emerging technology, military strategy, and special operations while working to establish the Applied Design for Innovation graduate curriculum.

As a General, **Jonathon Riley** commanded 1 Mechanised Brigade in the Balkans, the UK Joint Task Force in Sierra Leone and MND (SE) in Iraq. Senior coalition officer in U.S. CENTCOM and DCOM I.S.A.F. in Afghanistan, he has also been Director General and Master of the Armouries and Director of the Higher Command and Staff Course. He holds three academic degrees, including a PhD, and has published 30 books as well as numerous articles and essays.

Andrew Sharpe left the British Army as a Major General. His service included operational commands across the globe. His final posts included Assistant Chief of Defence Staff for Concepts and Doctrine, and running the Chief of Defence Staff's Strategic Advisory Panel. He holds an MA in International Studies from King's College London and a PhD from Trinity College Cambridge in Strategic Leadership. He is the Director of the CHACR.

Andrew Stewart is Head of Conflict Research at CHACR. Previously Director of Academic Studies at the Royal College of Defence Studies and Principal at the Australian War College, he is an Honorary Professor at the Australian National University and a Visiting Professor at King's College London. He is a widely published author with a focus on military history, diplomacy and conflict.

Professor **Matthias Strohn**, M.St. (Oxon), DPhil (Oxon), FRHistS is the Head of the Historical Analysis Programme at the think tank for the British Army, CHACR. He is also a Visiting Professor in Military Studies at the Humanities Research Institute, University of Buckingham. In his military role, he serves as Head of the German Military Delegation in the UK (R.).

Professor **Jonathan Trevor** is a noted researcher in the field of management, a published author, a consultant, a public speaker, and an educator specialising in strategy and organisation. He is the Associate Dean for Practice and Affiliates and Professor of Management Practice at the Saïd Business School of the University of Oxford.

Major **Luke Turrell** was a Chief of the General Staff (CGS) Fellow in 2021, followed by Executive Officer of CHACR and is now a member of the Directing Staff at the Land Command and Staff College in Shrivenham. He holds a Master's degree from King's College London and has served on operations in Iraq, Afghanistan and globally.

Acknowledgements

This book draws upon original research carried out for the British Army. The editors are grateful to Major General Paul Griffiths CB, Assistant Chief of the General Staff, and the officers who form the CHACR Management Board.

Also, to QinetiQ for its support in the production and publication of this book.

Finally, there has been a significant role played by Andy Simms, editor of *The British Army Review*, both with his expertise shown in the reading of the text and the design and production of the cover artwork. His critical and invaluable input is very much appreciated.

Foreword

General Sir C. R. V. Walker KCB DSO ADC Gen
Chief of the General Staff, British Army

A few years ago, as a brigadier working closely with the CHACR as the British Army's Head of Strategy, I encouraged them to publish their first book. It brought to a wider audience some of the CHACR's foundational thinking that the Army had considered as it went through a period of reform and reduction. That book was called *How Armies Grow* (and if you have not yet read it, I commend it to you). I am therefore absolutely delighted, now as the Chief of the General Staff, to be writing the opening words of their latest book *Storm Proofing*, which acts as an excellent companion volume to *How Armies Grow*, providing readers with another layer of depth on the subject. This book offers a very clear train of thought: the world is neither safe nor stable (the 'coming storm'); armies need to be ready for it; steady, traditional force development might not be up to the task; so, deeper and wider thinking is required across all the components of fighting power – physical, moral and conceptual, if we are to be ready when the storm breaks. In an era of increased peril and reduced resource, armies will have to think and act differently if they are to remain ready to fight and win wars on and from the land. This book, which draws together a collection of views from a wide range of experts, offers practitioners, policy makers and academics alike a veritable smorgasbord of food for thought.

Introduction: Weatherproofing for the Gathering Storm

Andrew Sharpe

The political classes of Europe, the U.S., and much of the rest of those parts of the world that enjoy leadership by some form of democracy, have for the last 35 years at least (if not since the end of the Second World War) had the luxury of living in a world where conflict, and war, whenever it does rage, rages far from their electorates. Those politicians who have served, either in a military guise or a political one, during periods in which their nations have been engaged in armed conflict or warfare, have done so in a context where those wars have been fought at a distance from their own soil. The vast majority of their populations have experienced war remotely, through their television or computer screens or, more likely, their phones or other electronic devices, as a side interest to their daily lives. This fortunate generation, both leaders and led, have been lucky to conduct their lives and their business in a context in which war has been, therefore, far away – in terms of geography, in terms of time (by a generation or two, or three), in terms of the effect that it has (and thus interest that it holds) for the voting public, and in terms of the likelihood of it finding its way into their own countries.

Against that backdrop, regardless of the conflicts, hot and cold, that have raged throughout the other corners of the globe since the mid-1940s, many voting populations have therefore had the luxury of being increasingly introspective (nationally and personally) and increasingly expectant of ever-higher levels of comfort and of support when it is needed (or wanted, even). The 'Cold War Generation' were led by the 'War Generation'. The proximity of large-scale conflict and suffering meant that the consequences of war were understood. A collective conscious or subconscious, therefore, also understood that a return to such a state of affairs should be avoided at all costs – including at the cost of an ever-increasing expectation of domestic prosperity, wellbeing and comfort; and thus the costs and demands of avoiding war were accepted. The 1990s brought with them thinking such as Francis Fukuyama's *The End of History?* and an idealistic sense of security and international relations positivity, such that liberal governments across the world dipped deep into their treasuries to reap the 'peace dividend' and pour much-needed resource into the wellbeing of their domestic populations. This came at the expense of paying their burdensome defence and security insurance premiums. War, and its demands and effects, became increasingly remote from the top of agendas, both governmental and personal. Whereas, among the great offices of state, the holder of the foreign portfolio had long been seen as first among the equals that sat round the cabinet table (after the prime minister or president), the closing decade of the twentieth century and the opening decades of the twenty-first century have seen the kudos of that position slipping fast below that of the holders of the treasury and the home/domestic portfolios. At the same time, the holders of the defence portfolio found themselves slipping below those of the occupiers of the offices of state that concerned themselves with welfare, health or education. The security of the governed population may still be the first duty of governments (in the university text books, at least), but let us be honest with ourselves, that security has increasingly been taken as a safe(ish) assumption, rather than a first priority. And, within this calculation, the notion that war could return to within direct reach of the nation(s) seemed remote.

Those of us who walk the streets of Whitehall, or the corridors of the Pentagon in Washington, or the Hexagone Balard, and in governmental circles throughout capitals all over the world have heard, for a long time now, a very similar mantra often repeated. It goes something like: '…it is safe to assume that we will be able to foresee the development of conflicts such that we will have 10 years to prepare ourselves for conflict at scale…'.[1] The contributors to this book (who have approached the preparations that they feel need our consideration from a very wide variety of standpoints) are all likely to agree on one single thing. Such an assumption is not 'safe' in either sense. That is to say that it cannot be taken as an obvious, or even, now, likely 'given' that war is distant and its outbreak predictable. Nor can such an assumption, which concerns the safety and security of all of us, be safe to make. It is not safe to decide not to put time, effort and resource into being able, immediately and effectively (enough), to head off threats, expected and unexpected, as they approach; it is not safe to assume that such threats can be deterred without making credible, visible, efforts to ensure that opponents' cost/gain analyses will be tilted in our favour; and thus it is not safe to decide not to spend the appropriate money on an insurance policy to cover events should the worst happen. A previous CHACR publication entitled *How Armies Grow* raised similar concerns,[2] and expressed a view on how history can provide us with steers, for militaries, governments and populations in general, if under-resourced and unready militaries are called upon to step up to the mark when required. This book takes that thinking a step further.

Clausewitz posits that war has an unchanging nature and a changing character. One of the cornerstones of his argument on the former is that war is, first and last, a human experience. War is, ultimately, about the decisions that humans make. This applies as much in the war cabinet's discussions and decisions as it does in the visceral world of the infantry squad. Tactical fights end because humans either die or are disabled such that they cannot continue, or, as history tells us occurs more often than not, because humans

---

1   Or, if not 10 years, whatever timescale the cynical observer would say that analysts have calculated the nation will need to be ready if so challenged.
2   Matthias Strohn (ed.), *How Armies Grow: The Expansion of Military Forces in the Age of Total War 1789–1945* (Barnsley: Casemate, 2019).

decide that they no longer wish to fight and opt for flight (or capitulation) instead. Strategic fights end because humans make cost/gain analyses and, with varying degrees of logic and emotion applied, decide that they wish their own people (and others' people) to continue to be killed or disabled to service their strategic ends, or that compromise or capitulation are better options.

At the same time, most military doctrines agree that fighting power is comprised of three components: the physical, the moral and the conceptual. These three components are, to varying degrees, also very much centred upon the human element thereof. Certainly, the moral component is almost entirely about the emotions and emotional decisions of humans. The physical component of fighting power is as much about equipment, and thus technology, as it is about the flesh and blood elements that comprise fighting forces. The conceptual component is, ultimately, about the decisions made by humans, but it is, increasingly, also about the informational gathering and processing capability of machines. Much of the force development thinking, of most defence organisations (globally), whether published or conducted behind closed doors, seems, currently, to contain a more-than-significant element of the influence of technology upon the practical prosecution of warfare. Whether it is the domination of the close-to-ground combat space by unmanned aircraft systems, drones or flying robots by any other name, or the collection, processing and delivery of information by artificial intelligence (AI), or any other aspect of the increasing tempo of the march of technological advance, non-human influences predominate twenty-first century thinking in this respect.

This book will not examine the doctrinal or developmental conclusions of the concepts developers in terms of warfighting models. It will not examine, in detail, the trajectories of AI-enhanced decision processes. It will not attempt to explain, in any meaningful detail, the science of this technological advance. But what it does do is explore the breadth and depth of the gaps in readiness that need to be addressed if nations are to be genuinely ready for twenty-first century warfare, at scale; and, thereby, it asks whether they are genuinely able to deter such war, or, if deterrence fails, successfully conduct it to a favourable conclusion. Thus, it will speculate upon whether the relationship between human and machine has become (and will increasingly be) such that the traditional understanding of those three components of fighting power (physical, moral and conceptual) needs revision. It will ask whether the deeply engrained way that soldiers look at warfare is still helpful in the twenty-first century. And, ultimately, it will ask whether the leisurely timelines that defence allows itself, and its supporting industry, to operate under in the generation of capability, set against the pace of change, are now dangerously confusing the notion of delivery 'on time' (against their own measure of timetable) with delivery in a timely (and therefore useful) manner. It will examine these overarching questions in three sections.

First, we consider the moral component of fighting power. What makes ordinary people do the extraordinary things that lead them to prevail in war? How do humans interact with each other to form the sinews of battle? Why do most armies (or their fighting infantry element at least) base their most basic building block of human cohesion upon an eight-to-ten-person squad that has remained unchanged since Marius reformed the Roman legions? How have machines (tanks and other armoured fighting vehicles, or helicopters, for example) changed that human dynamic through the restrictions of crew sizes? What is the different dynamic that manifests itself between single humans in machines remotely controlled by distant other people, from groups of humans pressed together in adversary and controlled on the spot by a confused and frightened but determined and focused fellow human? In the visceral world of close combat, many decisions and outcomes turn on the instinctive reading of the body language of friends (and enemies) – how will the lack of body language of machines change this important dynamic of warfare? How different will the decision-making process of a corporal in charge of seven machines in harm's way be from a corporal in charge of seven fellow humans in harm's way alongside them? What will all of this mean for the fight/flight decision-making at the tactical level? Or, by extension, at the strategic level? Napoleon famously observed that, in war, the moral is to the physical as three is to one. While military thinkers may be tempted to dance on the head of a pin in debating the exact ratio of proportions in this aphorism, few would disagree with its meaning or spirit. But what will it mean if machines, without a moral component of fighting power, increasingly make up our order of battle? How, in short, will the march of technology effect the moral component of fighting power?

Second, we consider the physical component of fighting power. For much of the history of war the term 'division' when applied to the formational structure of an army, was merely a noun based upon its verb-root. In other words, at random shapes and sizes, an army was 'divided' into 'divisions' to suit the tactical, practical, control or leadership expediencies of each unique set of tactical or operational circumstances. The word 'division' did not automatically conjure up in a military mind a standard formational model. For much of military history there was, therefore, no commonly understood formula for a 'division'. No set and standard wiring diagram leapt into the military subconscious when the word was used. Post-Napoleonic European reforms and, ultimately, the First World War, have, however, given the word not only a capital letter to make it a formal formational title, but also have delivered a fairly universal understanding of the sort of wiring diagram that ought to come with the use of the word on an order of battle. And this has set itself in military minds despite the wildly different realities of the various actual 'divisions' on the ground (whether through national differences, functional differences, national smoke-and-mirrors to meet international commitments, or, simply, attrition by combat causing a difference between map-room perceptions and physical realities). The French Revolutionary and Napoleonic Wars also delivered to Western, and then global, military thinking the concept of the corps – the operationally manoeuvring all-arms mini-army. They also formalised, at least in European Continental models, if not in the stubborn minds of British soldiers, a common understanding of the term regiment and, below that, battalion. The catch-all military term 'company' (which, originally, simply meant a group of fighting men of whatever size, from tens to thousands, could be appropriately mustered) also took on a specificity, as did the term 'captain', which ceased to mean simply 'the person in charge' (of a company, or endeavour, of indeterminate size) and became associated with the leadership of a now-determined-in-size company (which is why most armies in the world, stand fast again the stubborn British, still have their companies commanded by captains). But, and it is a significant 'but', the language of the force developers is increasingly removing traditional meaning from these accepted understandings of what is contained, in theory and on paper, within these given units and formations. Technology, tactics, techniques, procedures, doctrine and concepts are using the terms increasingly loosely. Is a twenty-first century brigade combat team, for example, anything like a Napoleonic, or, for that matter, Second World War brigade, in terms of numbers of people, or of units, or of variety of composition, or of command relationships with other formations, or of doctrinal application, or any other of a myriad relevant questions and circumstances? Or, likewise, division? Or corps? This second strand will, therefore, examine whether the march of technology, and its influence on the character of traditional units and formations, is such that this widely accepted (and applied) method of structuring, measuring, organising, task-organising and delivering the physical component of fighting power is still useful and relevant. Or is now the time for a really dramatic rethink in this respect?

Third, we will look at the conceptual component of fighting power, through the specific lens of command and control. This section we, perhaps tritely, have entitled for ourselves *Coup d'oeil or Coup d'AI?* Perhaps nowhere else is the march of technology so widely discussed in military circles as it is in terms of the already apparent and likely future impact of machines, and AI in particular, on the gathering, processing, dissemination and delivery of information. Headquarters sizes are a hot topic of discussion: why have they become so big; will machines process data faster and better than humans and thus replace humans; will military battle staffs become increasingly small and automated; how and by whom (or by what!) will decisions be made? And who or what will decide what is ethical? Terms such as the delivery of 'decision superiority' through the clever use of superior AI are bandied around. It seems self-evident, however, that idiots will still make idiotic decisions, regardless of the speed, width, depth and quality of data presented to them. Indeed, there is much evidence to suggest that those given to vacillation and prevarication will tend to default more to those tendencies if they feel that more and better information may be available to them shortly – and if the seizing and holding of the initiative is to remain a key component in the successful prosecution of warfare at any level, which we would argue it will, then is it a 'given' that such flows of machine-processed data are automatically helpful to all decision makers? This third strand will, therefore, sit alongside the first two strands and examine what machines are likely to mean for the conceptual component of fighting power, especially in terms of their influence on the planning and command functions of operational and tactical execution.

Wrapped around these three strands sits a context of increasing risk and urgency. Throughout the early 2020s, despite the world circumstances to which thinking people were daily exposed, the UK Ministry of Defence was still discouraging public conversations that suggested that we were at 'a new 1930s moment'. War talk, especially by soldiers, was considered unhelpful. Prudent and quiet contingency planning was considered useful, but anything more strident was frowned upon, whether from the cautionary statements of senior serving officers or the more strident and urgent considerations of retired or armchair generals, think tanks, academics and commentators. As conflicts multiply and become increasingly hard to wish away, however, governments (in the UK and more widely) are increasing the rhetoric, and are openly urging all to take the growing threat to stability, security and prosperity seriously. The context is now so self-evidently uncomfortable that defence is beginning to re-enter the mainstream debate in a way that it has not since the Cold War. But how likely is it to generate the leverage required to be ready, rapidly, resiliently and at scale, if the storm breaks?

Churchill's 'Gathering Storm' may well be rumbling away in the distant foothills once again and the wider polity is beginning, just beginning, to notice the predictions of the long-range forecasters. Russia, expansionist and at war, regardless of the longevity of Putin, looks highly unlikely to change its eternal spots and suddenly become a model global citizen. China, expansionist and aggressive, regardless of the longevity of Xi, is equally unlikely to change tack in the face of what it sees as the hollow and hypocritical stridency of its opponents. Iran, ever the architect of instability, continues flexing its muscles and stirring conflict and disruption in the Middle Eastern cauldron, despite a string of setbacks. And the pariah that is North Korea has found new support and solace in its interaction with all three. Against that background the security guarantee that has been provided to counterbalance all of these threats, from a strong and engaged U.S.A., is no longer a guarantee.

Thucydides famously stated that humankind would only ever go to war for one of three reasons: fear, honour or interest. All of these elements are abundantly clear, in all sorts of shades, in the modern international context. More importantly, perhaps, we believe that he omitted the fourth reason: 'by mistake'. Miscalculations, sometimes fuelled by the perceived weaknesses or lack of resolve of opponents, whether of readiness or expectation on one side, or of willingness and intent on another, seem to underlie so many of humankind's more bellicose behaviours. Our context is such that we cannot afford to put our trust in hope and assume that the happy circumstance of modern life as we know it will trot on uninterrupted, simply because the suffering and strife to which we are daily exposed by our media feeds will remain distant, present only to us if we care to dwell upon what is happening far away.

The events of the last 10 years, globally, offer every indication to even the most casual of observers that 'safe assumptions' about defence and security priorities are no longer safe in either sense. Thirty-five years on from the euphoria of the end of the Cold War it is clear that the increasingly inter-connected world is not a safe place – for any country. Diseases, whether jumping from bats to dogs and people, or escaping from research establishments, have demonstrated their ability to devastate populations and econo-mies globally. The accepted standards of international security have been shattered on a grand scale as a major power has shown contempt for international rules and norms and invaded, with the intent to conquer and subdue, a neighbour for the first time since the end of the Second World War. The conflicts of culture, political doctrine and dogma, and economic and power interests are rubbing up against each other in a way that has not been seen for decades. Alliances are growing and building, and becoming more powerful but more unstable as they do so, both internally and relative to each other. Nationalism and introspection, the cornerstones of nation-selfish politics, are becoming ever more popular in democracies, demagogueries and dictatorships alike. Climate change, and all of its side-effects, from resource shortages to population movements, is having a destabilising global effect.

And all of these causes are delivering tangible symptoms. Cyber-attacks on everything from businesses to national infrastructures, by one state against another, have become daily norms on a grand scale. Industrial and international espionage are both back on the rise. Evidence of election interference in competing nations is commonplace. Civil aeroplanes being shot down through error or poor judgement is not unusual. Global centres of instability are as unstable as they have ever been – the dynamics of Israel, Iran, Palestine, Lebanon, Syria, Iraq and Yemen are not only sending shock waves through the Middle East, but have evident consequences not just for Russia and for Turkey (and thus for NATO), but also for almost every corner of the globe. That recent beacon of East Asian stability, South Korea, is clearly not stable. Undersea cables, the global nervous system, are being interfered with by hostile actors. Islands are appearing on Pacific reefs and submarine drones are being landed by fishermen as far apart as Taiwan and the Philippines. The withdrawal of the last French garrisons from Chad and Cote d'Ivoire are not just a marker of the end of several centuries of European colonialism, but also one of the last pockets of a vacuum that is already being filled in Africa, in a different guise, by Russia and China's brand of neo-colonialism. And all of these are merely the physical acts of competing nations, let alone the policy acts, both delivered and proposed, that have been or are likely to be actioned over the next few years. None of these are friendly, constructive, stabilising or positive occurrences. Nor are they unnoticed. The tectonic plates of international relations are rubbing up against each other and the seismographs are registering. Those reading the seismographs are growing in agreement, number and volume – surely now there are too many Cassandras for Apollo's curse to hold them all in check?

So what? So, in short, the chapters of this book seem to suggest that the change in how we think about force development, in all of its guises, from the first glimmering new concepts through to the doctrinal wrap around newly acquired physical capabilities, may need a very, very radical rethink. Our armed forces need to re-set to deal not only with the self-evident battlespace circumstances of now: if NATO nations were compelled to leap into the fight alongside Ukraine for example, or alongside another, closer, ally who was the victim of a land grab, now, how *would they* breach the triple-lined Russian defences in the Donbas and southern Ukraine, or elsewhere, now, with what they have got, in order to break the stalemate? They must also re-set to deal with the very different battlespace circumstances that the increasingly steep curve of technological change is thrusting upon us. Our thesis is that this needs a soup-to-nuts rethink. And, importantly, that the urgency of circumstance suggests that this rethink cannot be done at a comfortable, unhurried and restrained rate (of 10-year policy-led programmes, long-term forecasts, finance-driven realism constraints, and Whitehall or Pentagon measured pace and measured tones).

The experience of much of the Western World's militaries over the last 25 years has been of wars of choice, fought remotely, whose strategic outcomes have had little or no direct effect on domestic populations. This experience has generated a certain way of thinking (and thus behaving) in an entire generation of political and military decision makers. So, perhaps we need to get a whole load of relatively 'new old ideas' out of the military mind in order to achieve two things. First, we might need to get some even older ideas back in again (like being genuinely able to fight and prevail in wars of no choice, at short notice, at a large scale, for example). And second, we might need to blend them with some brand-new ideas (in pace with the march of technology and at the expense of centuries-old default settings). Done together these two strands might help us to get close, quickly (and we can no longer afford to let traditional change or procurement paces and procedures hamstring serious national defence), to where we might need to be. The wisdom of Sir Michael Howard lives on – we know that, no matter what we guess is coming, and no matter how we guess we will best be able to deal with what is coming, we will be wrong. But we would do well to try to make a better guess than we are now, and better prepare ourselves in the breadth, depth and flexibility of our solutions and contingency solutions such that we are much more ready to prevail if (when?) the gathering storm breaks. Which may be sooner than we wish.

1

Storm Proofing: Meeting the Challenge of the 21st Century Land Domain

Shaun Chandler

'The problem which faces the reformer of armies in peace might be likened to that of an architect called on to alter and modernise an old-fashioned house without increasing its size, with the whole family still living in it (often grumbling at the architect's improvements since an extra bathroom can only be added at the expense of someone's dressing-room) and under the strictest financial limitations.'

Brigadier A. P. Wavell CMG, MC., 1930

Wavell visiting the contemporary British Army would see a busy building site with the architect's plans carrying the *Defence in a Competitive Age*[1] watermark visible through the *Land Operating Concept*[2] and the *NATO Force Model*[3] blueprints. Work is moving apace, but storm clouds are rolling-in from the East and the roof is not yet on.

On its surface, the contemporary land domain looks similar to that upon which much of military history has been written. However, as Daniel Kahneman warns in his examination of human cognition,[4] there is a tendency for decision makers to view a problem through a simplified paradigm based upon 'what you see is all there is'.[5] This same tendency, when applied to the land environment, introduces a cognitive dissonance that threatens to reduce the consideration of the application of land power to a series of ill-suited heuristics. Ill-suited when applied to a land domain that increasingly extends from the complicated to the complex. This complexity is characterised by the interplay

---

1   'Defence in a Competitive Age', Ministry of Defence (March 2021).
2   Major General James Bowder, 'The Land Operating Concept, A New Way of Winning', *The British Army Review*, 185 (Autumn 2023).
3   Brigadier David Bickers, 'Piecing Together a Picture of Our Future Role in NATO', *The British Army Review*, 186 (Spring 2024).
4   Daniel Kahneman, *Thinking, Fast and Slow* (London: Penguin, 2011).
5   'What You See Is All There Is' is a term introduced in Kahneman's *Thinking, Fast and Slow*.

of domains, both physical and non-physical, interacting within a battlespace that is ever more congested and connected – a battlespace that threatens to overwhelm the contemporary structures and procedures configured to fight and win on land.

This chapter seeks to consider the challenges of the contemporary land domain and the structure and attendant formations that may best meet them. Specifically, what do these structural changes tell us about the UK's approach towards the land domain in the early twenty-first century. Continuity, revisionism or change?

Considering the Contemporary Land Domain

> What is the main difference between the twentieth and twenty-first century? The major factor is the environment; the threat. The main factor is that we have lost our notion of the border. The threat has no border; it is not outside our border. In a permissive world without borders and linked by the internet, it is not just the ground on which we fight – but perception as well. Our terrain is not the same as in the twentieth century. There are many dimensions to this terrain.[6]

The canon of commentary and assessment of the future land operating environment is vast. In general, it broadly agrees that it will be complex. Certainly more so than a staff college table-top exercise would like.

Much of the training that creates and sustains an army seeks to address complication. Complication can be characterised as problems that are solvable; although that may require training of the solver(s). Whether it be learning to staff logistic estimates, manoeuvre mounted or dismounted across or through varying terrain, or drill across the parade square, the problem can be bound and visualised and, with training, the desired outcome can be achieved. Results are more likely to be repeatable with a bounded range of options and known variables. War, however, is complex. This increases exponentially as actors and, therefore, competition multiplies.

Complexity is often the sum of the parts in that it is the fusion of multiple complications, but it is also the play of chance and human factors. Increasingly, it is also the fusion of the physical and non-physical. Complex problems are invariably wicked, no neat solution presents, and any action is a compromise between varying possible outcomes relative to intention. Often, complex decisions are invidious; the whole problem cannot be fully understood yet a commander must balance the need for decisions and activity to occur at a speed of relevance against illusive understanding which invariably lags behind the rate of decision. Risk increases exponentially from the complicated to the complex. Or, in other words, from what you can see against what you cannot. The move

---

6   OF-6, Brigadier, Deputy Commander EMF I, French Army, interviewee 097, personal interview, 3 February 2016, quoted in Anthony King, *Command: The Twenty-First-Century General* (London: Cambridge University Press, 2019), p.297.

from single domain to multi-domain is congruent with an ascent from the complicated to the complex.

For ease of examination, we'll consider three interlinked factors which influence complexity and remain relevant to the design of land formations: space, mass and tempo.

Space

The battlefield has expanded beyond the soldier's survey to become a battlespace with a broadened zone of contest which now includes the space and cyber/electromagnetic domains. Regardless of which domain you fight in, but especially on land, there may well be as much activity that is unseen as is seen within your area of operations. Activity you may not have control over. This is not necessarily a revolution, but it certainly has the feel of a fast-paced evolution characterised by adjacent domains becoming increasingly intermeshed across the levels of war.

Cookie-cutting the battlespace into the deep, close and rear remains relevant in the land domain. After all, the land is still very much about people and geography. However, dependent on the character of the fight, and the level of formation, it can be difficult to apply this framework. When arrayed in a classic defensive framework or punching into an enemy's depth to secure a physical objective, shaping the deep, while winning the close, and protecting lines of communication to sustain through the rear, the geographical framework makes sense. However, securing an urban sprawl amidst a partial or non-compliant population with an active enemy manoeuvring across domains, can have a psychedelic effect on the traditional geographical framework.

Urban settlements compress space and generate density both physical and non-physical. In the former, the land domain becomes three-dimensional absorbing mass and constraining physical manoeuvre. In the latter, population density blurs traditional delineation between friend and foe and introduces a 'shade-shift' spectrum of actors who reside on a continuum of alignment in support of or in juxtaposition against one's intent.[7] These same actors are increasingly enabled through means and connectivity to communicate with an even wider spectrum of actors to broaden the arena of competition well beyond the visible city-block.

It is not just the geographical framework of close, deep and rear that is being stretched in all directions, but also the hierarchy of war as activity and attendant command and control. There is a blurring of war's decision-making hierarchy from the strategic to the tactical. As the non-physical has increasingly merged with the physical, and the battlefield has slipped the ties of geography to become the battlespace, the contest is no longer tied to a theatre but has expanded beyond to encompass the varied reach of the domains. Doctrinally we lack an information domain or framework which envelopes all domains; essentially an information space within which all domains reside. This doctrinal lacuna engenders a cognitive blind-spot as the decision-maker and staff visualise an incomplete

---

7   Shaun Chandler and Emile Simpson, 'Shade-Shift: A Post Operational Review', *The British Army Review*, 150 (Winter 2010/2011).

or disconnected battlespace. So, any contest within the land domain, especially at the operational level, must contend with an extended battlespace forming a competitive arena that is simultaneously physical and non-physical.

This broadened battlespace does not only challenge the physical paradigm of war; it also stresses the conceptual. Distinctions of war and peace are being challenged as they blur into a continuum of competition. The political contention at the heart of competing wills has become continuous which, while not new, is becoming ever more complex as actors multiply and thereby test conventional military structures. Aligning concepts of peace and war to the space of being at home or deployed is increasingly becoming at variance with reality. As contemporary paradigms of war and peace converge, structures are increasingly ill-suited to apply their means against an unrelenting threat. Especially a threat that can compete through emergent domains in spaces beyond the traditional bounds of war. As conflict is characterised as a continuous balance between non-physical and physical competition, the requirement to provide security is as urgent as the need to be ready to prosecute war. If competition is now both conceptual and physical, the space within which it occurs is poorly described by bounded paradigms of war. We cannot forget that conflict begins and ends in the mind.

Mass

Force elements are quickly blotted-up within complex terrain which makes itself felt by compromising the ability to manoeuvre through a combination of complex geometry and/or population density.[8] Adversaries can exploit this same environment to mitigate deficiencies in traditional mass by dispersing amongst the population and using terrain as a force multiplier. More complex, the mass of opinion and perception is likely to be more decisive in achieving any sense of victory than the mass of armed resistance. It is for this reason that high-intensity warfare is seen as a multinational endeavour and is a key factor influencing the UK's investment in the NATO Force Model – a burden shared and a collective sense of legitimacy.

Mass itself is an elastic concept. Is mass represented by tanks lined-up on the lawn or is mass the simultaneity of activity across time and space?[9] Or is it a sliding-scale that includes both as one moves from domain to multi-domain and domestic to expeditionary? Is it the case that those same arrayed 'tank' can be equally dispersed to provide effect across time and space or cohered to deliver force at a singularity? The 'three-block' nature of the modern battlespace and its increasing reach and lethality,[10] demands a degree of flexibility in task organisation and synchronisation that vastly complicates the job of warfighting.

8   Mike Davis, *Planet of the Slums* (London: Verso, 2006).
9   As SACEUR, General Dwight Eisenhower assessed that the defence of NATO's Central Region would require 96 divisions and 9,000 aircraft. Richard Simpkin, *Race to the Swift: Thoughts on Twenty-First Century Warfare* (London: Brassey's Defence Publishers, 1988).
10 Charles Krulak, 'The Strategic Corporal: Leadership in the Three Block War' in *Marine Corps Gazette*, 83:1 (January 1999), pp.18–22.

Surprise is often seen as an antidote for mass. An offensive mind-set is considered as a means to offset numerical disadvantage, but this is often short-lived, and the complexity of the battlespace will inevitably nullify any temporal advantage as the characteristics of the contemporary battlespace have a leaning towards attrition. This weighting towards attrition is driven by population mass/density and connectivity; acting as blotting-paper absorbing forces, this is a key reason why decisive outcomes are elusive when applying contemporary conventional force. NATO confronted with an enemy who have the offensive advantage to apply mass against its defensive mind-set is at a distinct disadvantage. Offensive capability is fundamental in deterrence to deter aggression, but NATO's defensive foundation weakens this. NATO cannot easily offset mass through threat. Lacking mass and, potentially domestic cohesion, it is also ill-placed to enter a war of attrition. However, those same land domain characteristics equally apply to the enemy and, as Russian forces have found in Ukraine, mass is quickly denuded as initial surprise and a war of movement on land translates to attrition. In this situation the tactical battlefield quickly becomes positional and manoeuvre is increasingly sought through multi-domain activity in the operational battlespace. While we rightly criticise Russia's aggression, we would do well to see past the politics to consider what its experience can tell us about our own approach towards the contemporary land domain.

Within the land battlespace the population is a factor too often ignored. Such omission will always prove costly. We generally fight where people live. Increasing population density and connectivity mean that as much as we may wish to fight on a reassuringly simple staff-table map, we cannot avoid finding ourselves situated amongst the people. Whether in the conduct of war or managing its aftermath, we would do well to pay close attention to the population. A successful offensive can all too easily transition to attrition as a hostile population sink a land force ever deeper into a quagmire.[11] If a population does not favour our presence, without care and resources beyond the conventional, it is only a matter of time before victory translates into defeat. Understanding the complex culture and political motivations of the human battlespace is as, if not more, important than understanding the enemy. Indigenous partnered forces are a mitigation, but building these relationships takes persistent engagement which too often is not an option, and the effect of such partnering is denuded if not supported by a sufficient sense of political legitimacy amongst the population. However, armed with our simplified heuristics of conflict, we too often find ourselves seeking to develop understanding and legitimacy when already embroiled and where the sum of our initial actions has already translated into malign effect. So, mass in the battlespace is as much about population density and resistance within it as it is about conventional force tables.

To fight in complexity requires enormous amounts of training and cost. Western armies, including the UK's, are struggling to maintain professional forces at the size

---

11   '...even the token use of armed forces against the nation instantly hardens public opinion behind the government. One enters a phase where the will to resist increases with the damage inflicted.' Simpkin, *Race to the Swift*, p.213.

necessary to deliver traditional mass. Inflow and outflow, or recruitment and discharge, simultaneously erode capability in terms of pure numbers, but also leak the hard-won expertise necessary to thrive in complexity. Remote and autonomous systems, or human-machine teaming, may assist in generating mass and offsetting the cognitive 'brain-drain' of personnel outflow.[12] Configuring highly networked and lethal teams that can as easily disperse as consolidate, promise simultaneously to assuage the mass dilemma while keeping pace with the land domain's runaway congestion and lethality. Nevertheless, beware the siren call of automation, infantry somewhere in the battlespace will be digging trenches long into the twenty-first century.

In meeting the demands of persistent competition, the distinctions between training and exercise and war are equally challenged. Increasingly, deployments on exercise are themselves acts of competition aimed at achieving effect amidst multiple audiences including adversaries. Every activity has friendly, neutral and hostile audiences intended or otherwise and while this is not new, the ability of media and communications to amplify that activity presents both opportunity and risk. As the audiences have multi-plied, the challenge of understanding how these activities will be perceived has become ever more challenging. Strategic empathy and deeper understanding of strategic culture require hard-won expertise, which is elusive as actors and audiences proliferate, trained staff are lost, and time for focused education is finite. The sum of activity is its own form of mass which must be synchronised to act at the cognitive centre of conflict. So, mass is also a challenged concept being stretched between physical quantity and activity affecting perception and cognition.

Tempo

The tactical can be seen as being largely contained within a domain; influencing and being influenced by other domains, but the bulk of activity being within the relevant domain. Tempo in UK doctrine has traditionally been used to consider activity relative to an adversary. However, it is perhaps more useful today to consider tempo as deci-sion-making and action relative to time and the competing decision-cycles of relevant actors. The sum of this decision-making relative to time and resource can be defined as activity. Such activity is neatly surmised in the OODA [Observe, Orient, Decide and Act] loop[13] which, while applicable across the levels of war, arguably increases from the complicated to the complex as one ascends the warfighting levels, reaching its apogee at the operational level. Here we encounter the fusion of tactical actions and strategic intent. Tempo, at any level, increases in complexity as actors and activities multiply, while decision-making time and available resource (options) dwindle. Commanders and their staff, presented with information at a rate that stresses their cognitive limits,

12   Kenneth Payne, *I, Warbot: The Dawn of Artificially Intelligent Conflict* (Oxford: Oxford University Press, 2021).
13   Frans Osinga, *Science, Strategy and War: The Strategic Theory of John Boyd* (Abingdon: Routledge, 2007).

must act with partial understanding while concurrently grappling to consider the effectiveness of decisions already taken. It is the integration of domains at the operational level which heightens the land domain's complexity as the contact surface area increases exponentially as domains interact. This is more Jomini than Clausewitz, and just as the former framed our initial approach to the operational level, a similar conceptual refresh is needed now.

The operational level seeks to cohere joint or, today, go further to integrate multi-domain activity that is as much non-physical as physical. At this level, activity across domains is fused to achieve the desired effects.[14] The activity may present in a single tactical domain and be coordinated by the domain's relevant tactical HQ, but the activity is most effective when planned and synchronised at the operational level. For example, firing a ballistic missile may be a tactical activity enacted in a single domain (potentially crossing others such as air and space), but the effects of that tactical action can quickly translate across the operational and strategic levels of war. In such a model, activities regardless of domain or nature (physical or non-physical) provide a power of combinations to achieve effect. The target is always someone's cognition to coerce decision-making. This is arguably the core concept behind effects-based operations.[15]

Effects are achieved through different courses of action (synchronised activity) which are distinguished by an admixture of kinetic and non-kinetic actions. This is further nuanced when one recognises that individual actions themselves can simultaneously be kinetic and non-kinetic depending on the target/audience. Regardless, the effect remains relative to the target (audience) and its effectiveness is dependent on the success or otherwise in achieving the desired change in condition (itself a representation of some influence on cognition). To talk of kinetic and non-kinetic *effects* is unhelpful and inhibits the manoeuvrist approach. Form follows function and an unhelpful conceptual distinction between non-kinetic and kinetic action and the domains that deliver them serves to undermine effectiveness. If we view the non-kinetic/kinetic and the non-physical/physical as distinct we are at risk of separating activities and structures in violation of the very nature of war.

Tempo can, therefore, be regarded as the rate and combination of activities to achieve effects in targets relative to capacity and need. The activity can be multidimensional, the measurement behavioural and/or physical, and the need driven by a combination of factors ranging from being relative to the actor(s) through to shaping the environment.

This multi-domain activity, conducted at unparalleled tempo, serves to compress the levels of war. It draws in audiences far beyond those intended, to broaden the battlespace well beyond that of the commander's purview, and to elevate the import of decisions beyond the complicated of a single domain into the complexity of multiple domains. This complexity is more than the challenge of multi-domain synchronisation to conduct

---

14   Synchronised and/or converged into a bespoke set unique to the desired outcome.
15   Edward Smith, *Effects Based Operations: Applying Network Warfare in Peace, Crisis and War* (Washington, DC: Command and Control Research Program, 2003).

activity; it is also the complexity of guiding and measuring effects against multiple audiences. Some of which may never have been intended and some of which may go unnoticed. Complexity builds exponentially with activity and the attendant cumulative level of friction is amplified by increases in space, mass and tempo.

The land domain then must be situated within a broader battlespace; the complexity of which can be measured through its characteristic space, mass and tempo. It is at the point at which multi-domain activity converges where we find the operational level and where situational awareness to enable decision-making to exercise operational art is most needed.

Aligning Form and Function – Chiselling Round Boulders[16]

> The Army will deliver a modernised, adaptable and expeditionary fighting force, centred around HQ Allied Rapid Reaction Corps as a NATO corps HQ, and 3 (UK) Division as a warfighting division, optimised to fight a peer adversary in a NATO context.[17]

A twenty-first century land operational formation is arguably still a work in progress but would lie (at a minimum) at the 3* level and may well be located (to some degree) in the firm-base as it would need enormous (and secure) data access, communications and processing capacity. It is the first level of command that can truly seek to manage the battlespace that envelopes the terrestrial battlefield.

At the core of a contemporary land formation must be the capacity to harvest and process vast amounts of data to support decision-making. Central to enabling this is a high-capacity data network, exploiting the electromagnetic spectrum and surrounding domains, to collect and pass information and coordinate activity. Autonomous and remote systems will likely play a key role here; collecting and processing big data with the decision-maker increasingly nudged onto the loop rather than in it. Artificial intelligence (AI) will, as a minimum, augment this process. While certain decision-making may ethically be best left with the human, AI may support the processing of data to inform decision-making or take on discrete unilateral decision-making (generating the tempo necessary to turn data into relevant activity). All of this serves to accelerate the land formation's OODA loop. As warfare becomes increasingly complex, AI offers the potential to mitigate the challenge of leveraging the finite timeframe of professional military careers, addressing the challenge of upskilling staff to grapple complexity while necessarily being committed to committing the bulk of their early careers to mastering the complicated tactical training necessary to understand their relevant tactical domains.

---

16 'Thus the potential of troops skilfully commanded in battle may be compared to that of round boulders which roll down from mountain heights'. Sun Tzu.
17 'Defence in a Competitive Age', p.19.

Of course, the more AI processes the data and interprets so as to inform human decision-making, the more it can be seen, vicariously, to be actually making the decisions. If one bases decisions and assessments upon the information one is presented, then the more that information is provided by AI, the greater the influence AI exerts over one's behaviour. As AI is a human construct, the algorithms that underpin it are as prone to error as human decision-making. Any bias, omission or lack of strategic empathy in the construct of algorithms will surely amplify those in the AI dependent human decision-maker with untold implications on the effectiveness of activity. Our tendency to fight the war we wish to fight as opposed to fighting the war we are in could, influenced by biased algorithms, be worsened rather than mitigated by AI. As we arguably experienced in Afghanistan, visual representations of blue arrows overcoming red enemy portrayed mission success but was at considerable variance to the progression of the actual conflict.

Tactically, and tethered to the land domain's battlefield, this all points towards a very different division to that of the twentieth century. It remains combined arms and capable of drawing-upon joint capability, but its area of operations is now nested within the battlespace. To exploit this, it needs the sensors and computational power necessary to capture and process data at the rate demanded by the conflict it finds itself in. In terms of automation, robotics and data processing, the division is likely to leverage these to help address the need for mass within space to generate tempo at the tactical level; this is very much about the sense-decide-shoot-assess cycle.

The ability to process multi-domain derived data to provide situational awareness to make decisions in relation to the land domain is likely to require automation. As the volume and rate of data open to collection is beyond human cognition, we must meet its demands of analysis through automation or willingly fight blind or, at best, partially sighted. This may be assuaged through computation to collect and fuse data and analytics, utilising AI, to interpret so as to make or inform decisions. This level of computation and decision-making is likely to lean towards the operational level and the corps owing to complexity – variety, volume and tempo.

To address the challenges of contemporary conflict we can but work within our means. There is no room for inefficiency. If we agree that it is at the corps level that operational multi-domain integration can most realistically be achieved and that the division can at best be network capable/integrated to leverage and deconflict tactical domain activity within the land domain, then the division should strive to achieve ever greater alignment within a corps construct. This, most practicably, means both 1 (UK) Division and 3 (UK) Division being formally aligned to the Allied Rapid Reaction Corps (ARRC) and/or interoperable with NATO's response forces. Concurrently, this also maintains sovereign capability in both formations and nurtures the knowledge, skills and experience necessary to fight on land across the tactical and operational levels of war.

Generating the mass necessary to warfight in the contemporary environment is a multinational endeavour. So, NATO interoperability and efficiency is essential. 3 (UK) Division is the UK's contribution towards NATO's need for traditional hard power on land. Armoured, mobile and survivable, its brigades are capable of packing a punch but also of doggedly holding ground. Aspiring to manoeuvre across the battlefield is right, but expectations of 1,000-kilometre surges into the enemy's depth are rightly tempered by robust NATO doctrine which assesses war as it is likely to be rather than we may wish it. For a division the battlespace against a peer-enemy is likely to quickly narrow into a battlefield cocooned within a much wider multidimensional battlespace. NATO is fundamentally defensive in mind-set and as such it is physically and conceptually configured to hold rather than seize ground. Such subliminal thought tends to narrow rather than expand the battlefield in war. It also hands the initiative to the aggressor.

If we accept that NATO will lean towards the defensive in war, there is nevertheless the opportunity for offence amidst competition and below the threshold of war. Complementary and addressing the need to persistently operate below or at the threshold of conflict, able to intervene at pace as a global response division or to shape the battlespace for warfighting intervention, is 1 (UK) Division. This division must be able to survive and operate dispersed and deliver shaping and decisive activities amidst competition; persistent reporting and engagement (in all its forms). Fully interoperable within a NATO battlespace, but also able to deploy its whole or force elements in pursuit of the national interest (for example, through the Combined Joint Expeditionary Force). It is, therefore, as important that 1 (UK) Division is as interoperable with 3 (UK) Division as it is within NATO.

6 (UK) Division was (re-)formed to deliver the Army's advanced capabilities; configured to compete upstream through forward partnering and influence operations. Its return as a formation was short-lived, but its capabilities remain essential. It is now being re-fashioned to include the formation of the Land Special Operations Force.[18] This is perhaps a reflection of the inherent tension of forming a division comprised of capabilities that are akin to strategic/operational enablers: Security force assistance, as persistent engagement, being a tactical activity with potential strategic effect, while its intelligence and influence capabilities sit closer to the operational/strategic boundary. The Land Special Operations Force has a role to play through persistent engagement below and beyond the threshold of war and as such resides most comfortably within or alongside 1 (UK) Division.[19] Finite intelligence and influence capabilities (as most recognisably held within 77 Brigade) are best leveraged at the operational level. As such, it suggests that these should reside at the corps level and practically aligned with the ARRC.

Fight Tonight… – *Deus ex Machina*

The war in Ukraine has come as a bucket of cold water waking the West to find that tactical land war remains similar to where we left it in the twentieth century. We moved

---

18   Colonel Hugo Lloyd, 'Sharpening a Specialism: UK's New Special Ops Force Prepares for NATO Spotlight' in *The British Army Review*, 186 (Spring 2024).
19   But ready to provide its capability across NATO; as per the assignment to lead the Special Operations Task Force in 2026.

on, it did not. Seeking the El Dorado of land war on the cheap, characterised by thinly dispersed jam and bold punches into the enemy's depth, is to attempt to sidestep the resource costs of being ready for war. This may be desirable, but it is also unattainable. If we must fight on land, tonight or tomorrow, we will find ourselves fighting in a high-density environment where complex terrain, comprised of clutter and population, drains mass. The fight will be across multiple domains both seen and unseen. Within this environment, land forces will simultaneously have to be dispersed and consolidated requiring an array of capabilities, from light to heavy, conducting tasks as diverse as advise and assist to combined arms manoeuvre. The 'man in the dark' is now the 'man in the light',[20] blinded by a white light of data that, rather than provide awareness to drive assured action, can paralyse if not funnelled and analysed at the appropriate level.

The corps must be able to exercise full control of and converge operational multi-domain activity within the land domain and nest within (as necessary) a Joint Force Command (JFC). It is the JFC which offers the best route to an operational-strategic interface. All of these formations must be technologically enabled to handle the complexity of contemporary conflict and to aid force protection and sustain digital capability. However, if we are not to paralyse tactical formations through a deluge of data, the corps and JFC (or, better, Integrated Force Command (IFC)) function within it must be matured at pace. This increased balance of activity at the corps-JFC/IFC levels may well constrain their deployability and tether them to their domestic firm bases or bases in the periphery; survivability and connectivity to enable utility must guide position.

Challenged by resources and needing to re-grow high-intensity warfighting competence, the British Army is today weighting its training model towards the sub-unit. This is necessary, but alone will not deliver the ability to fight and win on land. Rather, the need is as much about re-generating brigade and divisional competence at the tactical level and that of the corps at the operational. This latter aspect is most challenging; it is here the conceptual and resource challenges are most pronounced. Making this all the more difficult is the British Army's career structure. Officers spend arguably too much of their career at the tactical level mastering the complicated leaving little time and opportunity to rise to meet operational complexity.

Students passing through staff college over the period of campaigning have concentrated on the brigade, but they must now start to truly understand and master the higher formations and use them as a tool to grapple with complexity. Classrooms equipped with map-boards that tether the staff officer to a geographical paradigm encourage tactical solutions to operational problems. Most worryingly, they prize the physical over the non-physical thereby training in cognitive blind spots in relation to the decisive arena of perception. Where is the operational paradigm that bridges the physical with the non-physical? Without one we will plan and act in the tactical; struggling to integrate all our

---

20   Captain Basil Liddell Hart, 'The "Man-in-the-Dark" Theory of Infantry Tactics and the "Expanding Torrent" System of Attack' in *Royal United Services Institution Journal*, 66:461 (1921), pp.1–22.

actions to accentuate effects on actors and be in danger of fighting the war we wish as opposed to the one we are in. To reiterate, wars start and end in the minds of actors – this must be visualised through a common paradigm. Without such a paradigm, decisions will lack coherence and activity, rather than being notes to form a discernible tune, will tend towards white noise and defeat.

Failure to align the British Army's structure by developing its formations to meet the persistent and novel challenges of the twenty-first century land domain will quickly nullify any aspirations of manoeuvre and deliver only attrition. Wars are simultaneously fought at the tactical and the operational and, while the British Army is proven to be able to win at the tactical, its recent experience has been characterised by loses at the operational. While there has been much lamenting at a perceived death of strategy, and incoherence here has certainly been existential to success, it is the lack of operational gearing that has simultaneously enervated strategic realism and tactical action.

Armed with the Land Operating Concept and NATO Force Model blueprints and the skills necessary to exercise operational art in the twenty-first century land domain, there is a chance the British Army's roof will be on before the storm arrives. Continuity, revisionism or change? It is a bit of all three; when thinking of *How We Fight 26*, we would do well to think to the operational level whereas in considering how we approach the tactical we should consider *How We Would Have Fought 86*. We need to evolve our operational approach to the contemporary land domain to situate itself in the whole multi-domain battlespace while tactically re-generating the capability to fight at scale on the tactical battlefield. Two related, but differing challenges; the former leans towards the technical and the latter towards the physical, but both require considerable conceptual investment. In form this looks like brigades and divisions ready to fight joint at the tactical level and nested within a corps able to fight integrated at the operational level.

This conceptual refresh translated into capability will enable the British Army to fight and win in a land domain nested within a battlespace stretching beyond the physical dimensions of the battlefield and the cognitive limitations of the human decision-maker. The sum is a strategy informed by a realistic understanding of the ways and means necessary to achieve its desired ends. A strengthened operational bridge or a house with firm foundations and floors that house the tactical, operational and strategic levels; with staircases to allow its inhabitants to progress from floor-to-floor and all enabled with the wiring and plumbing to provide the data its needs to thrive. Storm-proofed to weather the tempest that approaches from the East.

2

Questioning the Modern Relevance of the Corps, Division and Brigade Levels

Armel Dirou

Napoleon inherited his military from the French Revolution. The new era that Goethe had imagined since the Battle of Valmy recognised the start of national armies, and with them numerous troops to field, lead and manoeuvre. After his victories during the campaigns in Italy (1796–1800), notably with the battle of Marengo on 14 June 1800, and Egypt (1798–1799), the divisional concept once theorised by Jacques, Comte de Guibert, in the early 1780s, which had proven highly effective during the French revolutionary wars, was no longer adequate. In addition, the rudimentary means of communication and the updates of advances in intelligence became more fragile due to the breadth of the contingents' deployment zones. 'There are many good Generals in Europe, but they see too many things; I see only one, and that is the masses. I seek to destroy them, of course the accessories will then fall by themselves.' To strike a sure blow, Napoleon methodically pursued the art of outnumbering this enemy mass on any given day.[1] In 1804 he created the Army corps headed by a corps commander and a small staff and comprising of two or three infantry divisions with their own divisional artillery, a cavalry division, a corps artillery unit, an engineer group and logistics units.

From the Army corps' first training ground near Boulogne on the Channel, where it looked at invading Britain in the summer of 1805 and to Austerlitz six months later, this invention effectively swept aside all of France's enemies. Each corps had its own marching orders for reaching the Rhine, crossing the Black Forest, and regrouping in the Swabian Jura; they would emerge grouped together at Ulm. These 'rivers', as the corps were nicknamed, fixed General Mack's Austrian forces while Marshal Ney's corps cut off the Austrian retreat and seized Elchingen – a compulsory crossing point on the Danube towards Vienna. The pursuit on either side of the Danube River demonstrated decentralised command at corps level. Later, at Austerlitz, Napoleon coordinated

---

1   *Maréchal* Ferdinand Foch, *Éloge de Napoléon* (Paris: Berger-Levrault, 1921), p.9.

the actions of his corps: while *Maréchal* Davout held the right wing at Tellnitz and Sokolnitz, attracting the main effort of Russian and Austrian troops as they were leaving Pratzen, Marshal Soult, responsible for the effort, cut off the centre of the coalition. Finally, *Maréchal* Murat with his cavalry corps, led the exploitation, while *Maréchal* Bernadotte and the Guard were kept in reserve. Meanwhile, *Maréchal* Masséna's corps in Italy attacked the Austrian occupying troops, preventing them from reaching the main theatre in Bohemia.[2] This corps' invention enabled great mobility, dispersal, distribution of command and the ability to assemble quickly and swoop down on an opponent. The Napoleonic era opened the national and industrial dimensions of war and highlighted the necessity to think about command structure and harnessing tactics to strategy. The Soviet leaders, inspired by their most famous military thinkers – Svechin, Tukhachevsky and Triandafillov, did so during the Second World War applying these command structures on different fronts.

These structures of command were applied successfully and proved their relevance during the Second World War and the Cold War. It was not until the collapse of the USSR and the preceding three decades of counterinsurgency and stabilisation operations that the role of this tactical organisation came into question. The question of relevance remained until the return of the great power competition and the war in Ukraine, which has seen the fielding of the largest armies since 1945. How can a tactical organisation inherited from the Napoleonic wartime era still make sense during the era of artificial intelligence and drones? The combat environment has profoundly changed because of the increased lethality of weapons (in terms of destructive power and range), the transparency of the battlefield, the increased mobility of units, data centric warfare and air power. Does this structure and organisation from the past, with corps, divisions and brigades, still make sense?

The Operative Level

An apocryphal sentence attributed to former French Prime Minister, Georges Clemenceau, during the Great War says that 'war is a too serious matter to be left to the military'. These words mean that the political leader is responsible for leading the war and defining the political outcomes, while the military wages the war and seeks to achieve the conditions to end it. Nevertheless, there can be a dual frustration: from the political side, the force cannot always produce the proper conditions to victory. And for the military, the political outcomes are sometimes unclear and remain blurred. Because 'war is nothing but the continuation of policy by other means' political stakeholders must remain at their political level to conduct the war in the

---

2   Claude Franc, 'La campagne de 1805 et Austerlitz: la genèse de l'art opératif', *Theatrum Belli*, 2 December 2023, https://theatrum-belli.com/la-campagne-de-1805-et-austerlitz-la-genese-de-lart-operatif/.

political, diplomatic and economic arenas.[3] Their vision must remain at the strategic level because war and combat are not the same in nature, as it is between strategy and tactics. 'Combat has its own logic through confrontation to achieve victory, whereas war has no logic of its own, since politics imposes its own.'[4] Indeed: 'The conduct of war …. consists in the planning and conduct of fighting …. It consists of greater or lesser number of single acts, each complete in itself, which …. are called engagements and which form new entities. This gives rise to the completely different activity of planning and executing these engagements themselves, and of coordinating each of them with the others in order to further the object of the war. One has been called tactics, and the other strategy.'[5]

Due to that difference in nature, the translation of strategic objectives into tactical actions requires a transfer matrix which is responsible for the conversion and the subordination of tactical operations to the goal of war. Dynamism and momentum are at the heart of tactics, which is a mix of both a sprint and endurance race. This is why I am using the adjective *operative*, whereas Svechin's concept is translated as *operational* art in the English version of his work.[6] This translation looks understated and does not cover the entirety of the meaning he developed around that idea. Etymologically, *operational* means to be ready for use; it is a state and expresses something quite static. *Operative* comes from the late fifteenth century French adjective *opératif*, and in turn from Medieval Latin *operativus*, meaning to produce the intended effect. This adjective indicates a notion of movement, a dynamic that corresponds to what Svechin theorised. The aim of operative art or operative command is not to be ready for use as the adjective operational suggests, but to order the means and maintain them in a tactical dynamic until the political aims of the war are achieved.[7] This is the reason why I will keep this translation to be as close as possible to Svechin's conceptualisation.

Svechin stresses the need to have a gearing, an operative command, that makes that linkage to avoid any divergence between strategic objectives and tactical realisations. If that structure does not exist, confusion rises and tactical actions will not further the war objectives. Napoleon was able to cumulate the functions of head of state, defining policy and conducting the war, and of a military strategist, who knew how to wage war. Few political leaders possess his genius or his military skills, therefore a gear or an interface is vital to link strategy and tactics, the latter being subservient to the former. 'Strategy pursues objectives, tactics solve problems,'[8] said Svechin, the theoretician of the operative art. It is for this reason these two areas must be led by different people.

3   Carl von Clausewitz, *On War* (Oxford: Oxford University Press, 2008), p.7.
4   Benoist Bihan and Jean Lopez, *Conduire la guerre, entretiens sur l'art opératif* (Paris: Perrin, 2023), pp.20–21.
5   Clausewitz, *On War*, p.74.
6   Aleksandr A. Svechin, *Strategy* (London: East View, 1993).
7   Bihan and Lopez, *Conduire la guerre*, p.72.
8   Svechin, *Strategy*, p.68.

During the Franco-Prussian War of 1870–1871, one of the main reasons for the French failures and final defeat arose from a failed command structure, whereas Moltke and his Great Headquarters were able to decipher and transcript in tactical words, the strategic and political objectives defined by Bismarck. On the French side, Gambetta, the Minister of War, dealt with tactical operations – the coordination of *francs-tireurs* units – but was unable to act on the political, diplomatic or economic areas, because he was overwhelmed by too many tasks. On the other hand, Moltke was the strategist who built the campaign plan and provided support to the corps in the *deep* and in the *close* while focussing his attention on the *rear*. He issued guidance to his corps commanders, asking them to be very careful of the French irregular units, whose *francs-tireurs* and partisans harassed the lines of communication. At his level of command, he was the sole commander having the widest and most accurate situational awareness. He coordinated the corps; he generated flows, facilitated the tactical engagements of German troops and secured his rear to which he dedicated 25 percent of his forces.[9] Throughout, he guaranteed that the tactical engagements met with the strategic goal of war, but he never interfered in the subordinate commands as one of the keys of success is what Germans call *Auftragstaktik,* and the British Army calls Mission Command. Bismarck, for his part, acted at his own political level as chancellor. Therefore, what we call operative level is not a third domain as strategy and tactics are, or something intermediate between them. According to Svechin, operative art is 'combining operations for achieving the ultimate goal of the war'.[10]

That command level in the land domain is the one that has all the resources needed to carry out operations, over the long term, until the political objectives are achieved. This vital interface between strategy and tactics is a necessary but not sufficient condition for success. The Battles of Ligny and *Quatre* Bras on 16 June 1815 highlighted this point clearly, as their consequences were fateful for Napoleon despite his victories. Having defeated Wellington around the crossroad of Quatre Bras and Blucher at Ligny, the Emperor was convinced that the Prussians would never recover. He overestimated the effect of his victory and delayed his actions, not launching Marshal Grouchy in pursuit of his enemy until around 11:00 a.m. the next day. Napoleon had lost the momentum that would have led him 10 years earlier to exploit the situation in depth. His late decision meant that Gneisenau arrived at Waterloo at the end of the day on 18 June, allowing Prussian troops to reinforce Wellington's cornered, but tenaciously resisting, British units. While his enemies had drawn lessons learned of their defeats by adopting the structure of the corps, the Emperor was defeated because he missed initiatives and did not exploit his previous action. He consequently lost the momentum.

9   Armel Dirou, *La guérilla en 1870, résistance et terreur* (Paris, 2e édition: L'Artilleur-Giovanangeli, 2021).
10 Svechin, *Strategy,* p.239.

Corps, Divisions and Brigades in Modern Warfare

Conceptual and theoretical reflections are difficult to implement when realised in an operational environment. It is not enough to have just a tool; the organisation must ensure that it works and is used to its best effect. Considering the operative command level, it is clear that it is multi-layered from joint aspects to the specific domains of air, sea and land. Many opinions were considered to establish whether some layers were still necessary based on the current reality of warfare. Shortly after the Second World War, the U.S. launched a study about the Modern Mobile Army (MOMAR), with the purpose of understanding the capability of the Army 'of conducting combat operations throughout the world in either a nuclear or non-nuclear environment and against a variety of enemy forces .... The corps was eliminated under the MOMAR concept'.[11] In the 1970s, following the Vietnam War, the U.S. Army decided to structure itself with 21 divisions, subordinated in different corps, which have remained their structure for tactical and logistical manoeuvre. Meanwhile in France, land forces were articulated around the 1st Army with two corps: one in Germany encompassing three divisions and one in France encompassing two divisions, gathering 50,000 and 40,000 soldiers respectively. Even though the strategic environment did not change in Europe in the early 1980s, the considerable reinforcement demonstrated by the Soviet Army led the French to reorganise with smaller divisions. In 1984, underneath the 1st Army, three corps were manned with smaller divisions, approximately 10,000 soldiers each, and an independent quick reaction force was structured like a corps. For the French Army, the corps was, and has always been, a fully capable manoeuvre echelon, because it centralises scarce capabilities lacking in the divisions to be used where and when it is tactically beneficial.

The radical change of strategic environment with the collapse of the USSR in 1991, and the promises of the so-called 'peace dividends', led to both an irrational dream of eternal peace and drastic cuts in defence budgets in Europe. The professionalisation of the armed forces also contributed to the downsizing of the Army format. The disappearance of the army level, stabilisation operations and the emphasis on counterinsurgency over some four decades have led to a loss of sight of the requirements of confronting a similar adversary, if not in a total war, then at least in a full-spectrum war. Then, manoeuvring only focused on limited commitments and was not seen in its holistic dimension. It therefore became difficult for the Army commanders to justify the need of a corps level, as troops could easily be led from Paris by the Permanent Joint Headquarters (CPCO)[12]. Such a request was and has been perceived as an Army's whim to preserve posts, underpinned by retrograde views on what modern combat must be. The Army has long been criticised for preparing for the last war rather than the next.

---

11   Robert A. Doughty, 'The Evolution of U.S. Army Tactical Doctrine, 1946–76', *Leavenworth Papers*, 1 (August 1979), pp.19–20.

12   The French equivalent of PJHQ is CPCO, *Centre de Planification et de Conduite des Opérations*.

The mirage of a high-tech force fed by data and info centric warfare led many to believe that digitisation would enable the army to be commanded directly from the strategic level. However, it seems that some constants have been forgotten, that Eastern rising threats remind accurately.

The complexity of modern warfare with the multiplication of assets, remote or not, the transparency of the battlefield due to the number of sensors and captors, cyber and electronic warfare, and the increased destructive power of weapons make the conduct of combat even more difficult than before. Such combat cannot be directed from Paris, or similar locations, because a long screwdriver is not a solution. If the strategic level is dealing with tactics, it does not carry out its own missions. With the disappearance of the army echelon in 1993, the corps is now the sole operative command level in the land domain of warfare that has all the combat, intelligence, joint coordination (maritime, air, space) and logistics resources at its disposal. That command structure has therefore no equivalent for planning campaigns, and coordinating actions in the deep, in the close and in the rear. Thanks to these capacities, the corps generates flows and is uniquely capable of acting as the transfer matrix between strategy and tactics. It directs operations as continuous, uninterrupted sequences until the political objective is reached, because its actions are sustained over time. In addition, the capacity to conduct operations in the deep requires 'resources that will allow to surmount any enemy resistance, both at the outset and during operations'.[13] Max Hastings' account of Konev's seizure of Silesia in January 1945 offers a perfect illustration of harnessing tactics to strategy: 'The broad principles of future operations were established. Zhukov would strike the main blow south of Warsaw, while Konev on his left sought to envelop the vast industrial areas of Silesia, rather than attack head-on against strong defences. Stalin was anxious to capture Silesia's mines and factories intact, and emphasised his wishes to Konev .... [The latter] had been ordered by Stalin to do his utmost to secure the area intact. The marshal launched his forces upon a grand envelopment, while simultaneously pressing the Germans frontally.'[14] The Soviet commander thus succeeded in achieving the political goal given by his head of state and defeating his adversary thanks to an appropriate tactical course of action. This is typically the role of the corps today because the corps commander will be responsible of a front in which he must subordinate combat to the war by 'combining operations for achieving the ultimate goal of the war'.[15] For these reasons, some compare the corps with a carrier strike group, because of the breadth of its responsibilities and capabilities from strategic to tactical level and its operative role. However, if the corps seems to be still a relevant command level, can we wonder whether division and brigade organisations are? Indeed, in the past, the model of the French division has been different and

13   Vladimir Triandafillov, *The Nature of the Operations of Modern Armies* (London: Jacob W. Kipp, 1994), p.90.
14   Max Hastings, *Armageddon, The Battle for Germany, 1944–1945* (New York: Alfred A. Knopf, 2004), pp.206, 360.
15   Svechin, *Strategy*, p.239.

evolved in accordance with the nuclear doctrine or the changes in the strategic environment. The Division 1959, named Division 59, was characterised by the reaffirmation of the brigade level, whereas the Divisions 77 and the 84 were downsized and had only regiments underneath. The Plan *Army 2000* led then to suppress the divisional level and to replace the divisions by brigades. Initially, the field army kept one corps and four division headquarters, named Force's HQs (EMF), dedicated to training and planning, and conceived to receive subordinate brigades in case of deployment. Two of them were disbanded in 2011. It is only recently, in 2015, that the two Force's HQs have been generated again to be operational division headquarters, each one with three brigades underneath. What is finally useful to carry out tactical combat operations: divisions, brigades, or both?

As it has been mentioned earlier, the battlefield has considerably evolved, and the lessons learned from Ukraine highlight the vulnerability of troop concentrations. It is therefore necessary to increase their survivability by being dispersed. Deployed wider and deeper, the divisions are the tactical level of command that produces the effects requested by the corps on the battlefield. Given the breadth of their own area of responsibility, divisions require relays to coordinate their actions. The brigades are this coordinating echelon that is permitted by the capabilities of the command information systems, the mobility of units and their extended combat capabilities. Nevertheless, this dispersal must not undermine the application of the three principles of war, inherited from Marshal Foch: economy of means, concentration of efforts and freedom of action.[16] The second principle will be the most difficult to apply because of the dispersion. We then should consider that we must understand the concentration of efforts by the concentration of effects that our equipment should allow, through a manoeuvre of trajectories.[17] Thanks to the flows generated by the corps, divisions can produce effects on the field, and, because of the dispersal, brigades are needed as coordinating echelons for tactical actions.

Given the number and multiplicity of units on the battlefield, the corps, division and brigade levels allow the management of complexity. The chain of command also allows agility, so the guns of a division can easily support a division to one of its flanks. Each command level allows this flexibility and so vertical command breaks horizontal organisation to mass effects. The importance of the corps lies in the fact that it is at the level of multi-domains actions aimed at shaping the battlespace, creating the conditions for engagement and degrading the land enemy's ability to operate, whereas the division seeks to condition the enemy's force ratio to allow the commitment of close combat brigades.

16   These principles of war are those doctrinally defined in the French Armed Forces whereas the British doctrine encompasses 10 principles of war.
17   Guy Hubin, *Perspectives tactiques* (Paris: ISC-Economica, 2009).

Conclusion

To the initial question, we can positively respond that Napoleon would recognise his invention 220 years on, even though he would be shocked by the transparency of the battlefield, the flows of information, and amazed by the joint aspect of warfare.

Even though we could make a comparison with a carrier strike group, a corps is more than a capability or an asset that owns all resources that its subordinate units do not control. It is the political-military tool for the coherence of war in the Land domain and a vital condition for tactical effectiveness and national sovereignty. That gearing enables the convergence of the strategic and tactical goals in the land domain. The French Navy and Air Force are conceived and organised around nuclear deterrence and state missions supported by coast guards and air space protection. That *ultima ratio*, which is the nuclear deterrence, cannot play its role however if it is not preceded and supported by reliable and credible conventional forces. The French Army is that latter part of defence and founds its credibility on operative and tactical structures – corps, divisions brigades – that permit France to remain a key player in the defence domain. This backbone of defence remains dependant on corps, divisions and brigades that are properly structured, manned and equipped – because a war starts on land and finishes on land. As part of the collective defence, the corps enables France to exert its strategic solidarity towards its allies and partners.

Finally, it is not unusual that strategy cannot get the expected political results from tactics. Such malfunctioning usually leads to protracted conflicts. It will therefore be interesting to study, after the conflict, the functioning of operative commands of both opponents in the war in Ukraine.

3

Weatherproofing? The Transformation of the German Army, 2011–2024

Michael Lanzinger

'…the *Bundeswehr*, the Army that I am authorised to lead, is more or less bare.' With these clear and drastic words, the Chief of the German Army, Lieutenant General Alfons Mais, described his frustration with the state of the *Bundeswehr* on the morning of the Russian invasion of Ukraine. Posting on the social media platform LinkedIn, he wrote:

> The options that could be offered to politicians to support the alliance are severely constrained. We all saw it coming and we were unable to get our point across, to draw conclusions from the annexation of Crimea and to implement them. It doesn't feel good! I am angry! …. When, if not now, is the time to leave the Afghanistan mission behind us structurally and materially and reposition ourselves, otherwise we will not be able to fulfil our constitutional mandate and our alliance commitments with any prospect of success.[1]

The post, unsurprisingly, proved a media sensation as it marked the first time a high-ranking German general had publicly articulated such a stark and unambiguous assessment. However, those versed in, or even responsible for, security and defence policy felt vindicated.

At the end of the Cold War the German population perceived itself to be encircled by friends and allies. Consequently, the *Bundeswehr*, along with other European armed forces, had to pay the 'peace dividend'. The warning shot of the annexation of Crimea in 2014 was heard and the right conclusions were drawn. Nevertheless, the requisite priority was not accorded to defence in respect of budgetary negotiations. It was taken

---

1   See https://de.linkedin.com/posts/alfons-mais-46744b99_du-wachst-morgens-auf-und-stellst-fest-es-activity-6902486582067044353-RZky.

for granted that nothing serious would happen. What could go wrong? And suddenly, on 24 February 2024, it became clear that we have a *Bundeswehr* that is excelling in crisis management missions abroad but can only to a very limited extent fulfil its contribution to national and alliance defence. The objective of this chapter is to provide a description, explanation and evaluation of the evolution of the German Army since the Cold War, and to examine its current preparedness for the new challenges of national and alliance defence.

Looking Back – How Did This Happen?

The last significant restructuring of the Army took place in 2011 within the context of a radically altered security policy environment. The likelihood of an immediate territorial threat to Germany and its allies was considered relatively low. Instead, 'out of area' missions dominated *Bundeswehr* and military thinking. Starting with the Balkan missions in the mid-1990s, the *Bundeswehr,* and in particular the Army, gradually lost its innocence. The reality of operations in Afghanistan shaped the prevailing mind-set. In accordance with the assessment of the then Defence Minister Peter Struck, Germany was defended in the Hindu Kush.[2] The 'HEER 2011' structure was therefore optimised for the 'most likely' scenario, namely the fulfilment of tasks in the context of international crisis management, under the constraints of tight budgetary resources.[3]

In this context, the conscription system was suspended in 2011 as it could no longer be justified on the grounds of the need for extensive personnel replacement in the event of national defence. Conscripts have been excluded from deployments and, consequently, they have only been trained in basic skills. In consideration of limited resources, the role of conscripts was increasingly perceived as a burden. Although, as it later turned out, they constituted an excellent recruiting pool for long-serving personnel and reservists, this advantage was negated by the considerable expense of an elaborate and costly training apparatus.

In 2011, the structure of the Army was determined by two principal factors: firstly, its commitments to NATO, and secondly, the requirement to ensure Germany's contributions to global missions and mission-equivalent obligations within the framework of NATO, the EU and the United Nations. The Army structure comprised two mechanised divisions, each with four combat brigades, a light division with special forces and an airborne brigade with the capability for evacuation operations. This structure was designed to provide the contingents for foreign deployments and simultaneously fulfil NATO commitments.[4]

2   See https://www.bundesregierung.de/breg-de/service/newsletter-und-abos/bulletin/rede-des-bundesministers-der-verteidigung-dr-peter-struck--784328.

3   Inspekteur des Heeres, 'Die Neuausrichtung des Heeres, Zweite, vollständig aktualisierte Auflage', July 2014.

4   Inspekteur des Heeres, 'Die Neuausrichtung des Heeres…'.

However, the constrained financial framework forced painful compromises. Consequently, certain capabilities were significantly reduced and entire branches of the Army, such as Army Air Defence, were disbanded. Similarly, reductions were implemented in combat support and command support troops, for example, within the artillery branch. In addition, other capabilities were consolidated across the entire armed forces, thereby removing them from the direct control of the Army. This fragmentation resulted in the implementation of complex planning and preparation processes, a notable lack of cohesion in operations, and, as a consequence, a tendency towards micromanagement at the highest levels.

A lack of equipment was another major challenge. A concept presented as 'dynamic availability management' resulted in a 'structural shortage management' system. In principle, units should maintain a stock of 70 percent of required equipment, with the remaining 30 percent being supplemented as required, for example, for operational or training purposes. This resulted in units being 'relieved' of their major equipment in preparation for their operational missions, thereby enabling other units to be temporarily 'fully equipped' for certain training projects. The continuous planning process associated with this concept was characterised by the alternation between the provision of operational contingents with corresponding deployment-related preparation and follow-up and as well as combined arms training. In conclusion, the aforementioned challenges have resulted in a state of frustration and a gradual decline in the ability to conduct combined arms warfighting operations effectively.[5]

The annexation of Crimea by the Russian Federation in 2014 represented the first occasion on which the lack of capabilities for national and alliance defence was confronted with the new realities of an aggressive Russian foreign policy. The comforting assumption that it is possible to prepare for an armed conflict with long warning periods has proved false in retrospect.

Under the new slogan 'cold-start capability', there was a notable improvement in operational readiness, with a heightened focus on potential threats from Russia. It was acknowledged that, following the withdrawal of the majority of U.S. forces from Europe, it was of paramount importance to bridge the strategic gap created until the arrival of U.S. forces across the Atlantic at an early stage of a potential conflict.

NATO responded with the Readiness Action Plan. In 2015 the Army provided the first contingent of the Very High Readiness Joint Task Force (VJTF) with an armoured infantry battalion to protect NATO's eastern flank. In 2019 and 2023, Germany led the way as the lead nation with one combat brigade each as VJTF (Land). This was when the Army began to face embarrassing scrutiny. It did not go unnoticed by the public that the reinforced battalion had to gather around 15,000 individual parts from the entire Army, from armoured personnel carriers to night vision goggles. Even the second and third German rotations of the NATO spearhead faced the same major challenges. Both *Panzerlehrbrigade 9*, responsible for VJTF 2019, and *Panzergrenadierbrigade 37* (2022) had

---

5   Christian Dewitz, 'Mangelwirtschaft lähmt Ausbildungsbetrieb der Bundeswehr', *Bundeswehr-Journal*, 10 October 2014.

to rely on material from across the *Bundeswehr* for their missions. These restrictions have had a significant impact on the training and exercises of support units across the Army.[6]

Concurrently, the Army assumed the role of framework nation for the enhanced Forward Presence Battle Group (eFP-BG) in Lithuania in 2017. The objective of the enhanced Forward Presence forces is to reinforce deterrence vis-à-vis Russia. The eFP-BG acts as a tripwire, making it clear to Moscow through the temporary stationing of NATO units in the Baltic states that even a limited military attack would be seen as an attack on all NATO members. Furthermore, since September 2022, Germany has also provided a mechanised combat brigade as part of the enhanced Vigilance Activities (eVA) in Germany with corresponding readiness levels, which is permanently repre-sented in Lithuania with a forward command element (FCE).[7]

'Zeitenwende' – Turning Point

Russia's full-scale invasion of Ukraine on 24 February 2022, which violated interna-tional law, resulted in a fundamental transformation of German security and defence policy, which was subsequently designated a 'turning point'. In a special session of the German Bundestag on 27 February 2024, Federal Chancellor Olaf Scholz delivered an historic watershed speech in which he asserted that Putin's intentions extend beyond the invasion of Ukraine to the establishment of 'a Russian Empire.' Scholz underscored Germany's obligation to provide unwavering support to NATO, 'without ifs and buts'. In light of the new situation, it became imperative for Germany to extend support to Ukraine, dissuade Putin from pursuing his military agenda, and prevent the conflict from escalating and spreading to other European countries. He characterised this as a pivotal moment – a 'turning point' – in German foreign policy.[8]

The real historic turning point for the *Bundeswehr*, however, was the completely unex-pected announcement that the defence budget would henceforth amount to more than two percent of gross domestic product (GDP) and that the 2022 federal budget would also be endowed with a one-off special fund of €100 billion. The fund was to be allo-cated to essential investments and armaments projects for the *Bundeswehr*, including the acquisition of superior equipment and the expansion of personnel.[9] Only a relatively limited number of individuals were involved in this sensational decision. The remainder of the population was wholly astonished.

---

6   Thomas Wiegold, 'Die deutsche NATO-Speerspitze: With a little help from my friends', *Augen Geradeaus!*, Teil 3, 18 February 2021.

7   See https://www.bundeswehr.de/de/einsaetze-bundeswehr-anerkannte-missionen/efp-enhanced-forward-presence.

8   See https://www.bundesregierung.de/breg-de/aktuelles/regierungserklaerung-von-bundeskanzler-olaf-scholz-am-27-februar-2022-2008356.

9   See https://www.bundesregierung.de/breg-de/aktuelles/regierungserklaerung-von-bundeskanzler-olaf-scholz-am-27-februar-2022-2008356.

The German defence budget has always been tight, because promising to increase funding for the armed forces is a questionable strategy to win elections in post-war Germany. Consequently, the 2014 NATO decision in Wales, which established the two percent target for members, was only endorsed with considerable reservation. Despite the Russian annexation of Crimea, Germany increased its defence budget, yet consistently fell short of the NATO target. While the proportion of GDP allocated to defence spending was 1.2 percent in 2014, it remained significantly below the NATO agreement threshold of approximately 1.5 percent during the period spanning 2020 to 2022. In formal terms, this would not have constituted a breach of the commitments made in Wales, given that the agreement was limited to 'moving towards the two percent target within a decade'. It was not until the NATO summit in Vilnius in 2023 that this loophole was closed and the two percent mark was set as a binding minimum.[10]

Notwithstanding the €100 billion special fund, in 2023 – the year after the turning point – just 1.6 percent was achieved. It was only in 2024 that Germany joined the two percent club and was able to meet the NATO target for the first time with a share of 2.1 percent of GDP. This figure was calculated by taking into account the original defence budget, the special fund and the relevant expenditure of other individual plans. The total value of the 2024 defence budget is €90.6 billion. This represents a 55 percent increase in the budget compared to two years prior.[11]

The initial enthusiasm was quickly replaced by disillusionment when the exact conditions became known. As the special fund is formally a loan, the actual funding available was approximately €87 billion due to the impact of inflation and the forthcoming interest payments on the borrowing. In addition, the procurement process started too slowly and did not meet expectations. The *Bundeswehr* planners knew very quickly what they wanted. The requisite list of specifications was already available at the Ministry of Defence in March 2022. Nevertheless, the formal approval of the special fund by Parliament initially necessitated an amendment to the constitution. Following the amendment in June 2022, the Budget Committee finally made the funds available in November 2022. Consequently, the first expenditure from the special fund was not made until almost a year later, at the beginning of 2023.[12]

Special Fund – What Does this Mean for the Army?

The procurement plan entailed the utilisation of the special fund to address the identified deficiencies and ensure compliance with NATO obligations. It is therefore a common misconception that the *Bundeswehr* is being upgraded through the special fund. In fact,

10   Klaus-Heiner Röhl, 'Verteidigungsausgaben. Gerade so genug für die NATO?', *IW-Kurzbericht*, 19 (2024).
11   Bundesministerium der Verteidigung, 19. Bericht zu Rüstungsangelegenheiten, Teil 1.
12   Rolf Clement, 'Trendwende – Zeitenwende – Kehrtwende: die Sicherheitspolitik der Bundesrepublik Deutschland', *Österreichische militärische Zeitschrift*, 62:2 (2024), pp.139–145.

the fund is solely responsible for closing the gaps. By the conclusion of 2024, the entirety of the special fund's financial resources will have been allocated, leaving no further scope for additional projects. In 2023, Minister Boris Pistorius stated that existing gaps could not be fully closed by 2030 and that considerably more funding would be necessary to achieve this goal.[13]

The Army's already depleted inventory was further reduced in 2022 and 2023 as a consequence of the donation of military equipment to Ukraine. Since the commencement of the Russian war of aggression in 2022, Germany has transferred military equipment from the *Bundeswehr* inventory with an estimated replacement value of approximately €5.2 billion. The main items delivered from the Army's stocks were the self-propelled howitzer Panzerhaubitze 2000 (PzH 2000) and the MARS rocket launcher, as well as the Leopard 2 main battle tank and the Marder infantry fighting vehicle.[14]

A comparable situation pertains with regard to the second largest item in the 'command and control capability and digitalisation dimension' of the armed forces, which amounts to €20.7 billion. The Army will benefit from investments in the digitalisation of land-based operations, in addition to improvements in satellite communication with the introduction of two new satellites. The Army has a major capability gap here and it is vital to maintain command and control superiority on the battlefield through the digitisation of land forces.[15]

A total of €16.6 billion is to be allocated to the 'land dimension', which represents the primary focus of the Army. Investments will be made in the acquisition of 50 upgraded Puma infantry fighting vehicles, 123 heavy infantry weapon carriers on GTK Boxers, 2,054 airborne vehicles and 227 new generation snow vehicles. Furthermore, the special fund will be utilised for the development of the new Main Ground Combat System main battle tank.

The largest share of the special fund investments, amounting to €33.4 billion, is being allocated to the 'air dimension'. This will be used for the procurement of the F-35, CH-47F Chinook, Eurofighter ECR, Heron TP drones, a space-based early warning system, additional maritime patrol aircraft and the development of the Future Combat Air System. However, the 'air dimension' is not exclusively owned by the Air Force. The Army also has a role to play in this area, as evidenced by the procurement of the new H145M light support helicopter and the Skyranger ground-based air defence system. The special fund will be used to procure 62 helicopters at a cost of around €2.6 billion. The first of these have already entered service. Until a decision is made on the successor to the Tiger combat helicopter, the H145M will serve as a bridging solution for ground air support, particularly against armoured units.[16]

---

13   See https://www.tagesschau.de/inland/pistorius-bundeswehr-105.html.
14   See https://www.bundesregierung.de/breg-de/aktuelles/lieferungen-ukraine-2054514.
15   Alfons Mais, 'Es ist noch nicht alles gut, aber es ist deutlich besser', *Wehrtechnik*, Issue 4 (2023), pp.48–52.
16   'Bundesministerium der Verteidigung, Zeitenwendeprojekt: Bundeswehr erhält ersten Leichten Kampfhubschrauber', 18 November 2024.

The New Structure of the Army

The fundamental change in the security architecture is not merely a matter of addressing gaps in procurement through a concerted effort; it also entails a structural alignment of the *Bundeswehr* and, consequently, the Army with the emerging challenges. For the *Bundeswehr* to fulfil its role as a deterrent against a concrete military threat, it must be equipped with the capabilities required for effective warfighting in the context of the contemporary era.

The reorientation of the *Bundeswehr* is based on the Defence Policy Guidelines (*Verteidigungspolitische Richtlinien* or VPR), which were presented by the Minister of Defence on 9 November 2023. The VPR are derived from the National Security Strategy and define the strategic priorities for an integrated defence policy of Germany based on a defence policy assessment. The VPR thus provide a compass for the future orientation of the *Bundeswehr* towards its core mission of national and alliance defence.[17]

Warfighting capability is the benchmark for the operational readiness of a war-ready Bundeswehr. It is imperative that the *Bundeswehr* can assume a leadership role in such a scenario. The new quality of security threats, particularly the brutal reality of the war in Ukraine, has made it evident that structures and processes must be aligned with the scenario of engaging with an adversary that is at least equal in strength. 'We don't just want to win this conflict, we have to. This sets the pace.'[18]

The ability to fulfil its role in national and allied defence within the framework of NATO and the European Union is the determining parameter for the structure of the *Bundeswehr*. It is imperative that capabilities, structures and processes are aligned with the NATO Level of Ambition and EU requirements.[19]

The entire range of *Bundeswehr* missions must be covered by a single set of forces. The strategic-conceptual objectives delineate the 'national ambition' as a graduated, balanced set of capabilities that is alliance-capable across all dimensions. These requirements present a significant challenge for the Army, which has historically focused its structure on the provision of trained and equipped contingents for crisis response deployments.

Mastering the land dimension is of paramount importance to enforce one's will in armed conflicts across the entire spectrum of intensity. Consequently, the development and deployment of land forces in armed conflicts is of pivotal importance. Following years of prioritising international crisis management missions, the *Bundeswehr*'s land forces are now primarily focused on national and alliance defence.

In addition to providing support to Ukraine and contributing to the management of international crises, it is now imperative for the Army, as the primary contributor of land forces,[20] to establish large, cohesive units capable of conducting cold-start operations across the entire spectrum of tasks and intensities of land operations.

17   'Defence Policy Guidelines 2023'.
18   'Defence Policy Guidelines 2023'.
19   'Bundeswehr's Concept', 20 July 2018.
20   'Land forces' encompasses not only the Army, but also any other forces belonging to organisational areas that are specifically designed or deployed with the objective of directly conducting and supporting land operations.

It is essential that the units can meet the required NATO standby times from a standing start, without extensive personnel and material transfers, in a sustainable manner. Consequently, fully staffed and equipped large-scale units should be available for deployment in a cold start in the context of national and alliance defence.

To enhance the range of response capabilities and to maintain the balance between international crisis and conflict management missions and national and alliance defence, a novel construct will be introduced in three force categories: light, medium and heavy forces.

Light Forces

The light forces, under the command of the Rapid Forces Division (*Division Schnelle Kräfte* or DSK), comprise the special forces of the Special Forces Command, in addition to the two infantry brigades of *Luftlandebrigade 1* and the Dutch 11th *Luchtmobiele* Brigade with the necessary combat and operational support in a unique mix of capabilities. With the transfer of the mountain troops (*Gebirgsjägerbrigade 23*) from 10 *Panzerdivision*, the Rapid Forces Division has already assumed its new structure. The paratroopers constitute the nucleus of the Army's contribution as standby forces to national risk and crisis management. The light forces are part of the rapid reaction forces of NATO, the EU and of Germany.

In accordance with the DSK's overarching principle of 'ready for action – at any time – worldwide', the light forces can undertake a comprehensive range of missions at varying levels of intensity and with minimal delay, due to their exceptional air mobility capabilities. This renders them the forces of the 'first hour' in the operational area. Evacuation operations in Libya, Afghanistan, Sudan and, most recently, the deployment of forces for a potential evacuation in Lebanon serve to illustrate the versatility of these capabilities.

Nevertheless, the elevated degree of mobility that facilitates expeditious capability projection exacts a toll on enforcement and sustainment capabilities, largely due to the nature of their equipment. Such forces can only be deployed for a limited period within the context of a military operation, serving to create the conditions for subsequent operations.[21]

Medium Forces

The concept of medium forces represents a new approach within the German Army. In the current structure, there is a gap between the light forces, which are fast but lack the capacity to establish and maintain a firm position, and the heavy mechanised forces,

---

21   Thomas Liebe, 'Zur Kriegstauglichkeit der Division Schnelle Kräfte', https://hardthoehenkurier.de/zur-kriegstauglichkeit-der-division-schnelle-kraefte/.

which are relatively complex to deploy. It is the intention to address this discrepancy by introducing wheel-based medium forces in the future.[22]

The medium forces constitute the hinge between international crisis management and national and alliance defence. The combination of agility with cold-start capability and logistical robustness enables medium forces to bridge the operational gap between light and heavy forces, expand the military 'toolbox' and thus contribute to enabling free operation.[23]

The medium forces will be equipped in such a way that they are highly mobile with their wheeled vehicles on their own axles, allowing them to deploy by road and to engage in high-intensity combat. In the context of strategic or operational deployment, the units of the medium forces will be capable of independent, unassisted movement over distances of up to 400 kilometres per day. This implies that specific operational zones can be accessed with greater expediency and autonomy, facilitating the reinforcement of existing forces. In both defensive and offensive operations, new main efforts can be formed quickly or the enemy can be channelled effectively using strategic manoeuvres.

The medium forces brigades will be equipped with a range of wheeled vehicles, including infantry fighting vehicles, howitzers, mortar systems, armoured transport vehicles, engineer capabilities and other systems, all based on the GTK Boxer platform. In the heavy infantry weapon carrier variant, the GTK Boxer is equipped with a weapon turret housing a 30mm cannon and a machine gun, as well as the MELLS anti-tank system.

The medium forces will comprise the recently restructured *Panzerbrigade 21* and *Panzergrenadierbrigade 41*, in addition to the Franco-German Brigade. In conjunction with Panzerlehrbrigade 9, which will serve as a heavy brigade, these units will constitute part of the future structure of *1 Panzerdivision*.[24] The very ambitious goal is to integrate *Panzerbrigade 21* as the inaugural medium force brigade within the NATO Deployable Force Pool from 2026 onwards. The brigade will not be fully equipped with the weapon systems until such time as it attains initial operational capability. This implies that an infantry battalion and the associated support forces will be constituted in an interim structure by that time. From 2027, a complete medium force brigade will be made available to NATO in an interim structure. It is anticipated that the target structure for all medium forces will be achieved by 2030 or later. Furthermore, it is inevitable that a combination of wheeled and tracked systems will be employed in the first few years.[25]

22   See https://www.bundeswehr.de/de/organisation/heer/aktuelles/neue-kategorie-im-kampf-die-mittleren-kraefte-5594418.

23   Alfons Mais, 'Mittlere Kräfte: notwendige Erweiterung des Fähigkeitsspektrums der Landstreitkräfte und zukünftiger Motor der Modernisierung', *Das schwarze Barett* (2023), pp.6–9.

24   Marco Pfitzner, 'Mittlere Kräfte als neue Kräftekategorie des Heeres: Definition Mittlere' in *Newsletter Verteidigung*, Issue 24 (2023), pp.13–16.

25   Alfons Mais, 'Mittlere Kräfte…', pp.6–9.

Heavy Forces

The heavy forces are classically typified by their infantry fighting vehicles and main battle tanks, which are equipped with tracks for mobility. When deployed over long distances, these combat vehicles must be transported at significant expense, for example by rail, road or sea. The heavy forces comprise *Panzerbrigade 12*, *Panzergrenadierbrigade 37* and *Panzerlehrbrigade 9*. Following their deployment, which is scheduled to commence with initial operational capability in 2026 and full operational capability in 2027, the newly established ninth brigade of the Army, *Panzerbrigade 45*, will be permanently stationed in Lithuania.

The Army's current focus is on the *10 Panzerdivision*, known as 'Division 2025', which will be ready for deployment as a Tier 2 category in 2025 rather than 2027 as originally planned. In accordance with the NATO Force Model, Tier 2 is defined as forces that are to be deployable within a timeframe of 11 to 30 days. By committing this division, including *Panzerbrigade 12* and *Panzergrenadierbrigade 37* and the divisional troops to NATO, Germany is thereby assuming its obligations for national and alliance defence.

If required, an additional heavy brigade, *Panzerlehrbrigade 9* from the *1 Panzerdivision*, will be made available for Division 2025. It will only be assigned to the *10 Panzerdivision* for training and exercises as part of national and alliance defence. Consequently, the Panzerlehrbrigade 9 will continue to fulfil its existing duties within the context of international crisis management.

The Division 2025 structure, which is still in the process of being finalised, will see the *10 Panzerdivision* incorporating *Panzerbrigade 12*, *Panzergrenadierbrigade 37*, the Dutch 13th *Lichte Brigade* and the Franco-German Brigade. Furthermore, the new *Panzerbrigade 45* in Lithuania will constitute part of the Division 2025 structure. It has yet to be determined which of the brigades will remain in the division alongside the Franco-German Brigade but not be part of Division 2025. A definitive resolution has yet to be reached concerning the prospective responsibilities and the revised function of the Franco-German Brigade.

A noteworthy aspect is the decision to establish the new *Panzerbrigade 45*, which will be permanently stationed in Lithuania as a Tier 1 brigade. The brigade comprises three combat units: the *Panzergrenadierbataillon 122* and the *Panzerbatallion 203* and the multinational eFP Battlegroup Lithuania. The advanced party for the formation of the brigade in Lithuania started its duties in early April 2024, with the official commissioning scheduled for April 2025.[26] This decision is without precedence in the history of the German Army, and it will be the first time that an Army formation will be stationed permanently outside of Germany. It is regarded as a flagship project of the security policy turnaround and is a strong indication of solidarity with alliance partners. The brigade

---

26   'Bundesministerium der Verteidigung, Tagesbefehl zur Brigade in Litauen', 6 November 2023.

is designed as a heavy combat unit and will be under command of Division 2025. It is anticipated that the brigade will become fully operational by the end of 2027.

The deployment of forces is scheduled to take place between July 2026 and June 2027, contingent upon the availability of requisite infrastructure and logistical support. Subsequently, the initial training and exercise activities will commence. Until *Panzerbrigade 45* is combat-ready, the eFP Battlegroup will continue to be present in Lithuania and the eVA Brigade – currently *Panzergrenadierbrigade 37* – will remain as Forward Land Forces brigade on standby in Germany.[27]

Panzerbrigade 45 is scheduled to receive the most contemporary equipment. As early as 2023, an order was placed for the delivery of 18 Leopard 2 A8 main battle tanks, representing the latest generation of this type, to replace the 18 Leopard 2 main battle tanks that had been gifted to Ukraine. In July 2024, an order was approved for a further 105 Leopard 2 main battle tanks – at a cost of approximately €2.9 billion – which are to be transferred to *Panzerbrigade 45* between 2027 and 2030.[28]

Divisional Troops

In recent years, the majority of divisional troops have been stripped and the combat support and command support troops were significantly reduced in number. As a result, divisions are now being re-equipped with divisional troops, particularly in the form of reconnaissance, artillery, engineer, logistics and communications battalions. The army divisions are once again able to take the troop organisation required for the respective mission from the basic structure, allowing them to respond flexibly to the demands of the operational environment. This puts the division in a position to take up the fight in depth and create the conditions for the immediate operations of its brigades.

In addition to the division's basic structure, other capabilities, including nuclear, biological, chemical defence; military police; operational communications and civil-military cooperation, are crucial and must be integrated in a manner that ensures the requisite range of capabilities is covered. It is of particular importance to note the integration of medical service support, which is achieved through the establishment of *fixed-couleur* relationships. This integration allows for the immediate subordinating of medical service support to Division 2025 in the event of an operation.[29]

Furthermore, the Army will provide a mixed helicopter task force in the form of a corps force for the Multinational Corps Northeast. This will be in an initial capability status and will be reduced in brigade strength from 2025. An expansion of the Aviation

27   'Litauen: Panzergrenadierbrigade 37 löst Panzerbrigade 21 ab', *cpm defence network*, 9 December 2024.

28   Martin Boldt, 'Ein Stolperdraht reicht nicht mehr: die deutsche Brigade in Litauen als Zeichen der Zeitenwende', *IF – Zeitschrift für Innere Führung*, 68:2 (2024), pp.56–59.

29   Erik Bohnet, '10. Panzerdivision – Der Weg zum einsatzbereiten Großverband', *cpm defence network*, 1 November 2024.

Brigade is scheduled to occur through a structural adjustment by 2028 and the integration of the new Light Combat Helicopter H145M, which is set to commence in 2025.[30] On 3 December 2024, the chiefs of the Army and Air Force agreed to combine their helicopter resources into an Aviation Brigade. The aim is to make more efficient use of resources, thereby improving readiness and responsiveness in the event of an alliance crisis.[31]

The Army Air Defence Force was decommissioned in 2012 as part of the restructuring of the combat support forces. In light of the renewed emphasis on the mission of national and alliance defence, it has become a crucial component. The close air defence system facilitates collaboration between the Air Force and the Army. The initial equipment of the air defence component of the Army will be the Skyranger 30 air defence system on GTK Boxer, comprising a 30-millimetre calibre automatic cannon and the Stinger guided missile.[32]

The IRIS-T SLM air defence missile system has been selected as the principal weapon system for the Air Force. This will result in the integration of the Army's mobile short-range air defence capabilities with the Air Force's medium-range and longer-range air defence capabilities. The entire planning of the new deployment is oriented towards the joint deployment of Army and Air Force forces. The system has been designed in such a way that it can be easily combined with existing air defence components or rapidly integrated into their units.

The initial procurement of a prototype and a further 18 series vehicles of the new anti-aircraft armoured vehicle is already planned. To achieve this, a task force will be set up in 2025 to coordinate and manage the new capabilities. By 2026, one unit will have been equipped with the Skyranger system. The force will then be gradually completed by 2028.[33]

Similarly, artillery is undergoing a period of renewed interest and development. Due to the *Bundeswehr*'s focus on stabilisation operations, the ability to fight with fire in the depths of space has been neglected in recent decades. Hardly any other branch of the German Army has shrunk as much as the artillery force. The Army has a total of five artillery battalions. In future the Army will have 10 of these in four different formations, probably by 2035. They will be assigned at the corps, division and brigade levels.

Each of the two divisional artillery battalions will be equipped with four firing batteries, enabling them to engage targets at a range of up to 150 kilometres while conducting reconnaissance. The initial deployment will consist of 16 MARS II rocket launchers. The second and third batteries will each be equipped with nine tube artillery systems. Until the arrival of the RCH 155, the divisional artillery battalions will be

---

30   Christoph Meier, 'Die Zukunft der Luftbeweglichkeit im Heer', *InfoBrief Heer: Publikationsorgan des Förderkreis Deutsches Heer*, 28:4 (2023), pp.6–8.

31   See https://x.com/Deutsches_Heer/status/1863918709791670520.

32   'Die Heeresflugabwehrtruppe wird jetzt neu aufgestellt', *Bundeswehr-Journal*, 3 May 2024.

33   Lars Hoffmann, 'Luftverteidigungsprojekt Nah- und Nächstbereichsschutz: Aufgabenteilung zwischen Luftwaffe und Heer ist jetzt offiziell', *Europäische Sicherheit & Technik*, 72:3 (2023), pp.56–58.

equipped with the PzH 2000. In the current circumstances, the Rapid Forces Division is obliged to operate without artillery. A corps artillery battalion will then be equipped with three firing batteries, each comprising 12 MARS II 'Future Long-Range Indirect Fire System' rocket artillery systems. It should be capable of reconnaissance and engagement of targets at a distance of at least 300 kilometres.

The German MARS II and PzH 2000 artillery systems donated to Ukraine have proven their effectiveness and thus their continued importance for fire support. The majority of losses incurred by both parties can be attributed to the use of heavy artillery. In particular, when enemy air defences or bad weather preclude the deployment of fighter aircraft, armed drones or combat helicopters, artillery provides a reliable and effective means of fire support for combat troops, irrespective of the electromagnetic spectrum. This experience demonstrates the significance of artillery as an effector, namely its capacity to achieve crucial effects at the depth of the battlefield.[34]

The seven brigade artillery battalions are subdivided into four heavy artillery battalions, equipped with the PzH 2000 of 10 *Panzerdivision*, and three medium artillery battalions, with the RCH 155 of 1 *Panzerdivision*. Each battalion will be equipped with three firing batteries, comprising nine howitzers in total. The seven brigade artillery battalions will be capable of reconnaissance and engagement of targets at up to 70 kilometres.

It is anticipated that the artillery force will comprise 289 tube artillery systems, PzH 2000 and 76 rocket artillery systems MARS II in the future. The operational lifespan of the 98 PzH 2000s is to be extended beyond 2040 as part of a mid-life upgrade. In addition, the maximum combat range is to be extended to 75 kilometres under the designation 'Future Medium-Range Indirect Fire System – PzH 2000'. Nevertheless, the project is not yet supported by budgetary funds.[35]

Furthermore, the subsequent procurement of 22 additional PzH 2000 howitzers is scheduled to continue until the end of 2026. These howitzers were previously gifted to Ukraine. Furthermore, the contract includes an option for the purchase of an additional six PzH 2000s. Nevertheless, the Army has stated that it requires a total of 121 systems.

The RCH 155 wheeled howitzers are being procured in collaboration with the UK Ministry of Defence. The British Army has selected the RCH 155 as part of the Mobile Fires Platform programme. The total requirement of the German Army for RCH 155 wheeled howitzers is 168 systems. The initial delivery of systems is scheduled for 2029. Nevertheless, only a preliminary allocation in the mid-double-digit range has been designated for budgetary resources. Ukraine will receive the initial delivery of 54 RCH 155s as part of Germany's military support.[36]

---

34   Waldemar Geiger, 'Mehr Rohre und mehr Reichweite: die Zukunft der deutschen Artillerie' in *Europäische Sicherheit & Technik*, 72:8 (2023), pp.32–35.

35   Robert von Dombrowski, 'Neue Aufgaben für die Artillerie', *cpm defence network*, 30 March 2024.

36   Waldemar Geiger, 'Keine Zeitenwende bei der Aufstellung neuer Artillerieverbände', *Hartpunkt*, 31 March 2024.

The 35 MARS have undergone modernisation to the MARS II standard. It was decided that the five MARS II rocket artillery systems gifted to Ukraine should be replaced with the Israeli PULS (Precise and Universal Launching System) rocket artillery system, which has a range of 12 to 300 kilometres.[37]

Recruitment

As a consequence of demographic change, declining birth cohorts and a labour shortage that now extends far beyond the skilled worker sector, the problems of recruiting new personnel represents a persistent challenge. The number of military personnel has remained relatively static for an extended period, with the current figure standing at approximately 182,000 soldiers and an Army share of approximately 61,000. This figure has been below the target of 184,000 for several years and considerably below the 203,300 active servicewomen and men planned by 2031. The 203,300 personnel, based on NATO commitments, are comprised of 190,800 regular and professional soldiers and 12,500 volunteers engaged in military service. Moreover, the plan calls for the recruitment of 60,000 commissioned and 200,000 un-commissioned reservists.

In addition to the annual regeneration quota of over 30,000 individuals, this would necessitate an annual increase of approximately 3,000 individuals from the present until 2031. These figures appear to be entirely implausible when viewed in light of the outcomes of recent recruitment efforts. Furthermore, the current NATO plans are purported to set a target of 'well over 272,000' soldiers.

The number of applicants in 2022 and 2023 was approximately 44,000, which is below the number of applicants prior to the Russian war of aggression against Ukraine, when it was 53,000 and 57,000 per year.

Consequently, new advertising campaigns were initiated on numerous occasions, and new recruitment incentives were introduced. However, the success of these initiatives was limited. A more decentralised approach is now being pursued, giving commanders more responsibility.

The latest initiative, which still requires parliamentary endorsement, proposes the introduction of a 'new military service' in lieu of the current 'voluntary military service as a special civic obligation'. The objective of the new military service is to expand the reservoir of available reservists and is to last between six and 23 months. The length of military service is to be determined on an individual basis. Nevertheless, all other potential forms of service, including temporary and professional soldier roles, will remain in effect.

In addition, it is imperative to modify the compulsory military service regulations. A mandatory survey is to be introduced for men, in which they are asked to indicate their willingness and ability to perform military service. For women and individuals

---

37   Clemens Speer, 'Die Zukunft der Artillerietruppe –Rüstungsprojekte & Organisation', https://suv.report/die-zukunft-der-artillerietruppe-ruestungsprojekte-organisation/.

identifying as other genders, responding to the questions is optional. Only those who have indicated their willingness to perform military service will be invited to undergo an assessment.

Conclusion and Summary

There is no denying that the current threat to our security in Europe is real: 'A Russian attack on NATO territory is no longer an abstract possibility, but a tangible danger.' In a period of between five and eight years, Russia has rebuilt its armed forces in a way that would enable it to attack NATO territory. It is therefore imperative that a credible deterrent is provided to prevent war.[38] The war of aggression against Ukraine, which expanded in February 2022 and continues to be fought, has served as a catalyst, accelerating the process the army had started. This war demonstrates that land forces continue to play a pivotal role in modern warfare.

In conclusion, fundamental decisions have been reached and it can be stated that the Army is undergoing a transition to a new structure that will enable it to effectively address the current security challenges and meet its NATO commitments. As a result of this reorientation, the German Army will become the backbone and primary guarantor of Central European security.

This development is, in parts, a return to 'classical' German thinking, stressing the importance of the Army and the land domain for a country that finds itself in the middle of Europe. The resulting strengthening of the land component, an ambitious process which has been initiated with great effort, has as its the cornerstones Division 2025 and the permanent deployment of *Panzerbrigade* 45 in Lithuania. The German Army of the future will transform, but it will not be characterised by a fundamentally new organisational design.

At the same time, the special fund has established the requisite conditions to facilitate tangible advancement over the forthcoming years, leading to the comprehensive provisioning of the Army's units and formations. A number of unfortunate decisions that were taken in 2011 have now been rectified. Yet it was evident from the outset that the special fund would prove inadequate for the complete closure of the capability gaps that have emerged over the three decades of the 'peace dividend'. Given it is projected to be nearly depleted by the end of 2027, the subsequent financing will have to be sourced from the defence budget in its current form. It is currently unclear where the additional €30 to €40 billion required for the defence budget from 2028 onwards will be sourced. Consequently, Defence Minister Pistorius, who has argued that Germany should allocate at least two percent of its gross domestic product in the long term, remains adamant that only an incremental increase in the defence budget will ensure the fund's long-term viability.

---

38   General Carsten Breuer, the German Chief of Defence.

Notwithstanding the encouraging indications of recent years, the path ahead remains lengthy and challenging. As early as 2023, the Chief of the German Army explicitly cautioned that the operational readiness of the division promised by Germany from 2025 could only be achieved to a 'limited extent'. The operational readiness of the second division, which the *Bundeswehr* intends to provide from 2027, is also 'unrealistic', given that this division will not have received the requisite large-scale equipment by that time. Without further action, he said, 'the Army will not be able to sustain itself in high-intensity-combat' and will be limited in its ability to fulfil its obligations to NATO.[39] Germany undoubtedly has the economic capacity and financial resources to shoulder this responsibility. The pivotal factor is the willingness of responsible and accountable politicians to act. But trouble is coming and, under the circumstances, measures are being taken. No other choice exists, and the words of the Roman writer Flavius Vegetius are timelessly true: 'If you want peace, prepare for war'.

39   See https://www.bild.de/bild-plus/politik/inland/politik-inland/bundeswehr-general-heer-kann-aufgaben-nicht-glaubwuerdig-wahrnehmen-83509072.bild.html.

4

The Historical Evolution of Corps and Division in the British Army: Discontinuities and Continuities

Paul Latawski

For more than two centuries the corps and division have been an important part of the British Army's order of battle and a major factor in its warfighting success. From the Napoleonic wars to the Boer War, the corps and division were somewhat ephemeral military entities insofar as they only existed in the British Army in wartime. By the twentieth century, the corps and division were on their way to becoming established formations in peace as well as war. The corps in the period of the two World Wars between 1914 and 1945 remained a formation raised in wartime, but during the Cold War found a permanent place in the Army's order of battle. The division, however, enjoyed greater permanence as it became an established part of the British Army in the run-up to the First World War and has been part of the order of battle ever since. Without a doubt the World Wars of the twentieth century provided the British Army with a substantial body of wartime experience that decisively shaped the conceptual foundations in the employment of both corps and division in the service. The core of this operational experience was against peer adversaries in conventional warfighting. Although the first half of the twentieth century was central to the development of these formations, in the broader sweep of the last two centuries, the British corps and division did in fact operate in multiple environments and against a range of conventional and unconventional adversaries thus providing a diversity of warfighting experience. The Cold War brought limited operational employment for both the corps and division, but new challenges emerged driven by new technologies. From this historical experience, what discontinuities and continuities can be identified in the more than two centuries of the corps and division in the British Army?

Historical Experience: The British Corps and Division in War and Peace

The Long Nineteenth Century

In the British Army, the corps and division entered the order of battle later than in Continental European armies. Sir John Moore's operations against Copenhagen in 1807 saw the earliest employment of a divisional organisation in the British Army. It was the Duke of Wellington, however, in the Peninsula campaign, who established the division as a standard formation in the British Army structure. On 18 June 1809, Wellington created one cavalry and four infantry divisions.[1] Between 1809 and 1814 Wellington employed a maximum of 10 divisions in the Peninsula campaign. His force was made possible by incorporating a Portuguese brigade in seven of his 10 divisions and for a time into an eighth division.[2] The integration of Portuguese brigades was pioneering as it created, for the first time, British-led multinational divisions. Wellington also established the Army's first corps on the eve of the Battle of Waterloo by mixing Hanoverian, and Dutch-Belgian troops with their more experienced British counterparts. This first British Army corps did not function as a tactical entity as Wellington controlled his divisions directly and had multinational integration as the main reason for its existence.

The remainder of the nineteenth century saw divisions employed in only a few conflicts: the Crimean War (1853–1856), intervention in Egypt in 1882 and the Boer War (1899–1902). The British Army fielded six divisions in the Crimean War, in Egypt three divisions and in South Africa one corps and 12 divisions.[3] All of these divisions existed only for the duration of the conflict. These nineteenth century wars were limited conflicts in terms of geographical scope and scale. Without the driver of a general European conflict which would have required British Army structures more akin to other European powers, the place of the corps and division was more the subject of discussion rather than action. As early as 1852, Prince George, the Duke of Cambridge, argued for the introduction of a 'divisional system' integrating all arms in the formation.[4] By 1875, the division entered the Army organisation, albeit on paper, as the division and corps became part of mobilisation arrangements. This reform was the result of the influence of the Prussian Army's campaigns in the 1860s and 1870s, which saw the efficient

---

1   *General Orders: Spain and Portugal: April 27th to December 28th, 1809,* vol. I (London: 1811), pp.70–71.
2   Malyn Newitt, 'The Portuguese Army', in Gregory Fremont-Barnes (ed.), *Armies of the Napoleonic Wars* (Barnsley, South Yorkshire: Pen and Sword Military, 2011), pp.221–222.
3   Material on nineteenth century drawn from research for Paul Latawski, 'Part 4: A Historical Perspective of the Division in the British Army' in, *Army Field Manual, Volume 1, Part 1A: Divisional Tactics* (London: Ministry of Defence, 2024).
4   'Observations on the Organisation of the British Army at Home', December 1852, in Colonel Willoughby Verner, *The Military Life of H.R.H. George, Duke of Cambridge* (London: John Murray, 1905), p.39. See also Giles St. Aubyn, *The Royal George 1819–1904: The Life of H.R.H. Prince George Duke of Cambridge* (London: Constable, 1963), pp.57–58; Hew Strachan, *Wellington's Legacy: The Reform of the British Army, 1830–54* (Manchester: Manchester University Press, 1984), pp.160–161.

mobilisation of large formations for war.[5] In the case of the corps, the memorandum of Edward Stanhope, then Secretary of War, defined the role of the British Army and the creation of two (paper) corps for home defence, with one of the corps to be deployable overseas. This would eventually evolve following the Boer War into six army corps commands with geographical areas assigned to be the basis of mobilisation of the corps.[6]

Stanhope's mobilisation scheme would be tested by the outbreak of the Second Boer War (1899–1902). Although passably successful in assembling the formations for service in South Africa, the real challenges rested in their employment. The British Army's insurgent Boer opponents precluded the singular corps and the 11 divisions from operating as complete tactical entities in a conventional force-on-force manner. Instead, these formations served in an area security role that presaged some of the post Second World War insurgencies. The character of the conflict in South Africa led to a span of command problems caused by corps commanders not utilising divisional headquarters and struggling to control the myriad lower-level formations and units.[7]

Overall, the South African war represented a culmination in the development of the corps and division in the nineteenth century. The shortcomings of this British formation model persisted throughout the nineteenth century and into the early years of the twentieth century. The weaknesses of this model stemmed from the fact that the corps and division were not standing organisations but sprang to life only at the outbreak of war. With each conflict the corps or division was thus an operational reinvention. The British experience of the nineteenth century in terms of the development of the corps and division was a story less of innovation than of belated emulation of wider European military trends regarding the organisation of armies. The experience of the Boer War, however, set in train reforms in the British Army. Richard Burdon Haldane, who became the Secretary of State for War in December 1905, established six large infantry divisions and one cavalry division as a permanent peacetime formation. These regular divisions would be augmented in wartime by the mobilisation of 14 divisions of the new Territorial Force.[8] Under the Haldane reforms, however, the corps remained something to be improvised after the outbreak of war.

The World Wars 1914–1945
The period of the two World Wars saw unprecedented wartime expansions of the British Army making it comparable to other major Continental European powers. This in turn

5   A. W. Preston, 'British Military Thought, 1856–1890' in Harold E. Raugh Jr. (ed.), *The British Army 1815–1914* (Aldershot: Ashgate, 2006), pp.383–384.

6   John K. Dunlop, *The Development of the British Army 1899–1914* (London: Methuen, 1938), pp.307, 314.

7   Testimony given by Maj Gen Sir H. E. Colville on 26 February 1903, in *Minutes of Evidence Taken Before the Royal Commission on the War in South Africa*, Volume II, CD.1791 (London: His Majesty's Stationery Office, 1903), pp.289, 294.

8   Edward M. Spiers, *Haldane: An Army Reformer* (Edinburgh: Edinburgh University Press, 1980), pp.81 & 106.

led to the numbers of corps and divisions growing enormously in line with wartime force expansion. At the start of the First World War, the British Expeditionary Force started from the modest base of only one shadow corps headquarters and seven divisions in its order of battle to expand by war's end to a force that at its maximum extent numbered 28 corps and 85 divisions (excluding Dominion and Imperial formations). After an interwar interlude where once again the corps disappeared, the divisional numbers were reduced to four and then later five peacetime regular divisions with territorial divisions numbering 14 and by the 1930s 12. The British Army's rearmament programme saw the number of divisions increase by September 1939 to two armoured, seven regular infantry and 24 first-line and second-line territorial divisions upon which to build the wartime force. The British Army would eventually raise 14 corps and 46 divisions augmented with the Dominion and Imperial formations in the Second World War.[9]

The First World War triggered major development of the operational responsibilities of both the corps and division in the British Army. At the onset of the war the corps served as an administrative entity and controlled a limited range of corps assets. As the war progressed, however, assigned corps troops grew in number including engineer, signals, logistics and other specialised units. It would also in due course have a role in air-land integration as it acquired observation and reconnaissance capability. The shift to indirect fire during the First World War gave the corps a critical function in delivering more sophisticated fire planning for the utilisation of firepower resources on the battle-field.[10] In the course of the war, the corps acquired control of the artillery brigades with medium guns that gave the corps a significant capability to engage in the deep artillery battle. The composition of corps assets could vary according to the assigned task. The corps exercised tactical command and control over its subordinate divisions and in doing so acquired a key role in the planning and execution of operations.

The First World War represented a kind of military coming of age for the division in the British Army. The biggest change to the division, however, was in its organic fire-power. In 1914 the artillery in an infantry division consisted of 76 guns, but by 1918 the number had dropped to 48. On the surface this seemed like a regression, but the artillery did not disappear instead being shifted to centrally controlled units. What is more, the introduction of trench mortars, which numbered 36 in the division by 1918, went some way in offsetting the loss of artillery pieces. The most dramatic increase could be seen in the numbers of machine guns rising from only 24 in 1914 to 400 in 1918.[11]

9   Material on the World Wars and Cold War is based on research conducted for Paul Latawski, 'The British Corps and Division in the Twentieth Century: Historical Evolution and Doctrinal Context' in, Tim Bean, Edward Flint, James E. Kitchen, Paul Latawski (eds), *Orchestrating Warfighting: A History of the British Army's Corps and Divisions at War since 1914* (London: Routledge, 2024), Chapter 1.

10   Sanders Marble, *British Artillery on the Western Front in the First World War* (Farnham: Ashgate, 2013), pp.67–71.

11   A. F. Becke, *History of the Great War. Order of Battle of Divisions, Part 2A The Regular British Divisions* (London: HMSO, 1936), pp.7, 25–26, 30, 47–48, 53–54, 59–60.

With the corps and division such significant components of the British Army's order of battle, the issue of doctrine for their employment became a pressing issue, particularly as no formation specific doctrine existed prior to the outbreak of war. Instead, the omnibus *Field Service Regulations, Part I: Operations* covered a broad range of topics and was meant to be applicable at all levels in the Army.[12] This did not prove enough doctrine as the British Army faced a daunting wartime challenge of orchestrating combined arms offensive operations to break through layers of defensive trench systems. Remarkably, no doctrine would emerge for the corps during the war for its role in solving this problem. The division, however, acquired its first doctrine. From the first example of doctrine for the division (*Instructions for the Training of Divisions for Offensive Action*) appearing in December 1916 to the final wartime divisional doctrine (*The Division in Attack*) produced in November 1918, the focus was very tactical and formulaic for producing a set-piece combined arms offensive operation on very narrow frontages.[13] Although divisional doctrine for defensive operations (*The Division in Defence*) appeared in one wartime edition in May 1918, the overall focus on formation specific doctrine was very narrow in its offensive tactical function.[14]

The interwar period saw the corps disappear once again from the Army's order of battle and the remaining hollowed-out divisions atrophied despite the hard-won experience of war. Although much-reduced in numbers and financial resources, the British Army could at least in theory think conceptually about the future development of the corps and division. The picture between 1919 and 1939, however, was one more of conceptual drift than of dynamic innovation. While it is true that Britain did show early and impressive innovation with its experimentation with mechanised forces in the late 1920s, this effort did not bear fruit in useable formation doctrine. Indeed, the only divisional doctrine to emerge was *Mechanised and Armoured Formations 1929* and its successor *Modern Formations 1931*.[15] They were essentially experimental doctrine providing an exploration of ideas rather than something useable in war. With war looming in Europe, the Army set about comprehensively updating its doctrine, which would see the return of formation specific doctrine.

The Second World War once again witnessed the rapid expansion of the British Army leading to the large-scale creation of the corps and divisions for a global conflict. The function of the corps in the British Army followed the pattern of the First World War with the corps being allocated various amounts of engineering, artillery and specialist armour capabilities that it could allocate to the divisions assigned to the corps. The corps had a critical role in assigning heavy and medium artillery concentrated in AGRAs [Army Groups Royal Artillery]. Nevertheless, the assets directly owned by the corps

---

12   *General Staff, Field Service Regulations, Part I: Operations* (London: War Office, 1914).

13   See *SS135: Instructions for the Training of Divisions for Offensive Action* (London: War Office, 1916) and *SS135: The Division in Attack* (London: War Office, 1918).

14   *SS210: The Division in Defence* (London: War Office, 1918).

15   *Mechanised and Armoured Formations 1929 Provisional* (London: War Office, 1929); *Modern Formations 1931 Provisional* (London: War Office, 1931).

was limited, particularly in the European theatre with its central capability being the command, control and planning of its headquarters. The geographical scope of employment of the corps was wider than in the previous world war. This led to the expansion in the functions in corps operations. In the Burma campaign (1944–1945), the corps owned more assets of a kind that typically were held at the army level. The vast geographic distances made this necessary and gave the corps more autonomy of operations in the Southeast Asian theatre. The flexibility of the Second World War corps was also illustrated by the British intervention in the Greek Civil War in 1944–1945. The III Corps that deployed to Greece had an initial stabilisation mission that morphed into the Corps becoming a theatre-wide headquarters covering all of Greece and having under its command a second corps tasked with fighting an urban battle in Athens to suppress Greek communist insurgents.

During the Second World War, the British Army employed a greater variety of divisional types including armoured, airborne, cavalry, infantry and a 'mixed' division. The infantry division was the most numerous and enjoyed more mobility through motorisation and possessed more organic firepower. With the increased resources, however, came a major increase in the logistical requirements to sustain the Second World War division. The need for more sustainment was illustrated by the growth in the 'divisional slice' which amounted to 40,000 men in total.[16] The armoured and airborne divisions were new innovations to the British Army's order of battle. The armoured division underwent a bumpy road of development with its organisation undergoing nine revisions and its tank strength being reduced to create a better balance between its organic arms. The airborne division was a light scales formation lacking firepower and sustainability as it had to be transported into battle by air.

During the Second World War, no formal doctrine emerged for the corps mirroring the experience of the previous world war. The corps remained a formation of no fixed organisation and was allocated resources as necessary for the assigned corps task. There was, however, no lack of doctrine for the division produced during the Second World War. Generally taking the form of short pamphlets, the doctrine focused on separate functions for the infantry division such as the attack, defence and the advance.[17] Doctrine for the armoured division differed in being concentrated in one document and had a messier gestation, seeing a variety of publications before definitive doctrine emerged.[18]

---

16   Colonel H. W. Wilson, *Administrative Planning* (London: War Office, 1952), pp.62, 181.
17   For example, see: 'Operations, Military Training Pamphlet No.23, Part II – The Infantry Division in the Defence, 1942', *The War Office*, 23 March 1942; 'Operations, Military Training Pamphlet No. 23, Part IX – The Infantry Division in the Attack, 1941', *The War Office*, 21 July 1941; 'Operations, Military Training Pamphlet No.23, Part X – The Infantry Division in the Advance, 1941', *The War Office*, 22 September 1941.
18   The definitive wartime armoured division doctrine: 'MTP No.41, The Tactical Handling of the Armoured Division and its Components'; 'Part 1, The Tactical Handling of Armoured Divisions in July 1943'; 'Part 2, The Armoured Regiment in February 1943'; 'Part 3, The Motor Battalion in June 1943'.

Certain problems dogged doctrine for the armoured division with the most important being the poor practice of tactical level combined arms. The legacy of interwar doctrinal thinking that stressed the tank operating independently rather than in conjunction with other arms lingered in the wartime doctrine. Its resolution came more from experience on the battlefield rather than doctrine providing a template on how to practice combined arms integration.

The two World Wars saw an enormous number of corps and divisions raised. For the British Army such scale is unlikely to be seen again. This period was undoubtedly the most formative period in shaping the corps and division as warfighting formations. This is reflected in a variety of ways including changes to organisation and the creation of a body of doctrine. The corps and division were employed in a variety of theatres and environments during the two World Wars. The employment of corps and division was to concentrate force at the decisive point in their operations. Spatially this meant that operations occurred on limited frontages. This was particularly true in the European arena which saw the largest scale employment of the corps and division. Limited frontages allowed firepower to be concentrated on the battlefield. Even in the more fluid and dispersed theatres such as in Burma, concentration at the decisive point still occurred. This reality underlined the importance of the corps and division in delivering battle winning firepower at scale.

The Cold War

The Cold War ushered in a significant dichotomy in the type of formations required to meet likely contingencies. In Cold War Europe, the British Army faced a massive Soviet conventional military threat requiring the corps and division to be capable of conventional warfighting to underpin conventional deterrence. The sprawling global British security commitments, however, favoured infantry brigades that had characteristics more suitable for operating in more austere, less developed regions of the world and yet overmatching less formidable conventional or unconventional opponents. By the 1960s, the need for the overseas role of the brigade gradually disappeared, but that of the corps and division continued to the Cold War's end.

The Cold War saw for the first time the corps made part of the peacetime order of battle of the British Army. The creation of I British Corps in the British Army of the Rhine in late 1951 established a formation that remained in existence throughout the Cold War in Germany only being disbanded in August 1992. For a brief period, a second British corps (II Corps) was raised during the Suez crisis of 1956. It was from the outset a multinational headquarters integrating French staff officers. Judged a success in multinational integration, II Corps disappeared soon after the Suez crisis was over.[19] I Corps remained in northern Germany as part of the British-led NATO Northern Army Group (NORTHAG), occupying a sector in the 'layer cake' deployments in NORTHAG that

---

19   Stockwell, 'Report on Operation Musketeer', Annex B: Lessons and Recommendations, 1 February 1957, pp.4, 6, 7, WO288/79, The National Archives, London.

also included Belgian, German and Dutch corps throughout the Cold War. Given the static deployment of I Corps, it controlled on a more permanent basis assets designed to support its subordinate divisions and brigades. The composition of corps troops typically included a mixture of reconnaissance, artillery, air defence, engineer and signals units. As was the case in the two World Wars, longer range artillery was a key corps asset for delivering firepower to support subordinate formations.

The British Army retained more divisions after the Second World War than in the interwar period. In the early 1950s the British Army fielded three armoured and five infantry divisions better equipped and not so hollowed out as their interwar counterparts. Most divisions were based in the United Kingdom and Germany, with a few deployed to the Middle East and Far East.[20] This eight-division total gradually declined and, from the early 1970s to the end of the Cold War, the British Army consistently fielded four or five active divisions.[21] During the Cold War the number of division types gradually declined from three to one. In the wake of the Second World War, the British Army had airborne, armoured and infantry divisions. The airborne division was the first to go followed by the infantry division, which lingered longer because of the utility of its headquarters capability in internal security and counterinsurgency operations that persisted in the wider global arena. By the 1970s, the only division type was exclusively armoured. With increased firepower and effective combined arms organisation, the Cold War armoured division was operationally more relevant to meeting the Soviet threat in Europe. Moreover, growth in its combat capabilities meant that the Cold War armoured division delivered much more combat power than its Second World War counterpart.

The emergence of nuclear weapons on the battlefield during the Cold War had a profound effect on the employment of both corps and division. The corps and division, particularly when its assets were concentrated on the battlefield, was now a vulnerable target for tactical nuclear weapons. On the nuclear battlefield, formation survival required a more dispersed mobile force with redundant command and control capability. This new reality stood juxtaposed to the enduring need to concentrate force density and firepower necessary to defeat the large Soviet conventional armoured threat. The result of this changed threat environment was a conundrum that defied an easy solution if any at all.[22]

The Soviet threat in Europe was not the only kind of threat faced by the British Army. In November 1956, Britain and France mounted an intervention in Egypt that saw II Corps established for the operation. Although Suez was a political disaster

20   'Size and Shape of the Armed Forces', 30 October 1950, CAB129/42, The National Archives, London.

21   Data on the number of divisions taken from 'Statements on Defence Estimates', 1970–1983, The National Archives, London; International Institute for Strategic Studies, *The Military Balance*, 1972–89, see https://www.iiss.org/publications/the-military-balance/.

22   See Simon Moody, *Imagining Nuclear War in the British Army, 1945–1989* (Oxford: Oxford University Press, 2020).

in military terms, the II Corps was seen to have worked well as a multinational headquarters.[23] In the global arena, the British Army repeatedly conducted internal security and counterinsurgency operations. Some of these involved the use of divisional headquarters. In Palestine in the late 1940s, the 6th Airborne Division and the 1st Division served in this capacity with the 17th Division engaged in this role in Borneo in the 1960s.[24] The only conventional employment of a British-led division occurred in the Korean War (1950–1953) with the establishment of 1 Commonwealth Division. The Commonwealth Division was the only case of a British-led division being involved in conventional warfighting. Its uniqueness rested on its multinational composition, with its troops drawn from Britain, Canada, Australia, New Zealand, India and South Africa. Moreover, this coalition formation operated within a wider American-led coalition.[25]

The British Army entered the Cold War period with mature practice for the corps and mature doctrine for the division as a result of the experience of the two World Wars. The British Army received its first corps doctrine in the early Cold War period with *Command and Organisation of a Corps Headquarters in War 1950*. This corps doctrine essentially captured the Second World War experience. Similarly, early Cold War British Army doctrine for the division consolidated wartime lessons. Cold War corps and division doctrine, however, would eventually blur into 'formation' doctrine for both formations.[26] Divisional doctrine only reappeared in the last decade of the Cold War.[27] As formation doctrine developed from the 1960s onwards to the end of the Cold War, the issue of trying to blend conventional land operations with battlefield nuclear weapons dominated doctrine development. Resolving the problem of how to concentrate the warfighting strength of formations at decisive points for effect while having to stay dispersed to survive a nuclear strike was something that formation doctrine never found a workable solution to. Despite this unresolved conundrum, the British Army persisted in its attempts to develop its formation doctrine to meet the evolving challenges of the Cold War.

23   Stockwell, 'Report on Operation Musketeer'.
24   For a description of these operations, see General Horatius Murray, *'A Very Fine Commander': The Memoirs of General Sir Horatius Murray* (Barnsley: Pen and Sword, 2010), pp.212–223; R.D. Wilson, *Cordon and Search: With 6th Airborne Division in Palestine* (Aldershot: Gale and Polden Limited, 1949); 'Joint Report on the Borneo Campaign', 27 January 1967, Army Historical Branch, Ministry of Defence, London.
25   See Brigadier C. N. Barclay, *The First Commonwealth Division: The Story of British Commonwealth Land Forces in Korea, 1950–1953* (Aldershot: Gale and Polden Limited, 1954); Tim Carew, *Korea: The Commonwealth at War* (London: Cassell, 1967).
26   See for example *Land Operations. Part 3 of the 1964 Land Battle thus became Land Operations, Volume II: Non-Nuclear Operations, Part 1: Formation Tactics* (London: Ministry of Defence, March 1971).
27   *Army Field Manual, Volume 1, Part 2: The Armoured Division in Battle* (London: Ministry of Defence, 1983).

Conclusion: Discontinuities and Continuities

From the beginning of the nineteenth century to the end of the Cold War, the corps and division underwent an evolution that saw both formations become established fixtures in the British Army's order of battle. This journey, however, has both its discontinuities and continuities. The first among the discontinuities is that of scale. In the nineteenth century both the Napoleonic and Crimean wars saw sizeable numbers of divisions fielded. The peak in scale of both the corps and division occurred during the two World Wars. The Cold War saw the British Army order of battle possessing a single corps, but more numerous divisions. Contrasting this legacy with the 30-plus years since the end of the Cold War, the British Army has been effectively reduced to a single corps (albeit a multinational NATO one) and two divisions, of which only one can be realistically fielded at any given time.[28]

The second discontinuity resides in formation role specialisation. The corps emerged in the two World Wars as a formation focused on the tactical battle mostly in a confined spatial arena with the wider battlespace management the responsibility of army and army group levels. In contrast, the post-Cold War corps not only must be capable of conducting the tactical battle, but it must be reconfigurable to operate in wider operational contexts subsuming a role that earlier would have been the purview of the army or theatre level. In the case of the division, the story is one of multiple divisional types being reduced to a single organisational type. What is more, the single type does not necessarily follow a standard pattern on deployment as illustrated by the British Army divisions deployed in the two Gulf Wars (1990 and 2003). Thus, formation role specialisation has been replaced by the bespoke formation tailored to the operational deployment.

The third discontinuity is in the realm of the spatial employment of the corps and division on the battlefield. Throughout the nineteenth century to the end of the World Wars in the middle of the twentieth century, corps and division were fought in a concentrated manner on the battlefield. The Cold War, however, marked a rupture in this practice. The advent of nuclear weapons and greater accuracy and lethality of conventional weapon systems created a requirement for the corps and division to fight in a more dispersed manner to survive. In the post-Cold War era, this problem is only likely to be exacerbated as persistent surveillance makes the battlefield more transparent. Armed uncrewed aerial systems and long-range precision weaponry, such as rocket artillery, will require formations to disperse and hide while they fight.[29] This creates an imperative

---

28   See *Defence in a Competitive Age* (London: Ministry of Defence, 2021), p.20; *Future Soldier Guide* (London: Ministry of Defence, 2021), p.14.

29   Ben Barrie, 'Russia's War in Ukraine: What are the Emerging Military Lessons', in Nigel Gould-Davies (ed.), *Strategic Survey 2022: The Annual Assessment of Geopolitics* (London: International Institute for Strategic Studies, 2022), pp.39–40: https://www.iiss.org/globalassets/media-library---content--migration/files/publications/strategic-survey-2022/strategic-survey-2022_military-lessons-russia-war-in-ukraine.pdf.

for the division to find new means of survivability while concentrating force to achieve decisive effect.

Turning to elements of continuity, the first and most important was the need to underpin the employment of the corps and division with a conceptual framework – namely doctrine. On the surface, the story of formation doctrine is not one of coherent development. It was not until the First World War that formal doctrine emerged for the division and not until after the Second World War that it emerged for the corps while the interwar period was something of a void in producing formation doctrine. By the end of the Second World War, however, these problems had been largely rectified. British Army doctrine since then has evolved with changing technologies and lessons from armed conflicts. The continuous development of corps and division doctrine remains vital if these formations are to retain a place in twenty-first century warfare.

The second continuity is the importance of the corps and division to deliver firepower on the battlefield. If there is an enduring lesson from the evolution of the corps and division from the two World Wars onwards it is their vital role in delivering concentrated firepower. The fires capabilities of corps and division were the key to success against peer adversaries in the first half of the twentieth century. The requirement for formation dispersal from the Cold War onwards does not alter this key role. What has changed is that the corps and division deliver firepower over a wider area and with precision. Concentration is now about using the mobility of fire to achieve scale of lethality when required at decisive points rather than physical proximity.

The third and final continuity concerns the British Army's historical experience of multinational British-led corps and divisions. During the Napoleonic wars the British Army created a multinational corps and multinational divisions. In the Cold War, II Corps during the Suez operation and the 1st Commonwealth Division in the Korean War are other examples of British-led multinational formations. After the Cold War, Britain would deploy the British-led multinational Allied Rapid Reaction Corps in Southeast Europe in the 1990s and Afghanistan in the 2000s. Similarly, a British-led multinational division operated in stabilisation operations in Bosnia between 1995–2004.[30] An important historical role of British multinational formations is to augment British mass. With the British Army experiencing a steady decline in numbers of troops in the post-Cold War period, multinational composition of a British-led corps and division may have become a necessary means to maintain credible formation warfighting capability.

---

30   Michael Clarke and Andrew Duncan, 'Replacing SFOR in Bosnia: Options for DFOR in 1998', *Centre for Defence Studies*, London Defence Studies 43 (December 1997), pp.4–9; NATO, 'NATO Handbook', *Public Diplomacy Division* (2006), pp.145–147.

5

Thinking About the Nuclear Battlefield:
Lessons for the British Army from the Early Cold War?

Andrew Stewart

The continuing war instigated by Russia in Ukraine has raised questions and concerns about the character of future conflict and how it is changing. Much attention has focused on the role played by unmanned aircraft systems (UAS), one element of a technology enabled approach to battle which has saturated the modern operating environment with sensors and detection. General Valery Zaluzhny, then Ukraine's commander-in-chief, explained in an October 2023 interview with *The Economist* that '… sensors can identify any concentration of forces, and modern precision weapons can destroy it'.[1] Another commenter has agreed arguing this 'drastically enhances lethality on the land battlefield, as it puts an end to the safety of the rear, as it questions the very principles of stealth in every domain, of concealment, of concentration of forces, of tactical surprise…'[2] With it appearing to have become an almost impossible space in which to operate, understanding the modern battlefield and its newfound transparency – and finding the means to mitigate against its effects – represents a key challenge for land forces.

Discussion of how a new weapon system or tactical approach creates an 'empty battlefield' is most commonly first associated with the Franco-Prussian War. The impact of an increased concentration of firepower, enhanced range and greater accuracy and the resulting stalemate – and tactical crisis – this produced on the Western Front further fuelled the

---

1 'Ukraine's commander-in-chief on the breakthrough he needs to beat Russia', *The Economist*, 1 November 2023.
2 Guillaume Garnier and Pierre Néron-Bancel, '"At the Other Side of the Hill": The Benefits and False Promises of Battlefield Transparency', *Focus stratégique – Ifri*, 118 (May 2024); Franz-Stefan Gady, 'How an Army of Drones Changed the Battlefield in Ukraine', *Foreign Policy*, 6 December 2023, https://foreignpolicy.com/2023/12/06/ukraine-russia-war-drones-stalemate-frontline-counteroffensive-strategy/.

debate.[3] Manoeuvre was restored to the Second World War battlefield, most notably by the German Army and Air Force employing a highly effective joint and combined approach. This, at least in part, was subsequently attributed to time spent during the interwar period assessing the failings of the previous war and then identifying key lessons which were adopted through doctrinal and organisational change. But the August 1945 atomic raids against Japan pointed to, what to many, seemed the introduction of a new decisive weapon system and a significant adaptation to how future wars would be fought. Much of what had been learned during the course of the war was now arguably useless.

Responding to the potentially huge impact of technological change was not the only consideration for British military planners as they struggled to match resources to requirements. Faced with the reality of the post-war world, notes prepared for the head of the British Army Field Marshal Bill Slim, in advance of his April 1952 Kermit Roosevelt lectures in the United States, explained the problem that had emerged in attempting to balance the requirements of 'end of Empire' irregular warfare while preparing for a possible hot, shooting Cold War. Following the war's end, the British Army was effectively split into two parts. The first was an active regular force stationed at home or abroad, initially at least intended in part to act as an occupation force in Germany but also as garrison forces across the British Empire/Commonwealth. The other was the auxiliary, the reservists, militia and volunteers supplementing a regular cadre.[4] In a period of constrained budgets, the focus for regular forces – the 'petrol feet' according to one description – was European security and the Soviet threat.[5] This meant leaving reserve formations – the 'brown knees' – and their often second-rate equipment to deal with the rest and, according to Slim's prepared notes, meant 'taking a risk with our eyes open'.[6] This seemed to echo Slim's own views; in 1947, as the first post-war Commandant of the Imperial Defence College, he had warned that conventional forces alone would not be enough to defeat Russia and there was a need to ensure that 'realism not be allowed to degenerate into defeatism.'[7] As could perhaps be argued remains the case now, managing Britain's defence posture and strategic commitments and finding some measure of balance between competing requirements is not for the faint hearted.

3   James J. Schneider, 'The theory of the empty battlefield', *The RUSI Journal*, 132:3 (1987), pp.37–44; Randy Noorman, 'The Return of the Tactical Crisis', *Modern War Institute*, 27 March 2024, https://mwi.westpoint.edu/the-return-of-the-tactical-crisis/.

4   'General notes on post-war planning: Conference with Cs-in-C at the Staff College, Camberley, 16 September 1945', Joint Services Command and Staff College Archives, Shrivenham. The actual 'secret' conference was convened in October to discuss the Army's future needs; 'British Generals Meet', *The New York Times*, 11 October 1945.

5   Allan Mallinson, *The Making of the British Army: From the English Civil War to the War on Terror* (London: Transworld Publishers, 2011), p.523.

6   'Notes for CIGS Lecture to the U.S. National War College', n.d.; they were most likely prepared by his MA, Lieutenant-Colonel Charles Harington, WO216/953, The National Archives, London.

7   'Imperial Defence College – General Policy', Chiefs of Staff Committee, COS (47) 153rd meeting held on Wednesday, 10 December 1947, DEFE4/9, The National Archives, London.

Thinking About the Next War

Despite the challenges which existed in the years following the end of the Second World War, this did not mean that the question of how to fight on and survive the new conventional nuclear battlefield was ignored. Patrick Blackett – who won the Noble Prize for Physics in 1948 – was a naval officer during the First World War, a senior scientific adviser during the next, a pioneer of operational research and one of the most influential defence commentators in the early Cold War years. Writing more than 60 years ago, he argued that: 'Traditionally, Britain has been averse to thinking about war in between fighting wars; once they are over, we tend to forget them until the next time.'[8] This is a reasonable argument to make when considering the wider span of British military history but he was not quite correct on this occasion. What has been referred to as 'the speculation phase' of the late 1940s and early 1950s was taking place around him in what is an illustrative example of the value of adopting an intellectually informed approach in the face of an apparently intractable problem.[9]

As the British Army thought about the possible impact of these new weapons, there were some wide-ranging discussions in journals and the media. These also extended into political and public interventions and a leading voice in the debate was Field Marshal Viscount Bernard Montgomery. Having led the British Army prior to Bill Slim's appointment, from April 1951 to September 1958 he held the position of deputy commander of NATO's European forces (DSACEUR) and made his focus turning it into a credible military force. He identified another key consideration in 1955 when he referred to 'a revolution in military affairs brought about by scientific advances in the development of nuclear weapons and the means of delivering them', one which would force changes in warfare. He warned of a resulting increased tempo and the possibility that decisive military operations could begin almost immediately.[10] This followed his mapping of the nuclear battlefield, in a RUSI speech the year before, as he identified the key requirements for conducting successful land warfare.[11] First, there had to be what he termed 'M-Day troops', 'trained and equipped to the highest pitch: mobile, hard hitting, offensive troops of magnificent morale, very highly disciplined, under young

8   P. M. S. Blackett, *Studies of War: Nuclear and Conventional* (London: Oliver and Boyd, 1962), p.115.
9   Simon Moody, *Imagining Nuclear War in the British Army, 1945–89* (Oxford: Oxford University Press, 2020), p.18. He recorded nearly 100 articles in the leading military publications: *The RUSI Journal*, *The RUSI Journal India*, *Army Quarterly*, *British Army Review*, *Journal of the Royal Artillery*, *Royal Engineers Journal*, *Royal Armoured Corps Journal*.
10   Field Marshal Viscount Montgomery, 'Organization for War in Modern Times', *The Journal of the Royal United Services Institution*, 100:600 (November 1955), p.510.
11   Field Marshal Viscount Montgomery, 'A Look Through a Window at World War III', *The Journal of the Royal United Services Institution*, 99:596 (November 1954), pp.513–514; Simon J. Moody, 'Was There a 'Monty Method' after the Second World War? Field Marshal Bernard L. Montgomery and the Changing Character of Land Warfare, 1945–1958', *War in History*, 23:2 (2016), pp.210–229.

and active commanders' who would 'stand firm' during the opening phases of the next war. Behind them the 'Post M-Day' reserve forces 'well organised, capable of being mobilised in echelons, and each echelon receiving sufficient training in pace to ensure it is fit to fight at the time it is needed'. Supporting these he mentioned only two other requirements, 'a sound logistic and movement organisation' and, within each NATO member state, an effective Civil Defence body.[12] Wars, he seemed to be arguing, could still be fought and won.

Not everyone was so certain that the nuclear battlefield could be tamed. Another regular writer on the character of war, most notably on the role of airborne forces, was the Austrian born Czech officer, Lieutenant Colonel F. O. Miksche. In considering 'these extremely powerful weapons', he cautioned that 'on account of their special character it is difficult accurately to compare them to the conventional ones'.[13] Nonetheless, in a lengthy analysis he examined in some detail how they might be used considering both the attacking and defending forces' organisation, equipment and tactics. Ultimately, he determined there were too many unknowns at that stage of their development. His analysis did, however, extend into speculating that tactical weapons could have such an impact that ground combat would only take place with 'a completely guerrilla-like character' and 'in this case, it would be futile to speak of concentrations, breakthroughs or envelopment.'[14]

Discussion about the potentially enormous destructive effects was a major theme. Beatrice Heuser notes that attempts were made in the first decade of the Cold War to make some distinction between tactical and strategic as part of promoting ideas of a more graduated deterrence and some form of limited nuclear war.[15] The British strategist Basil Liddell Hart disagreed arguing, in 1955, that expanding strategic nuclear arsenals and the development of the hydrogen bomb made conventional forces irrelevant and unnecessary. By this stage nuclear forces existed as a deterrent or, in the event of this failing, any conflict would be resolved rapidly in 'a suicidal manner'.[16] Unsurprisingly NATO planners disagreed arguing that expansion of nuclear arsenals actually made conventional forces more decisive and a future was envisaged where 'active wars are fought by regular armies.'[17] Others contributing to the public debate agreed. As part of a

---

12   One recent examination of the British Army has argued that, in the early stages of the Cold War, 'the uncomfortable realities and implications of employing tactical nuclear weapons in terms of likely losses, the psychological impact on morale and discipline, and collateral damage to civilian populations were avoided if not ignored'; Ian F. W. Beckett, *The British Army: A New Short History* (Oxford: Oxford University Press, 2023), pp.174–175.

13   Lieutenant Colonel F. O. Miksche, *Atomic Weapons and Armies* (London: Faber, 1955), p.111.

14   Miksche, *Atomic Weapons*, p.218.

15   Beatrice Heuser, *The Evolution of Strategy: Thinking War from Antiquity to the Present* (Cambridge: Cambridge University Press, 2010), pp.371–375.

16   Letter to Editor (from Basil Liddell Hart, 'Planning for Defence, Implications of the Hydrogen Bomb'), *The Times*, 3 January 1955.

17   Colonel Robert C. Richardson III to General Schuyler, 18 January 1955, NATO Archives (declassified – PDN(2012)0008).

wider discussion about the future role of the tank, another writer argued that while the problem with tactical nuclear weapons was 'over killing', the real question was how this could best be used. The conclusion was that tactical nuclear weapons would 'probably be confined to long-range action against columns, or concentrations of tanks in areas well to the rear' most likely dropped by aircraft or long-range missiles.

Some of the conceptual work was more innovative than others, a notable example being a 1955 hypothetical study of the likely impact of nuclear weapons as they might have been deployed in May and June 1940 by Anglo-French forces when faced with the German invasion of North-East France. With its focus on 'a critical defensive position', this represented the first major attempt to assess the use of nuclear weapons at the tactical level.[18] Although flawed in so much as it failed to consider in any real detail the potential for escalation and the use of more strategic weapons, it highlighted some innovation in the conceptual process. Some of the contributions could also be imaginative in other but more speculative ways such as a 1947 article anticipating the role of infantry. Projecting nearly 20 years in the future, this concluded that the main object of military forces would be to disable atomic bombing bases, there would be no large, motorised formations and no practical role for tanks and armoured vehicles. 'The pride of place in battle' would go to 'fast-flying, lightly although expensively burdened airborne soldiers', specially equipped infantry operating in an air assault role. Even here there was some wisdom to be gained from the discussion of what personal attributes would be needed from these future soldiers. The writer concluded that the two most important qualities needed by the future infantryman 'apart from the age-old military essential – courage' would be 'agility rather than endurance and the ability to fight in small isolated groups without the psychological encouragement of large numbers of comrades within his view.'[19] When considering the potential requirements for operating in the future transparent battlespace, this would appear to retain much relevance.

Irresistible Force Meets Immovable Object

It has been argued that, ultimately, the conclusion to all this reflection and debate was a lack of any meaningful outcome beyond a conclusion that the nuclear battlefield was simply an evolution to 'conventional war but with much bigger explosions.'[20] In 1952 a Chiefs of Staff working party concluded the manpower and conventional weaponry strength of the Soviet Union and its allies could be offset by employing tactical 'low-yield' atomic weapons. The year before, in October 1951, 'Surprise Packet', the first big

---

18   Maurice Kirby and Matthew Godwin, 'Operational Research as Counterfactual History: A Retrospective Analysis of the Use of Battlefield Nuclear Weapons in the German Invasion of France and Flanders, May–June 1940', *Journal of Strategic Studies*, 31:4 (2008), pp.633–660.

19   P. H. H. Bryan, 'The Infantry of 1965', *The Army Quarterly*, LV (October 1947/January 1948), pp.225–234.

20   Moody, *Imagining Nuclear War*, p.12.

home exercise since the end of the Second World War which was conducted in southern England and involved nearly 30,000 troops, had as the primary target for the attacking force their opponent's nuclear weapon depot.[21] Tactical weapons represented a means to possibly reduce large conventional forces which were almost impossible to sustain financially while also avoiding the devastation of another long, attritional war. Indeed, the resulting *Global Strategy Paper* was predicated on the thesis that the development of nuclear weapons made total war no longer possible. Hence a reliance on deterrence and the threat, if this failed, of nuclear retaliation, but at least initially at a tactical level.

Moving forward, even if planners could conceive of an actual battlefield and some attempt at manoeuvre, this capability, or more accurately the potential for its introduction on the battlefield, although entirely untested and existing only at the conceptual level, had a huge impact on operational thinking. And as one writer put it, the outcome was 'two dominating and conflicting requirements' for army planners, 'the need for dispersion and the ability to concentrate in order to effect a decision on enemy ground forces'. This was acknowledged by Lieutenant General Sir Dudley Ward, Deputy Chief of the Imperial General Staff, who argued in the September 1956 edition of *The British Army Review* that nuclear weapons offered 'a constant threat to the enemy if he attempts to concentrate his strength.'[22] Major General Lewis Lyne, who had been military governor of the British zone in Berlin, also concluded it was now more difficult to concentrate an all-arms force, using this as the basis to argue there remained a role for tanks and armoured personal carriers – the latter an especially critical platform to many writers of this period – as part of an increasingly likely dispersed and mobile armoured campaign.[23] In the United States, Pentomic thinking agreed and extolled effective dispersion the key goal. If there were 'no lines of entrenchment, no masses waiting in reserve, no roads jammed with trucks moving to the front …. no front only a battle area …. to a depth of 100 miles or more, [with] small mobile units deployed at intervals measured in miles instead of yards', then there was no target for tactical nuclear weapons.[24]

Despite the considerable intellectual investment, there was a noticeable lack of any supporting doctrine to provide the conceptual anchor. Colonel John Frost, best known for his role during the Battle of Arnhem, produced an unofficial version which again

---

21   Major General B. T. Wilson, 'Some Salient Features of the United Kingdom Manoeuvres, 1951', *The Army Quarterly*, LXIII (October 1951/January 1952), pp.153–156.

22   'New Look for NATO's Divisions', *The Economist*, 29 October 1955, pp.393–394; F. O. Mischke, 'Crisis of the Divisional System', *An Cosantóir* (Irish Defence Force), October 1956, pp.492–499; Captain N. A. Shackleton, 'Armoured Infantry and Atomic War', *Canadian Army Journal*, April 1956, p.10; Lieutenant General Sir Dudley Ward, 'Divisional Organisation', *The British Army Review*, 3 (September 1956), p.4.

23   Brigadier C. N. Barclay, 'The Future of the Tank: Part I', *The Army Quarterly*, LXVII (October 1953/January 1954), pp.45–46; Major General L. O. Lyne, 'The Future of the Tank: Part II', *The Army Quarterly*, LXVII (October 1953/January 1954), p.179.

24   A. J. Bacevich, *The Pentomic Era: The U.S. Army Between Korea and Vietnam* (Washington, DC: National Defense University Press, 1986), p.67; 'The Pentomic Division', *Time*, 4 January 1957.

emphasised the importance of armoured personnel carriers – protected by thermal shields – to move infantry around the battlefield. It was only in 1958 that a short booklet was issued – *The Corps Tactical Battle of Nuclear War*, nicknamed 'The Purple Pamphlet' due to its cover – which for the next 10 years constituted the only clear doctrine.[25] Within this, land forces were strong in tanks, most of the infantry were carried in armoured vehicles and nuclear artillery was the principal arm. With an emphasis on employing a major defensive obstacle in the first instance – the River Weser supplemented by demolitions and minefields – before conducting offensive mobile operations, the initial aim was to identify axes of enemy advance, create a delay and, through the resulting potential bunching in a rear area, present a target for the tactical weapons.

Even with this doctrine, the nuclear battlefield remained a problem to be overcome, one for which it was not clear any real solution ever actually presented itself. With General Officer Commanding 1st (British) Corps, General Sir Harold Pyman anticipating he would be outnumbered at least 3:1 (infantry) and as high as 5:1 in tanks, it was envisaged a battle on the line of the Weser – Teutoburg Hills would last for a maximum of 30 days; another estimate was that any fighting would last no more than five days. With further strikes against enemy forces forming up, the plan was to develop an armoured counterstroke but with no reference to any fall-back position, success was measured in how long the Warsaw Pact forces would be delayed. Using tactical weapons to breach NATO lines followed by rapid moving armour and mechanised infantry, a Soviet 1961 exercise concluded the whole of Western Europe could be conquered within 10 to 15 days.[26] That same year 'Spearpoint', the largest exercise of its kind up to that point in the Cold War, highlighted that NATO could not halt a Warsaw Pact advance without nuclear support.[27]

The reality was that until at least the mid-1960s and the idea of a 'Flexible Response' strategy, conventional forces – including the British Army of the Rhine – effectively remained a tripwire, a sacrificial trigger which it was hoped would fight long enough to impose sufficient cost on their opponent and create the conditions for a negotiated settlement. The focus remained a static forward defence on NATO's eastern Europe periphery, in which there seemed little practical thought on how to fight a long-sustained conflict. Much greater emphasis was placed on the significance of conventional forces during the last decade of the Cold War, as demonstrated by the reforms to the British Army implemented by the then General Sir Nigel 'Ginger' Bagnall, as Commander of 1 (BR) Corps, and his apparent refusal to simply passively absorb the blow of the opposing

---

25   Col. J.D. Frost, 'An Organisation for Battle', n.d., Basil Liddell Hart Papers, LH15/5/283, Liddell Hart Centre for Military Archives, King's College London; Hugh Beach, 'The Nuclear Battlefield', in Douglas Holdstock and Frank Barnaby (eds), *The British Nuclear Weapons Programme 1952–2002* (London: Frank Cass, 2003), pp.41–43.

26   David French, *Army, Empire, and Cold War: The British Army and Military Policy, 1945–1971* (Oxford: Oxford University Press, 2012), pp.232–233.

27   Beach, 'The Nuclear Battlefield', p.38.

Soviet shock troops and the resulting destruction of his forces that this would produce.[28] Alongside Air-Land Battle with its emphasis also on creating the conditions for battlefield manoeuvre, there nonetheless remained considerable limitations in operating in a high-technology 'killing field' environment with high rates of material loss and critical limitations imposed by the levels of available munitions and the challenge of how to fight a long, sustained conflict.[29]

Towards the Modern Battlespace

The thinking about the nuclear battlefield following the Second World War's conclusion was one example in a much longer process, trying to anticipate the field of battle and what form it might take, and which continues today. Montgomery himself noted the study of war: 'reveals a thread of relentless change. In fact, change is inevitable from time to time…'.[30] In the timeline of subsequent speculation, by the end of the Cold War the battlefield had become 'spacious, fluid and non-linear', nearly a decade later and it was already transparent and with ever greater volumes of information and generally reduced troop densities which afforded opportunities for manoeuvre.[31] As the war in Ukraine has once more demonstrated, in all this informed discussion, the latter is the key recurring point. As a 2001 discussion concluded, on 'a battlefield saturated with precise, long-range, and destructive fire, which is likely to characterise symmetrical wars between two or more highly technological adversaries, it will be more difficult to manoeuvre and attack'.[32] The recent employment of unmanned vehicles apparently operating in combined fashion independent of any actual troops – what has been termed as the Battle of Lyptsi – could represent the next move forward and the inevitable response to the transparent battlefield. As ever, existential threat and the associated abandonment of fiscal responsibility appears to be driving military transformation.[33]

This example also reiterates that alongside any discussion of manoeuvre sits the equally vital one about the impact of technology. A former Chairman of the United States Joint

28 Major Luke Turrell, 'Mission Command in the British Army', CHACR, In Depth Briefing, 67 (November 2023), p.3.
29 John Pay, 'The Battlefield since 1945', in Colin McInnes and G. D. Sheffield (eds), *Warfare in the Twentieth Century: Theory and Practice* (London: Unwin and Hyman, 1988), pp.213–234.
30 Montgomery, 'A Look Through a Window at World War III', p.517.
31 Richard N. Armstrong, 'Battlefield agility: The soviet legacy', *The Journal of Soviet Military Studies*, 1:4 (1988), p.511; Dick Applegate, 'Towards the Future Army', in Brian Bond and Mungo Melvin (eds), 'The Nature of Future Conflict: Implications for Force Development', *Strategic & Combat Studies Institute*, 36 (September 1998), pp.81–82.
32 Avi Kober, 'Has battlefield decision become obsolete? The commitment to the achievement of battlefield decision revisited', *Contemporary Security Policy*, 22:2 (2001), p.99.
33 Mick Ryan, 'The Battle of Lyptsi: Robotic Land Combat', *Futura Doctrina*, 22 December 2024, https://mickryan.substack.com/p/the-battle-of-lyptsi-robotic-land?utm_source=substack&utm_medium=email.

Chiefs of Staff warned in 2017 that the pace of technological and strategic change has 'accelerated the speed of war, making conflict today faster and more complex than at any point in history'.[34] Yet, assessing nascent technologies and implementing suitable responses has traditionally taken time and the current period still feels like it is dominated by a lot of guesswork – and a good measure of hyperbole and armchair pondering – which has the potential to prove distracting. Nonetheless, there is much to be gained from an intellectual 'Phase 0' in which new ideas are proposed and nurtured by 'Ginger Groups' based on informed assessment of current battlefield developments. Not least as speculation grows about the Russian use of tactical weapons. Drawing on leaked files and ambiguous political statements from Moscow, there is continuing discussion about its doctrinal approach to this capability and its potential use as part of its war against Ukraine. What has been termed as a strategy of 'fear inducement', following on from its various earlier iterations throughout the Cold War, is now once again something for NATO planners to anticipate and which will require a credible counter.[35]

This chapter is intended as no more than a condensed overview of a complex process, how to respond to potentially significant change across an operating environment. Viewed through an applied history lens, there do, however, seem clear parallels between the modern debate about the changing character of conflict and those of the early Cold War years relating to the implications of the new nuclear battlefield. Some of the debates remain familiar, most notably with enduring discussion about the role of armour. Then, as now, other common themes included the role of technology, combined arms manoeuvre, logistics and sustainment and survivability, specifically in reference to the concentration and dispersal of forces. Added to these were such considerations as ratios, notably rates of fire and 'force to space', and even a specific focus on the organisation of armies, including the size and structure of the division and whether this was the most appropriate formation for operations in an increasingly lethal environment.[36]

Looking to the past will continue to provide valuable insights when storm proofing for the future.

Alongside well practised informal learning and passing along of knowledge through personal networks, long employed by the British Army, there are numerous files in the National Archives at Kew which document the challenges encountered during key

34   Jim Garamone, 'Dunford: Speed of Military Decision-Making Must Exceed Speed of War', U.S. Department of Defense website, 31 January 2017.

35   Kristin ven Bruusgaard, 'The paradox of nuclear strategy', *Engelsberg Ideas*, 27 August 2024, https://engelsbergideas.com/essays/the-paradox-of-nuclear-strategy/; Michael Evans et al, 'Will Russia Use Nuclear Weapons? Putin's Option Explained', *The Times*, 26 September 2024; Fabian Hoffman, 'Why Putin's nuclear threat is not a cause for panic', *The Spectator*, 26 September 2024; Harrison Kass, 'Putin Isn't Bluffing: Could Russia Test a Tactical Nuclear Weapon?', *The National Interest*, 25 November 2024.

36   Roger J. Spiller, 'S. L. A. Marshall and the ratio of fire', *The RUSI Journal*, 133:4 (Winter 1988), pp.63–71; B. H. Liddell Hart, 'The Ratio of Troops to Space', *The RUSI Journal*, 105:618 (1960), pp.201–212. At the time of writing, examining questions relating to future structure and design remains a major ongoing CHACR research activity.

operations and campaigns and some of the responses that were developed.[37] This more formal 'lessons learned' process expanded throughout the early Cold War period with detailed studies on the conventional fighting during the Korea and the Suez operations and a huge amount of study undertaken on the Falklands conflict. This process has continued to evolve and become well established and today there exists a vast volume of literature related to how military organisations can learn lessons, whether it be from studying the battles and wars they have fought or through analysing the experiences of others.[38] As part of this process it needs to be accepted that these lessons first need to be identified before they can be learned. As a senior NATO analyst noted recently, although there has been some improvement in collecting them there is still 'a habit of "setting them to one side" and not doing anything with them'.[39] The warning offered by the official study of the Falklands campaign must also be acknowledged and a need for caution in drawing lessons from historical examples which may, in many respects, be unique.[40] Nonetheless, looking at the challenges that would have faced the British Army of the Rhine at the dawn of the tactical nuclear age and comparing them with those presented by today's transparent battlefield, it could be argued there is at least one cautionary tale which can be identified from both.[41] While warfare remains a Clausewitzian contest of wills, it can also be seen as a highly lethal game of hide and seek in which it is never enough to offer up as a strategy for victory simply outlasting an opponent.

37   The landings and subsequent fighting in Sicily and Italy are a particular focus, not least as these were used to help shape planning for the subsequent June 1944 invasion of France.

38   Tom Dyson, 'A revolution in military learning? Cross-functional teams and knowledge transformation by lessons learned processes', *European Security*, 29:4 (2020), pp.487–488.

39   Leading to an entirely new category, 'Lessons Admired'"; Ms. Jacqueline Eaton, Principal Operational Research Analyst (PORA), '20 Years of Lessons Learned: An overview of two decades of Lessons Learned', NATO Lessons Learned Conference, Lisbon, 4–5 May 2022.

40   'The Falklands Campaign: The Lessons', presented to Parliament by the Secretary of State for Defence by Command of Her Majesty, December 1982 (London: HMSO, 1982), p.15.

41   Andrew Stewart, 'An Active Edge: The British Army, NATO and the Cold War', *British Army Review*, 186 (Spring 2024), pp.28–33.

6

Army Fitness Means Capabilities First, Structure Second

Jonathan Trevor

Unfit organisations are incapable of performing their purpose. When their purpose, their raison d'être, is so vital as the British Army's, for example, fitness is perhaps the most essential concern of all, organisationally and nationally. But what does 'business' fitness mean in practice, whichever business we are concerned with, i.e. the business of commerce or the business of government? And what does it look like for the Army specifically? How is it achieved and maintained? What is the role of leadership in the process? My academic work and its application to organisations of every variety in every sector, including the Army, have sought to shed light on these questions.

These issues are a core aspect of strategic leadership and the focus of this chapter. In the context of the Army (and other services), they are directly relevant to force development and future-proofing to ensure that the Army can continue to perform its vital purpose in the future, taking advantage of all opportunities (such as alliances, new technologies and innovation) and countering all threats (such as adversaries, but also including the external economic, social and legal factors that all organisations face). In Army leadership discussions, when considering force development, one consistent theme that emerges is the shape of the Army – its structure. How should we structure the British Army to be fit for purpose now and in the future?

Form Follows Function

When thinking about organisational structure, the first thing that often springs to mind is an organisational chart. Organisational charts are engineering schematics illustrating boxes connected by wires intended to convey how all the impersonal pieces of an organisation, often groups of people or roles, are related to each other. Another way to think about structure is that it is an essential element of how individuals and groups (think teams, groups, departments, divisions, et cetera) formally and informally *cooperate* to create value greater than could ever be achieved alone. Cooperation is – should be – the fundamental organising principle of any structure, whether through vertical coordination of effort or horizontal collaboration.

Militaries were one of the few examples of organising work at scale before the Industrial Revolution ushered in large commercial businesses and government departments. The legacy of military language is still pervasive today. The terms 'officer', as in chief operating officer, and 'rank', as in rank and file to refer to workers, are just two examples. A 'division' is another. The term 'division' arose centuries ago from mobilising disparate individuals to form a coherent military fighting force. A division was simply an ad hoc grouping of people separated, or 'divided', from others by their task and to be formed and disbanded as a group as required. Over time, divisions became established and evolved to become brigades, regiments, battalions, squads and so on, each reflecting an identity centred on its specialised role, function and ways of working as part of, eventually, a professional army – the British Army.

In many cases, taking inspiration from or simply stealing military principles of organising work at scale, late nineteenth century and early to mid-twentieth-century commercial organisations divided their labour to encourage task specialisation. This, in turn, created efficiencies that enabled firms to grow fast and large by offering their products more affordably to customers and creating mass markets in the process. This dominant form of work organisation is often called the U-form organisational structure.

The U in U-form stands for uniform – in name and nature. The essential attributes were top-down management control, singular product focus (i.e. specialising in one thing alone), impersonal treatment of customers and staff, hierarchical organisational structure, formal procedures and rules, and precise planning formulated by the 'thinkers' (for which read managers, or officers) to be implemented by the 'doers' (for which read workers, or rank and file). Maximising economies of scale through the efficient execution of superior strategy was the primary definition of success.

The next iteration in organisational structure extended a singular product (or business) focus to multiple products and multiple businesses, each representing a different division of the same firm, typically. Enter the M-form organisation – M for multi-divisional. In the quest for growth, managers looked to exploit commercial opportunities in adjacent industries and markets, capitalising upon their superior management skills to steal a march on parochial non-traditional competitors. The middle of the twentieth century onwards saw the blossoming of corporations structured as multi-divisional conglomerates. Some of these continue today. But many of the most famous conglomerates – including the most famous of all, General Electric (GE) – have gone under or split apart.

GE used to be the most valuable and admired company in the world. A titan of American (and by extension, international) business, GE at one point manufactured everything from aircraft engines to light bulbs; it ran hospitals and financial services (the ill-fated GE Capital). Its chief executive officer, Jack Welch, was lionised and revered. The principle was that GE's superior management competencies (often referred to as the 'GE Way' and the subject of best-selling books and considerable emulation by aspiring others) meant it could succeed at virtually anything. But today, GE is worth a mere fraction of what it once was and was recently split into three. GE, as it was, no longer exists.

Instead, it has been largely replaced at the top of the corporate scoreboard by technology sector newcomers, such as Amazon and Google, which brings us to our final phase and the most recent iteration of dominant organisational structures – the network.

Management scholars distinguish two broad epochs in work organisation — the Industrial Age (described above) and the Information Age. The latter corresponds to the late 1970s and onwards but gathered steam in the new millennium. The standard presumption is one of simple succession between the two. Information Age firms would inevitably succeed their industrial forebears at the apex of economic value creation. This has occurred to a large degree. The world's most valuable companies at the time of writing are all technology companies (think Microsoft, Apple, Amazon, et cetera). Industrial giants like GE have been eclipsed.

The Information Age ushers in a new form of organising, too. It is often referred to as a post-bureaucratic organisation in scholarly circles and as a network-based organisation or organisational ecosystem in the popular press. In form, network-based organisations are the antithesis of the Industrial Age hierarchy. They are informal (not formal), values-based (not rules-based), flexible (not rigid), networks (not hierarchies), personal (not impersonal), organic (not mechanistic), rely upon external resources primarily (not internal), and are horizontally (not vertically) integrated. The idea is to maximise innovation outcomes rather than efficiencies.

However, it would be wrong to think that only organisations structured along post-bureaucratic lines have a future. The industrial hierarchy, the multi-divisional, and the network represent different approaches to work organisation and organisational structure. Each represents a distinct form to achieve a particular function. Each possesses advantages and disadvantages. What is true is that each iteration of how organisations are structured – whether U-form, M-form, post-bureaucratic or everything in between – has been enabled by technological advances, with profound economic, social and political implications.

Technology is forcing change again by challenging the assumption that roles occupied by people (bankers, doctors or soldiers, for example) are the primary means through which an organisation's work is performed. Technological automation is nothing new, of course, but integrating human and machine capabilities for *all* tasks for enhanced performance will become the dominant concern for how work is organised in the near future.

Concerning warfighting, the U.S. military already distinguishes between 'self-directed' and 'self-deciding' systems in its *Unmanned Systems Integrated Roadmap*. Semi-autonomous self-*directed* systems perform tasks independently of human control according to a planned programme. However, self-*deciding* systems operate with complete autonomy, independent of a 'human in the loop', the machine deciding for itself the best course of action in 'unforeseen situations' according to inputs from its sensors and its ever-advancing cognitive capabilities.[1]

---

1   D. Petraeus and A. Roberts, 'Conflict: The Evolution of Warfare from 1945 to Ukraine', *The U.S. Army War College*, 54 (2024), p.169.

Organisational leaders should make careful and intentional choices about how their organisation is structured, which resources they should invest in, and how to align the moving parts of their enterprise to be fit for purpose. However, many organisations are manifestly not fit for purpose. Why, and what can we do about it?

A Structure Can Have Its Own Life

A common reason organisational structure can become misaligned with strategic requirements is that it is often self-perpetuating. Management writer Peter Drucker famously said (or at least it is most commonly attributed to him) 'culture eats strategy for breakfast'. He could also have been writing about structure. A common interpretation of Drucker's statement is that the values, beliefs and behaviours that represent an organisation's culture frame the strategy choices of its corporate executives, whether they consciously appreciate it or not. And the stronger an organisation's culture – the more committed individuals and groups are to it – the more influential it is over how they perceive their world and their choices.

Strategising is a reflexive activity. Separating agency from structure and choices from prevailing norms is hard, despite our best intentions. Organisational structure, like culture, serves to 'structure' how we view the organisations we lead and the choices we make, even to the extent that attempts to transform an organisation may serve to reproduce and reinforce its existing values and practices unwittingly.[2] Ideally, it should be the other way around. Culture and structure (as the form of an organisation) should follow strategy (as the function of the organisation). The form should follow function, and culture and structure should be designed explicitly to support strategy implementation.

The point is that how organisations are structured and why they are structured the way they are is often not the result of reason or rational planning. This is especially a perennial risk in large, long-established, inwardly focused, monopolistic, complex organisations with elaborate symbols, pervasive social rituals, and intangible and taken-for-granted cultural norms. Sound familiar?

In such cases, including many storied private sector firms, the choice of organisational structure might be classified as non-strategic (and non-rational, technically) because it is not a choice at all. It merely reproduces the status quo despite being billed as something new. Or, an organisation's structure can be emergent (not planned), accidental/unintended (instead of purposeful), unstructured (not systematic), informal (as opposed to explicit) and inconsistent (as opposed to uniform). These are not bad qualities per se. Indeed, all these qualities are inevitable to some degree, especially in large, complex

---

2   The antidote to 'structuration', to coin the phrase popularised by the sociologist Anthony Giddens, is to bring in an external perspective to challenge group norms (which can become groupthink in the extreme) and the prevailing status quo. Indeed, bringing an external perspective to proceedings is part and parcel of the CHACR mission.

organisations operating under high uncertainty. However, they are not strategic in the strict sense of the word and its meaning, i.e. deliberate, far-sighted, evidenced, systematic, et cetera.

Emergent organisational properties can introduce randomness into organisational systems, meaning that strategies go unimplemented or are implemented poorly, or unintended consequences occur despite the best leadership intentions. The goal of all leadership – especially systems leadership – should be to create and maintain organisations that are fit for their purpose. This is a strategic concern in which organisational structure is just one (albeit an important one) feature of organisational design. It is a critical means to achieving the organisation's ends. How should we approach it?

A Strategic Approach

Adopting a capability-led perspective is a robust way to align organisational structure strategically. As noted earlier, there are many different forms of organisational structure, not just U-Form or M-Form (to name just two). Which is the correct one? It depends upon requirements. Such an answer assumes a contingency approach to organisational design. There is no one-size-fits-all solution to every requirement. There is no best practice; the only choice is to select a form of organisational structure from many different options that best fits the requirements. So, what are the requirements, and what are the associated structural options?

My research has attempted to shed light on this question as part of a broader concern with aligning businesses (including governments and public sector organisations) to be fit for purpose and high performing.[3] I identify four principal requirements through which leaders can meaningfully choose between different strategic approaches, including their approach to structuring their organisation. As illustrated in Figure 1, we can use a simple two-dimensional framework to make sense of a capability-led approach in the context of market requirements.[4]

In the first dimension, the x-axis, leaders must choose between organisational stability or agility. Stability enables standardisation, repetition, reproducibility and consistency of operation. These organisational attributes, in turn, enable predictability and efficiency as outcomes. In a stable market environment, *stability*, as an organisational capability, enables executives to confidently match market demand with predictable volume (i.e. supply), quality and cost. Such matching strategies were the hallmark of yesteryear's successful company and corporate executive career and remain so today for many businesses.

---

3   For more detail, refer to Jonathon Trevor, *Re:Align: A Leadership Blueprint for Overcoming Disruption and Improving Performance* (London: Bloomsbury, 2022), Chapter 2.
4   Trevor, *Re:Align*.

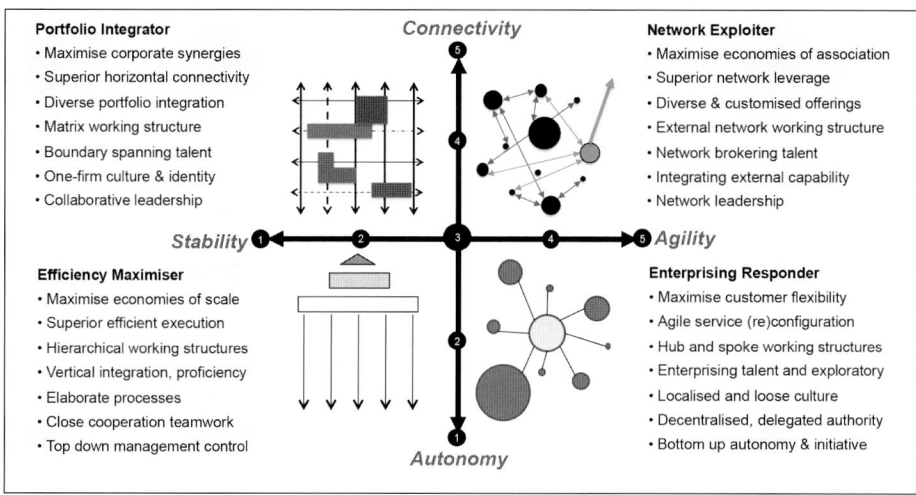

Figure 1: The Strategic Alignment Framework
Source: adapted from J. Trevor, *Re:Align: A Leadership Blueprint for Aligning Enterprise Purpose, Strategy and Organisation* (London: Bloomsbury Publishing, 2019) © Jonathan Trevor 2019. All Rights Reserved.

But, of course, the external environment today is much more volatile, uncertain, complex and ambiguous (i.e. the popular VUCA thesis) than it was in the middle of the previous century. Agility must, therefore, also be considered a core organisational requirement for many businesses, government agencies and non-profit enterprises. In extreme cases, agility enables organisations to customise their offerings to market and even personalise their products and services to individual customers' preferences. Agility permits teams to be agile around the needs of their customers and be creative and flexible in how they respond to demands.

In the second dimension of the framework, the y-axis, leaders must choose between autonomy and connectivity. Autonomous organisations are self-sufficient and rely upon their own resources and capabilities to offer competitive products and services to the marketplace. Autonomy is associated with simplicity, control, speed and strategic focus. There are few(er) distractions or tricky external relationships to navigate; autonomy permits leadership teams to pursue their own internal logic and be masters of their own destiny, as much as is possible in regulated environments. However, autonomous organisations are bounded by their own resources. Moreover, autonomy is often a feature inside and out – even different internal teams and departments are often separated structurally to permit freedom to specialise and focus on domain-specific performance.

Conversely, connectivity enables organisations to exploit synergies internally (think between teams or departments, for example) or externally (think between partnering organisations). By strategically prioritising and developing connectivity as an organisational capability, leaders can supercharge horizontal (as opposed to simply vertical coordination) collaboration between structurally separated individuals, teams, business units and organisations. All of these enable a whole organisation to be much more valuable than the sum of its individual parts. This is because value can reside between and not simply within different organisational units (think business verticals), but only if there is connectivity between them. However, connectivity comes at a cost – specifically, higher transaction costs. Collaboration is difficult and costly if it is not necessary.

Stability, agility, autonomy and connectivity can be developed – they are acquired capabilities. However, they are also competing values across the two dimensions. Agility comes at the cost of stability, and vice versa. Equally, simplicity and self-sufficiency (i.e. autonomy) are sacrificed in the interest of synergies (i.e. connectivity). Developing either stability or agility, as well as autonomy or connectivity, should be a proactive strategic choice. It is the choice to be capable in one way and not another according to a judgement by an organisation's leadership.

The framework helps us identify four distinctive strategic approaches to competing and winning in competitive marketplaces or, for that matter, battle spaces. In order of sophistication, but also complexity, these are:

> *The Efficiency Maximiser:* This strategic approach emphasises stability and autonomy to achieve superior efficiency. Key attributes include standardisation of practice, close cooperation in teamwork (as opposed to wide-ranging collaborations), consistency of standards, and firm rules with little tolerance for variation. Top-down supervision of performance against pre-defined targets is the dominant style of leadership. While it most closely conforms to the principles of the Industrial Age bureaucracy (the ideal type of which is technically the most efficient form of organising work, according to the sociologist Maximillian Weber), the Efficiency Maximiser remains highly relevant today. Indeed, many of the world's most successful product-based organisations conform to a model in which maximising economies of scale is as important today as it was a hundred years ago. Structurally, the Efficiency Maximiser resembles most closely the top-down, vertically integrated Industrial Age hierarchy (but can be multi-divisional), with close spans of control and vertical integration up and down the established hierarchical organisational structure.

> *The Enterprising Responder:* This strategic approach emphasises autonomy but agility instead of stability. Enterprising Responders succeed through their ability to adapt, reconfigure and customise their products and services to the changing requirements of different markets or even individual customers. Customisation, not standardisation, is the name of the game. It is achieved by ensuring high levels of autonomy in operations. Enterprising Responders are characteristically informal, relying for success upon decentralised decision-making, flexible working patterns, outcomes-based management and highly enterprising talent. Structurally, the Enterprising Responder typically takes the form of a hub and spoke configuration. Independent 'front-line' units (i.e. those closest to customer interaction in a commercial setting) are organised into often independent teams (the spokes), with

a relatively weak relationship with a coordinating central function (the hub). The spokes often act independently of each other and maybe only share some form of financial relationship with the 'centre'. Operational autonomy is sacred and fiercely protected. Many expertise-based organisations, such as law firms, consultancies, professions and universities, fit this mould.

The Portfolio Integrator: This strategic approach emphasises horizontal connectivity between individuals, teams, divisions and organisations as its defining capability. Horizontal connectivity can take many forms, but the most common is cross-departmental collaboration to pool resources, share knowledge or collaborate to offer customers an enhanced portfolio of goods or develop some form of innovative product or service. Portfolio Integrators are highly aligned, vertically but also horizontally, permitting the sharing of ways of working, corporate values, easier mobility of talent, and one-firm culture. Structurally, Portfolio Integrators resemble a matrix, with either fixed or open teams working across vertical boundaries on a permanent or temporary basis according to threats and opportunities imposed by the external environment.

The Network Exploiter: This strategic approach emphasises connectivity and agility as key capabilities. Instead of exploiting economies of scale solely, Network Exploiters, as the name suggests, are focused on exploiting economies of association. By leveraging networks of external resources (think partners, collaborators and allies), they can offer customers an enhanced variety of personalised products and services than if relying upon their internal resources alone. Similarly, in purely capability terms, Network Exploiters are able to leverage the intellectual capital of potentially thousands of partnering organisations to supercharge their innovation capability. The ability to forge diverse connections with other organisations, each with their own interests, capabilities, and idiosyncratic ways of working, as well as nourish and leverage connections to pool knowledge strategically, are critical success factors. Structurally, Network Exploiters resemble networks, with multiple nodes (perhaps representing a partner or an ally) and a hub in which knowledge is curated through deliberate knowledge creation, exchange and application across the whole ecosystem and aligned to market opportunities.

Which is the best approach of the four described? Again, of course, *it depends*. Each approach possesses advantages and disadvantages. No one approach is better than the others.

The two risks for any organisation are, firstly, choosing the wrong approach from the four available options (and bear in mind there are wide degrees of variation within each quadrant of Figure 1). The second, and what I observe very frequently across all sectors, is the failure to choose any approach at all and sleepwalk into the middle (a three score in Figure 1). The middle is not the most capable or a 'best of all worlds' option. It is the opposite. Organisations in the middle might be described as jacks of all trades and masters of none; they are not distinctively good at anything. They have no clear direction or priorities. Uncertainty or a lack of confidence within their leadership has resulted in mediocrity with no potential for improvement.

Can this framework be meaningfully applied to the Army? Very much so – it is an annual exercise on the Army Generalship Programme. When thinking about the Army overall (or any other organisation), or a specific element of it, and in the context of external threats and opportunities, consider: First, what are the requirements for organisational stability or agility? Second, what are the requirements for autonomy or connectivity?

Can you score both requirements on a scale of 1 to 5 using Figure 1 as a guide? How you define your 'unit of analysis', to use academic-speak, is important. In the case of the British Army, say, you could choose between Field Army or Home Command. Or, better yet, between different activities, such as infantry; artillery; explosive ordnance disposal; logistics; air assault; engineering; special forces; medical; signals; intelligence, surveillance and reconnaissance; military intelligence; estates, et cetera. Even these are sweeping categories. Each can be broken down further, depending on how forensic you wish to be in your analysis.

At the same time, can you use the same questions to map the approaches of known competitors (or adversaries)? What are their capabilities? What are they trying to win at? Is it a scale play or an agile response doctrine, for example? How about partners and suppliers? What about the Ministry of Defence? What about civilian institutions? Once scored, can you further differentiate between short-term (say this year), medium-term (say 2 to 3 years) and long-term (say 5 to 10 years)?

Once the mapping exercise is complete, what can you observe from the results? How would you describe your current approach? Do all of your team agree with your assessment? Is your approach the same as your competitors? Consider further: are you fighting the same fight or, adopting a so-called 'Blue Ocean' strategy, could you find an advantage by changing your approach to warfighting (for example) and embracing distinctiveness?[5] Does everything you do fit neatly into one approach (i.e. one quadrant on the framework) or do you do many different things simultaneously? Are requirements changing over time? If so, how?

How should the Army realign to change with them? What happens to effectiveness and performance if it cannot? And why would that be? Is it because of external factors, such as funding constraints and the political landscape? Or is it due to internal factors, such as culture, people and leadership? If it is the latter, are you your own worst enemy?

If you are, you are not alone. My experience of organisations generally suggests that internal factors are the greatest barriers to effective strategic realignment. However, external factors typically get the lion's share of executive attention, possibly because they are abstract and more comfortable to discuss. Remember, 70 percent of all change

---

5   W. Chan Kim and Renee Mauborgne, *Blue Ocean Strategy: How to Create Uncontested Market Space and Make the Competition Irrelevant* (Boston, MA: Harvard Business Review Press, 2014).

programmes fail to meet expectations due to internal and not external factors, according to the consultancy McKinsey & Co.[6]

Leadership Considerations

Howsoever you might have answered the questions posed above, it is almost certain that Army leadership, like all leaders everywhere, will have to develop and double down on three critical leadership skills. These are:

Ambidexterity: the ability to nourish and maintain multiple different operating approaches, systems and models (or different quadrants of the framework, if you like) simultaneously without imposing a one-size-fits-all management imprint on all or allowing cross-contamination between them.

Versatility: the ability organisationally to move successfully and rapidly, if needed, from one quadrant to another according to the changing requirements of the external environment.

System-level thinking: that is, to think of the Army as one enterprise, aligned behind one well-understood purpose, but with many different moving parts (i.e., a system of systems) that should be complementary but will likely find themselves in conflict without an overall strategic scheme or if they are operationally managed poorly.

Conclusion

So, in conclusion, consider what enters your mind when you look at a military wiring diagram and see the terms 'division' or 'brigade'. Do fixed images of utility, equipment and numbers of people, ranks, and military units automatically aggregate in your subconscious? If the answer is 'yes', you could consider whether this is because these long-accepted terms and structures retain their relevance and effectiveness or whether we have, despite our best intentions, allowed accepted norms to draw us into point number 3 on the framework. To abuse an over-used cliché: the easy thing is to talk about new ideas in military minds. The hard thing will be to decide, *deliberately*, to get the old ones out.

---

6   See https://www.mckinsey.com/featured-insights/leadership/changing-change-management.

7

Exploring the Human Challenges of Human-Machine Teaming for Military Applications

Leo Blanken, Justin Davis and Cecilia Panella

Introduction

The future of warfare will assuredly involve the integration of increasingly intelligent machines into military organisations, to include both 'smart robots' (cyber-physical systems with autonomous or artificial intelligence (AI)-enabled sensing, processing and actuation) or 'smart advisers' (cyber systems that include such processes but are incapable of physical actuation). If this integration is done successfully, it is hoped that the resulting human-machine teams would allow Western militaries to achieve mass, precision strike and scalable effects with a shrinking number of human operators. Considering recruiting problems and casualty aversion in many Western societies, this option is increasingly attractive. Given the current trajectory of technology, the only question remains – how deeply and how soon will this human-machine teaming occur?

Current attention is largely focused on the technical aspects of this challenge, such as the maturing of technologies and manufacturing of the resulting systems at scale. Much less attention is being placed on the human aspects of the challenge at the individual, organisational, and systemic levels. This chapter explores the impact of such teaming at these three levels, arguing that now is the time to conduct thoughtful analysis around the intentional design of these socio-technical systems. The three following topics should be included in such efforts: (a) the emotive response of humans to machines and their interfaces at the individual level; (b) the construction (and deconstruction) of martial identity and military culture at the organisational level; and (c) the shaping of international norms on the use of human-machine teaming at the international system level. Unravelling these complex topics now is critical, as the pace of technology may soon overtake planning around the human aspects of future battlefields.

Human-Machine Teaming as a Socio-Technical System

Militaries worldwide are currently (and justifiably) fixated on unmanned systems. Though discussion around such systems has been brewing for decades, the war in Ukraine has shown that the successful integration of these systems is already impacting warfare in significant ways.[1] Given this confirmation of the ready application of unmanned – and increasingly autonomous – systems, the race is on to field them.[2] In the United States, for example, this race for battlefield autonomy has three foci: research and development (R&D), acquisition and scaling. R&D has become an area of real concern for the United States for most cutting-edge technologies, as the private sector is now driving technological progress and China is superior at leveraging the market through its civil-military fusion of research efforts; this has put the U.S. Department of Defense (DoD) in the uncomfortable position of playing technological 'catch up.'[3] Acquisition is a second major area of concern.[4] The conflict in Ukraine, for example, is displaying a dizzying pace of technological change as both sides adapt continuously, with a particular focus on unmanned systems.[5] Many observers note that the U.S. DoD acquisition process is frankly unable to match this speed of change.[6] The final concern in the U.S. national security community is the capacity of the defence industrial base to produce these systems at the scale necessary

1   T. McCormick, 'Lethal Autonomy: A Short History' in *Foreign Policy*, 24 January 2014, https://foreignpolicy.com/2014/01/24/lethal-autonomy-a-short-history/; S. L. Pettyjohn, 'Drones Are Transforming the Battlefield in Ukraine but in an Evolutionary Fashion' in *War on the Rocks*, 5 March 2024, https://warontherocks.com/2024/03/drones-are-transforming-the-battlefield-in-ukraine-but-in-an-evolutionary-fashion/.

2   R. O. Work, 'Principles for the Combat Employment of Weapons Systems with Autonomous Functionalities. *Center for New American Security*, 28 April 2021, https://www.cnas.org/publications/reports/proposed-dod-principles-for-the-combat-employment-of-weapon-systems-with-autonomous-functionalities.

3   A. Fritz, 'China's Evolving Conception of Civil-Military Collaboration', *Center for Strategic and International Studies*, 2 August 2019, https://www.csis.org/blogs/trustee-china-hand/chinas-evolving-conception-civil-military-collaboration; 'China Leads U.S. in Global Competition for Key Emerging Technology, Study Says', *Reuters*, 1 March 2023, https://www.reuters.com/technology/china-leads-us-global-competition-key-emerging-technology-study-says-2023-03-02/.

4   *Defense Resourcing for the Future: Final Report*, Commission on Planning, Programming, Budgeting, and Execution Reform (Arlington, VA: 2024).

5   U. Franke and J. Soderstrom, 'Star Tech Enterprise: Emerging Technologies in Russia's War in Ukraine', *European Council on Foreign Relations*, 5 September 2023, https://ecfr.eu/publication/star-tech-enterprise-emerging-technologies-in-russias-war-on-ukraine/; J. Askew, 'Drones and Robots: How the Ukraine War is Driving Technological Innovation', *Euro News*, 27 September 2023, https://www.euronews.com/next/2023/09/27/drones-and-robots-how-the-ukraine-war-is-driving-technological-innovation.

6   P. Scharre, 'Preserving U.S. Military Advantage Amid Rapid Technological Change', *Center for New American Studies*, 12 March 2024, https://www.cnas.org/publications/congressional-testimony/preserving-u-s-military-advantage-amid-rapid-technological-change.

for modern warfare.[7] China's industrial capacity to manufacture high-tech systems, for example, dwarfs that of the United States and there is no easy solution to this problem.[8]

Though these concerns of R&D, acquisition and scaling are all important technical aspects of the problem, they fail to address the more human concerns of fielding human-machine teams on the battlefields of tomorrow. This emphasis on the physical challenges of new technology, however, tends to: 'neglect the interaction of a changing material world with the values, practices, and emotional responses of individuals and institutions. These are just as important as technology – arguably more so.'[9] Humanity's journey on this planet has been shaped to no small degree by the things we have constructed. From vehicles to tools, to weapons to toys, the things our societies make, in turn, help to make our societies. Militaries, in particular, have paid close attention to new technologies as relative advantage in the quality and quantity of material often plays a central role in determining outcomes on the battlefield.[10] What is often neglected in stories of technological change, however, is that outcomes are jointly determined by creators and creations; humans and things interact – in what are referred to as socio-technical systems – to cure diseases, land people on the moon and win wars.[11] Humans not only build things and determine their usage, but also socially construct the cultural meanings and identities around them and this impending process of social construction around human-machine teaming offers important opportunities for strategic planning.

Given this, we offer some thoughts around the human aspects of such teaming in military organisations. More specifically, we explore ways forward by structuring the topic along three levels of analysis: the individual, the organisational and the systemic. Thinking in terms of designing may be helpful here, using Herbert Simon's expansive definition: '[e]veryone designs who devises courses of action aimed at changing existing situations into preferred ones.'[12] This mode of enquiry entails both objective analysis and the empathetic engagement of these human considerations in its problem-solving

7   J. Clark, 'Defense Innovation Official Says Replicator Initiative Remains on Track', *United States Department of Defense*, 26 January 2024, https://www.defense.gov/News/News-Stories/Article/Article/3657609/defense-innovation-official-says-replicator-initiative-remains-on-track/.

8   S. G. Jones and A. Palmer, 'China Outpacing U.S. Defense Industrial Base', *Center for Strategic and International Studies*, 6 March 2024, https://www.csis.org/analysis/china-outpacing-us-defense-industrial-base.

9   L. Blanken, 'The Weird and Eerie Battlefields of Tomorrow', *The Strategy Bridge*, 25 August 2020, https://thestrategybridge.org/the-bridge/2020/8/25/the-weird-and-eerie-battlefields-of-tomorrow.

10   W. H. McNeill, *The Pursuit of Power: Technology, Armed Force, and Society since AD 1100* (Chicago: University of Chicago Press, 1982).

11   W. E. Bijker, T. P. Hughes and T. Pinch (eds), *The Social Construction of Technological Systems: New Directions in the Sociology and History of Technology, Anniversary Edition* (Cambridge, MA: The MIT Press, 2012).

12   H. Simon, 'The Science of Design: Creating the Artificial', *Design Issues*, 4 (1988), pp.67–82.

techniques; it is, therefore, well-suited for exploring these topics as a multi-stakeholder, collaborative enterprise.[13]

Intentionally designing the path forward for human-machine teaming is critical for at least two reasons. First, the technologies that are central to these capabilities are fundamentally dual use. This means that their employment in the military sphere will have important implications – normative as well as technical – for wider society. Second, even though these technologies are currently showing deep impact at the tactical level in conflicts such as Ukraine, they will begin to exert more pressure on the strategic level of conflict. One predictable way in which they will do so is by shortening decision-making cycles on the battlefield – a tightening of the 'kill chain'.[14] Given these implications of evolving human-machine teaming, it is critical to treat the phenomenon as a grand design challenge around a broad socio-technical system. Military expediency should be treated as one intermediate goal, but the wider context is to balance battlefield performance against the more fundamental aspects of security writ large: human, national and global. Getting ahead of these inevitable impacts is crucial, and savvy leaders should begin these efforts now.

The Individual Level

At the individual level, the dyadic interface between human and machine will be critical for effective teaming. The technical considerations around interface will be determined by the required tactics, techniques and procedures given anticipated future operational environments and mission types. This will, in turn, help to determine the range of operations that can be enabled by the human-machine team, as well as the scalability of the team (the ratio of human to machines, or '1:n'). Much work has been done to define and explore the issue of trust around human-machine teaming, but we argue that further human considerations need to be taken into account as well.[15] Such additional design efforts should focus on the subconscious reactions that operators have towards the machine itself as well as its behaviours.[16] We label this subconscious reaction the *emotive response* and we focus on how this emotive response will be driven by aesthetic choices around the appearance and interface of the machine.

---

13   P. V. K. Anderson and W. S. Mosleh, 'Conflicts in Co-Design: Engaging with Tangible Artefacts in Multi-Stakeholder Collaboration', *CoDesign*, 17:4, pp.473–492.

14   C. Brose, *The Kill Chain: Defending America in the Future of High-Tech Warfare* (New York: Hachette Books, 2020).

15   T. Ueno et al, 'Trust in Human-AI Interaction: Scoping Out Models, Measures, and Methods', *CHI Conference on Human Factors in Computing Systems Extended Abstracts*, 254 (2022), pp.1–7; S. Mehrotra et al, 'A Systematic Review on Fostering Appropriate Trust in Human-AI Interaction: Trends, Opportunities, and Challenges', *ACM Journal of Responsible Computing* 1:4 (2024), pp.1–45.

16   E. Eich et al, *Cognition and Emotion* (New York: Oxford University Press, 2000).

Shaping the individual's emotive response to a machine 'teammate' will hinge on the machine's form factor and interface.[17] This should be a critical consideration during the design process because it is part of human nature to emotionally categorise any entity that, through perceived agency, is distinguishable from a passive object: 'Sociability is our natural interface, to each other and to living creatures in general. As part of that innate behavior (*sic*), we quickly seek to identify objects from agents. In fact, as social creatures, it is often our default behavior (*sic*) to anthropomorphise moving robots.'[18] Emotive response, therefore, should be carefully considered here as the design of the machine and its functioning will drive the nature of the relationship that is subsequently developed within the human-machine team. Is the machine a disposable tool? A beloved pet? A valuable platform? Or a trusted collaborator? Do machines with four legs appear dog-like (endearing)? Would a machine with six, eight or many legs appear insect-like (repulsive)? Should efforts be made to anthropomorphise the appearance of machines?[19]

Consider also the current debates around the artificial voices selected as interfaces for AI tools.

> Voice interfaces represent a profound step forward: instead of expecting users to adapt to complex interfaces, we're teaching machines to understand our most intuitive form of communication. Yet, making voice interfaces feel truly human-like requires more than just recognising speech – it involves understanding cultural nuances, context, emotion, and ethical guardrails. The key is to determine what emotional response is desired and then carefully design machines and interface to achieve the desired effect.[20]

These choices around voice interface – particularly its gender – will be critical for military human-machine teaming. Research shows that females voices are perceived as being 'empathetic' and 'benevolent' while male voices are perceived as being 'dominant'.[21]

17   P. Saariluoma, 'Four Challenges in Structuring Human-Autonomous Systems Interaction Design Processes', *Autonomous Systems: Issues for Defence Policymakers*, (2015), pp.226–248.
18   H. Knight, 'How Humans Respond to Robots: Building Public Policy Through Good Design', *Brookings Institute*, 29 July 2014, https://www.brookings.edu/articles/how-humans-respond-to-robots-building-public-policy-through-good-design/.
19   J. Zlotowski et al, 'Anthropomorhism: Opportunities and Challenges in Human-Robot Interaction' in *International Journal of Social Robotics*, 7 (2015), pp.347–360; M. Mori, 'The Uncanny Valley: The Original Essay by Masahiro Mori' in *IEEE Spectrum*, 12 June 2012, https://spectrum.ieee.org/the-uncanny-valley.
20   S. Bora, 'Breaking the Silence: How Voice AI is Shaping the Future of Human-Machine Interactions' in *Medium*, 8 November 2024, https://medium.com/@sanjeeva.bora/breaking-the-silence-how-voice-ai-is-shaping-the-future-of-human-machine-interactions-9575fa1a3d44.
21   E. Blakemore, 'Why Do So Many Virtual Assistants Have Female Voices?' in *National Geographic*, 22 July 2024, https://www.nationalgeographic.com/science/article/female-voice-assistants-siri-alexa-woman.

Female AI interface voices for most applications are designed to appear supportive, but subordinate: 'They embody what we think of when we picture a personal assistant…. she gets you to meetings on time…. and delivers relevant information…. Nevertheless, she is not in charge.' This can be contrasted with IBM's Watson AI: '[it] speaks with a male voice…. IBM went with one that was self-assured and had it use short definitive phrases. Both are typical of male speech – and people prefer to hear a masculine-sounding voice from a leader, according to research – so Watson got a male voice.'[22] What would improve performance of human-machine teams in the stress of conflict? Should these voice interfaces be varied by conditions or by varying audiences? To what degree should these decisions around military machine interface reflect or confront broader societal debates around gender issues? At what points should AI's interface with the human user be considered subordinate (and therefore can be dismissed) or authoritative (orders to be followed)? This is a non-trivial consideration as split-second human decisions are often shaped by unconscious and subconscious reactions.

Besides the machine's human teammate, what other actors in the operational space should be taken into account during these aesthetic design considerations? At least two additional groups of individuals may be considered: enemy combatants and civilians. These other sets of individuals may also be considered distinct 'end users' that the machine is intended to impact. First, let us look at the outsized emotive response that a novel weapon system can have on enemy combatants. Consider the terrorised reaction of a German soldier to the introduction of tanks by the British on the Western Front in 1916: 'My blood froze in my veins. Crawling along the cratered battlefield were two mysterious monsters. The monsters approached slowly – limping, staggering, swaying – but no obstacle could stop them. They moved ever forward [as if by] supernatural force.'[23] Second, consider the civilian population in the human terrain of future conflicts.[24] The degree to which future wars involve 'a violent struggle…. for legitimacy and influence over the relevant population(s)' then the emotive response of the civilian population to the human-machine team will be paramount.[25] Given these two distinctly different additional sets of actors that will be impacted, what additional considerations should be taken into account in the aesthetic design of the machines? Should they be designed to strike terror? Should they appear to be reassuring? Balancing such aesthetic choices around machines to balance the emotive response of all relevant end users should not be neglected in the design stage.

22   C. Steele, 'The Real Reason Voice Assistants Are Female (and Why it Matters)' in *PC Mag*, 4 January 2018, https://www.pcmag.com/opinions/the-real-reason-voice-assistants-are-female-and-why-it-matters.
23   Quoted in Blanken, 'The Weird and Eerie Battlefields of Tomorrow'.
24   B. Connable, 'Human Terrain System is Dead, Long Live… What?' in *Military Review* (January-February 2018), pp.25–33.
25   Quoted in D. H. Ucko and T. A. Marks, 'Redefining Irregular Warfare: Legitimacy, Coercion, and Power' in *Modern War Institute*, 18 October 2022, https://mwi.westpoint.edu/redefining-irregular-warfare-legitimacy-coercion-and-power/.

The Organisational Level

At the organisational level, the integration of machines into existing bureaucratic structures and social dynamics will also be critical for effective teaming. One comparative advantage that military organisations enjoy over most other groups is the strength of their organisational culture.[26] Group identity, tradition and shared values are necessary to bind personnel together through the rigours and terrors of war and this cultural fabric is jealously guarded and carefully reproduced through symbols, language and institutionalised rituals. The design endeavour, therefore, should entail understanding how culture and incentives would need to be shaped to enable the successful integration of new technology. This will require both the understanding as to how the formal and informal aspects of institutions work together to produce outcomes and how designing the integration of human-machine teams at the organisational level will synchronise with design efforts at the individual level (treated above) and the systemic level (treated below).

Consider the disruptions created by the change in naval propulsion systems in the nineteenth century, during which navies changed from fleets of elegant sailing vessels to smoke-belching steamships.[27] This change in technology significantly disrupted sailors' culture, traditions and social hierarchies as much as it disrupted naval warfare. As one contemporary observer lamented the introduction of steaming ironclads: 'Those who know anything of sailors must see the charm of the life which animates them; and it is only surprising that any who confess their sympathy for the profession should be advocating the construction of engines (they cannot be called ships) devoted to all the grossness and barbarity of war, while they are deprived of everything attractive to a sailor.'[28]

This cultural disruption was reflected in the painful integration of the personnel dedicated to the new technology. 'The division between below-deck [engineers] and topside sailors was immediate and stark…. the topsiders always saw themselves as above the engine room operators. They were even known to belittle the engineers, calling them dirty, their job unimportant…. they didn't even hold naval ranks until [decades after their introduction].'[29] This example highlights two important facets of the challenge: changing cultural attitudes and building viable career incentives to onboard new technology.

Can military culture be actively shaped to accommodate new technologies? Symbology and aspirational ideal types are two key locations of organisational culture. Consider the symbology represented in the iconic scene from Francis Ford Coppola's film *Apocalypse*

---

26 P. R. Mansoor and W. Murray (eds), *The Culture of Military Organizations* (New York: Cambridge University Press, 2019).

27 D. Leggett, *Shaping the Royal Navy: Technology, Authority, and Naval Architecture, c.1830–1906* (Manchester: Manchester University Press, 2016).

28 Quoted in L. Blanken et al, 'America's Military is Choking on Old Technology' in *Foreign Policy*, 29 January 2018, https://foreignpolicy.com/2018/01/29/americas-military-is-choking-on-old-technology/.

29 E. T. Miller, 'The Men Who Sail Below' in *All Hands*, 26 September 2018, https://allhands.navy.mil/Stories/Display-Story/Article/1840591/the-men-who-sail-below/.

Now, in which the helicopters of the First Air Cavalry are taking off as a bugler plays the call for 'charge' while wearing the attire of a nineteenth century Western frontier cavalryman. In this case, the battlefield mobility afforded by a new technology (helicopters) was wedded effectively to a romantic aspect of the American military tradition (Westward expansion). This offers glimmers into how a military organisation might strategically shape organisational culture to adopt new technology effectively. Additionally, the ideal type within the organisation captures the touchstone for the membership. Can current warrior ideal types, such as 'the ace' or the 'the door kicker', be replaced by ideal types that are centred on the indirect efforts of enabling machines to create the desired effects? Perhaps an ideal type could be constructed that views the specialist in human-machine teaming as an 'orchestra conductor' or a 'football quarterback'.[30]

Beyond attempts to directly shape the culture through symbology and ideal types, many social scientists argue that organisational culture is best understood as a dependent variable that is driven by formal institutional incentives.[31] In this vein, the effective integration of human-machine teaming specialists would hinge on the rationalist-materialist incentives around recruitment, advancement and retention.[32] Beyond bonuses, awards and promotions, a key organisational design consideration here would be how this specialist career path would lead to higher command. The United States Navy, for example, has traditionally associated increased responsibility with the number of personnel that one manages. How might this 'scope of responsibility' metric be translated to machine teammates? It will require careful designing to weave together such material incentives along with aspirational cultural trappings to successfully integrate human-machine teams into existing military organisations. We would offer that a first principles approach to understanding operational risk, human task load, and holistic complexity with any given task or occupational speciality around human-machine teaming needs to be adopted before designing the attendant career incentives.

The Systemic Level

The employment of human-machine teams in combat will fundamentally transform the norms of warfare on the international stage. Past technological advancements, such as the strategic bomber, the submarine and chemical, biological and nuclear payloads, all drove similar transformations.[33] In response, actors shaped – and were shaped by – the

30   American football (apologies to British readers).
31   R. W. Jackman and R. A. Miller, 'Social Capital and Politics', *Annual Review of Political Science*, 1 (1998), pp.47–73.
32   R. Gibbons, 'Team Theory, Garbage Cans and Real Organisations: Some History and Prospects of Economic Research on Decision-Making in Organisations', *Industrial and Corporate Change*, 12:4 (2003), pp.753–787.
33   C. A. Ford, 'Rules, Norms, and Community: Arms Control Discourses in a Changing World', *European Union Conference on Nonproliferation*, 13 December 2019, https://2017-2021.state. gov/rules-norms-and-community-arms-control-discourses-in-a-changing-world/.

resulting norms that arose to shape and constrain such advancements. Actors should treat the transformative impact of human-machine teams as an opportunity to design system-level norms of behaviour; in fact, it will be critical to do so. We argue that shaping international norms around human-machine teams should be pursued with three attributes in mind: advantage, desirability and sustainability.

International norms are regularised forms of accepted (and expected) behaviour among system members and may be held in place due to two distinct mechanisms: internalisation over time or enforced through punishments for transgression.[34] The defining feature of social norms is their resistance to easy manipulation; this is because actors' behaviours both drive and are driven by the system's emergent normative arrangement of accepted behaviours in a jointly endogenous causal loop.[35] Despite the difficulty in strategically shaping international norms, game theoretic modelling provides some useful concepts and by identifying viable locations for the establishment of such norms.[36] Given this, strategies around norms formation could be approached by applying three tests of sustainability, advantage and desirability.

> *Sustainability* here refers to the likelihood of identifying, achieving and maintaining the desired norms – not only among allies but, critically, among adversaries. The Nash equilibrium solution concept within non-cooperative game theory provides the basis for such thinking as Nash equilibria are defined as outcomes from which no player has a unilateral incentive to defect. Such outcomes, therefore, provide natural locations upon which to build norms that are endogenously binding.[37] In other words, pursuing the establishment of norms around human-machine teaming that lie outside of Nash equilibrium conditions fails the sustainability test.

> *Advantage* here refers to paying attention to any distributional conflicts that may occur when sorting through potential equilibria. Nash equilibria can include outcomes in which one actor gains more than another. The 'Battle of the Sexes' class of games highlights this issue.[38] Imagine a husband and wife who would like to coordinate their evening to meet for a pleasant night out. They could meet at a hockey game (the husband's preferred choice) or the opera (the wife's preferred choice). Going to either event together is in equilibrium, while going to separate events is not. There is

34   G. Goertz and P. F. Diehl, 'Toward a Theory of International Norms: Some Conceptual and Measurement Issues', *Journal of Conflict Resolution*, 36 (1992), pp.634–664.
35   D. Dessler, 'What's at Stake in the Agent-Structure Debate?', *International Organisation*, 43:3 (1989), pp.441–473.
36   J. D. Morrow, *Order Within Anarchy: The Laws of War as an International Institution* (New York: Cambridge University Press, 2014).
37   L. Blanken, *Rational Empires: Institutional Incentives and Imperial Expansion* (Chicago: University of Chicago Press, 2012), pp.2–4.
38   This heuristic example reflects the gender roles of when it was introduced. See R. D. Luce and H. Raiffa, *Games and Decisions: An Introduction and Critical Survey* (New York: Wiley & Sons, 1957).

distributional conflict, however, as each 'date night' involves one actor enjoying their evening more than the other. This is referred to as a 'relative gains' problem and may lead to either absolute gains being foregone through the collapse of the equilibria or one actor putting other(s) at a strategic disadvantage through their asymmetric gain.[39] In other words, pursuing norms around human-machine teaming that significantly disadvantages any relevant actor(s) may be prone to break down .

Desirability would be where the preferred values and domestic norms of a society and its leadership would come into play. This would, most likely, be an attempt to reconcile the international norms of acceptable employment of military human-machine teams in a manner that is least inconsistent with domestic laws, standards and ethics. Though war, by its very definition, constitutes a qualitative break with domestic normalcy, nations – particularly democracies – often strive to pursue war in ways that violate domestic norms as little as possible.[40] In other words, within the subset of Nash equilibria (sustainable) that are not plagued by significant distributional issues (advantage), actors should look to pursue norms that are least divergent from domestic norms.

The evolution of strategic nuclear weapons provides a relevant comparison. The use of these weapons has been kept in check since 1945 largely because strategists were able to articulate significant value in the non-use of these weapons through the concept of mutual assured destruction.[41] The shared concepts, strategies and norms that regulated the non-use of strategic nuclear weapons among nuclear powers were created contemporaneously with the game theoretic logics explained above.[42] Though such analytic modelling does not create reality, it can help discipline and focus policy and strategy efforts towards desired outcomes.

What are the key attributes of human-machine teaming that should be considered when designing future norms? We argue that the central challenge will be the speed of kill chains. If war is determined to a large degree by the comparative speed of adversaries' OODA [Observe, Orient, Decide, Act] loops, and if '[f]uture enemies employ AI and autonomous systems to expedite targeting unconstrained by ethical norms', then machine-speed kill chains will rapidly defeat ones that are interrupted by human interference.[43] Though many experts advocate for a 'trust but verify' approach to machines

39   D. Snidal, 'International Cooperation Among Relative Gains Maximizers', *International Studies Quarterly*, 35:4 (1989), pp.387–402.
40   M. Howard, *War and the Liberal Conscience* (New Brunswick, NJ: Rutgers University Press, 1978).
41   L. E. Freedman, *The Evolution of Nuclear Strategy* (New York, Third Edition: Palgrave MacMillan, 2003).
42   H. D. Sokolski (ed.), *Getting MAD: Nuclear Mutual Assured Destruction, Its Origins and Practice* (Carlisle Barracks, PA: Strategic Studies Institute, 2004).
43   U.S. Army, *Army Futures Command Concept for Command and Control 2028: Pursuing Decision Dominance* (AFC Pamphlet 71–20–9), p.13.

and to 'keep humans in the loop', the speed of future conflict will most likely stress or break these injunctions.[44] Just as strategic nuclear weapons became 'too big' to be useful, machine-speed kill chains may become 'too fast' to be useful. As human-machine teams become more effective on the battlefield, it will be in the interest of each state to compete to make their systems more effective on the one hand, while simultaneously looking for ways to control their destructive impact on the other. If this is to be achieved, it will most likely be done through the strategic shaping of international norms or some clever tweak of deterrence strategy.

Conclusions

Getting the future of human-machine teaming right is not simply a technical challenge; the human elements of the story must not be neglected. Priming military and political leadership to begin designing this massive socio-technical system as soon as possible is necessary to achieving the best path forward. Here we offer some final thoughts on the topic.

The first challenge is 'who is the designer?' Our brief survey of the challenge space has not identified what single actor within a modern, Western military would be empowered to direct such a comprehensive endeavour. Given the broad array of topics covered here, the effort would need to be a collaborative effort among various military, civilian and private sector entities. Though daunting, such a collaborative design approach may have its own benefits. Mobilising heterogeneous stakeholders and engaging in an iterative process may allow militaries (and societies) to successfully 'muddle through' to the fruitful and responsible employment of human-machine teams.[45]

A second challenge will be mobilising the appropriate resources to rapidly prototype towards solutions in a cost-effective manner. We offer three suggestions. The first is the special operations communities. These military organisations have an established track record and intrinsic institutional attributes that lend them to being testbeds for such innovation efforts to benefit the wider conventional military.[46] Similarly, professional military education (PME) institutions should be more fully leveraged to study, experiment and wargame the future-machine teams. Beyond providing critical analysis on the challenges of human-machine teaming, the students at these PME institutions will become the leaders of tomorrow who will employ and manage human-machine teams

44   P. Lushenko, 'Trust but Verify: U.S. Troops, Artificial Intelligence, and an Uneasy Partnership', *Brookings Institute*, 22 January 2024, https://www.brookings.edu/articles/trust-but-verify-u-s-troops-artificial-intelligence-and-an-uneasy-partnership/.
45   C. E. Lindblom, 'The Science of "Muddling Through"' in *Public Administration*, 19:2 (1959), pp.79–88.
46   L. Blanken, 'The Future of Innovation in Special Operations Forces: Challenges and Opportunities', in James D. Kiras and Martijn Kitzen (eds), *Into the Void: Special Operations Beyond the Global War on Terror* (New York: Oxford University Press, 2024).

on the battlefield. Finally, advances in computer-based simulation in military training (termed 'Live, Virtual, Constructive' environments) will prove increasingly valuable for comparatively testing critical military tasks and combined operations, prior to their use in real world combat.[47] Critical thinking, creativity and rapid iteration will be necessary to co-evolve the human and technical aspects of this challenge.

In sum, exploring and debating these topics and trade-offs needs to be done before the pace of technological change overtakes the pace of thoughtful consideration. Framing the endeavour as the collaborative design of a complex socio-technical system provides an appropriate toolkit for knitting together technical and human dimensions, as well as synchronising efforts at the individual, organisational and systemic levels.[48] The time to get started is now.

---

47   A. Park, 'Live, Virtual, Constructive Called the Future of Navy Training' in *National Defense*, 29 November 2023, https://www.nationaldefensemagazine.org/articles/2023/11/29/live-virtual-constructive-called-the-future-of-navy-training.

48   G. Fischer and T. Herrmann, 'Socio-Technical Systems: A Meta-Design Perspective', *International Journal of Sociotechnology and Knowledge Development*, 3 (2011), pp.1–33.

8

The Impact of the 4th Industrial Revolution on Combat Cohesion

Warren Chin

'The art of war is subjected to numerous modifications to accord with scientific and industrial and other progress. But one thing does not change: the heart of man. In the final analysis, combat is a moral affair; in all the improvements concerning an army, its organisation, its discipline, and its tactics, all must concede that the human heart in the supreme moment of battle is always the essential question.'

Ardant du Picq, *Battle Studies*, 1880.[1]

Introduction

The unleashing of the Fourth Industrial Revolution is likely to be something of a Pandora's box. As a feat of technological innovation, it promises to revolutionise every aspect of human existence, including the conduct of war. Evidence of its importance in the military realm can be seen by how it is driving the latest arms race between the United States and China. In this competition for superiority, technological innovation, rather than weapons, has become the metric of victory – reflect on Vladimir Putin's observation that the state which wins the race in artificial intelligence (AI) will control the world. The speed and breadth of change induced by this revolution in the military realm are causing militaries to ask existential questions about how these technologies will change the conduct and character of war. Much of this debate has been pitched at the strategic and operational level of war, but it is important to remember that tactics impact on both.

---

1   Ardant du Picq (Roger Spiller, trans. & ed.), *Battle Studies* (Lawrence, KA: Kansas University Press, 2017).

Consequently, a theory of military operations that neglects tactics will likely encounter a rude awakening as thinking based in the ethereal domains of strategy and operations is challenged by the grim reality of battle. Recent neglect of the tactical level by those tasked within the military to gaze into the future of war has stemmed from two sources. First, imagining a future battlefield is not an easy thing to do, often the implications of technologies in war are not revealed in the lab but only when used at scale on the battlefield when they interact with other technologies and indeed human beings. Second, direct experience also encouraged our thinking about future war to neglect the tactical battlefield. One of the principal lessons learned from the Gulf War (1990–1991) was that technology enabled the dislocation of the enemy within the theatre of operations as a whole before the tactical battle began.[2] As a result, battle became little more than a case of forward units 'sweeping up the rubble' of an enemy destroyed largely by long-range indirect fire. Subsequent wars in Kosovo (1999), Afghanistan, (2001–2002) and Iraq (2003) revealed a continued focus on the operational domain of warfare prosecuted via a host of technologies. For a brief but painful moment our attention was again forced back to the tactical level of war as victories in Iraq and Afghanistan mutated into protracted insurgencies. However, the return of great power competition between states forced the lens of future war to refocus on the high end of the spectrum of conflict. But once again, battle was largely a footnote in these analyses which seized on the exploitation of technology to wage war via non-kinetic means. This new kind of war was described as grey zone war, hybrid war, unrestricted warfare. Within these scenarios, land battles were depicted as discrete operations fitting in within a broader grand strategy in which the outcome of the war was shaped principally by social, political and psychological forces.[3]

Underlying longer term visions of future battle was a hope that technology would and could sanitise a future war and erase the bloody horror of combat as more subtle means were found to defeat generic enemies. When battle was visualised, it was through this prism, and we struggled to describe future combat except through the logic of technological advance based on stand-off weaponry. This created an image dominated by machines empowered with AI. In this world of war, the fragile limitations of humanity meant flesh and blood no longer had a part to play in a duel now waged between machine intelligences operating in nanoseconds and employing a host of exotic lethal weapons.[4]

The logic underlying this vision has been challenged by the grim reality of the Russia-Ukraine War which began in 2022. This war is based on mass not precision, it is a war of attrition rather than one focused on psychological dislocation and by extension it is a protracted war that is assuming the characteristics of old-fashioned twentieth century total war. Bizarrely these effects have been attributed not merely to the incompetence

2   John Warden, *The Air Campaign: Planning for Combat* (Washington, DC: National Defense University Press, 1988).

3   Ofer Fridman, *Russian Hybrid Warfare Resurgence and Politicisation* (Oxford: Oxford University Press, 2018).

4   Robert H. Latiff, *Future War Preparing for the New Global Battlefield* (New York: Alfred A. Knopf, 2017).

of two Soviet-style armies embracing high tech, but rather to the unexpected combat outcomes created through the deployment of new and emerging technologies.[5] The most important technical evolution on the battlefields of Ukraine has been the creation of a 'poor man's' tactical reconnaissance strike complex consisting of a vast array of cheap drones, linked in the case of the Ukrainians, via homemade apps to provide accurate indirect fire. It is estimated that 86 percent of Ukrainian artillery targeting relies on the use of drones. This connectivity has allowed a targeting cycle which takes minutes not hours to initiate to destroy enemy forces. The combined effects of the old and the new on the contemporary battlefield has led to levels of lethality reminiscent of the casualties of the First and Second World Wars. One Ukrainian general observed during his army's offensive in 2023, that on today's battlefield 'if it moves it's killed'. As a result, the defining characteristics of this war are precisely the opposite of what had been imagined – positional and attritional in which mass rather than demassification of armies has become the imperative of war. Most important, mass now extends to new technologies employed in war. For example, it is claimed the Ukrainians lose 10,000 drones per month, with each drone having a life expectancy of six missions. To this end the Ukrainians are scaling up production to manufacture two million drones per year. Technology has also allowed the defender to maintain his front line with a lower density of troops. Today 350,000 Russian soldiers are arrayed on a front line of 1,200 kilometres, this is around 300 men per kilometre of front. In the Second World War, force concentrations were approximately 3,000 men per kilometre of front.[6]

In sum, the war in Ukraine has ensured that battle at the tactical level has been restored to its former position of pre-eminence. This can be demonstrated by the scale of losses inflicted in the forward edge of the battle area. In the first year of the war, the combined material losses on both sides equated to more than 11,000 major weapons platforms destroyed. The human cost has also been high and it is estimated that in the first two years of the war over 500,000 Russian soldiers were killed or wounded. Before becoming complacent and judging the belligerents as 'mere armed mobs' we should note that in a recent wargaming and simulation exercise conducted by NATO, brigades achieved their objectives but suffered 80 percent casualties. This, as Watling points out, is a staggering rate of attrition and no state possesses the resources to replace these losses.[7] While there are no official figures on cases of 'battle stress', the psychological impact of fighting in this setting is clearly recognised – at least within Ukraine's armed forces.[8] Much of what is described feels very similar to the experiences of soldiers in past wars, grinding battles

5   See Marla Karlin, 'The Return of Total War Understanding and Preparing for the New Era of Comprehensive Conflict' and Michael Horowitz, 'Battles of Precise Mass', *Foreign Affairs*, 103:6 (November/December 2024).
6   'Western Armies are learning a lot from the war in Ukraine', *The Economist*, 3 July 2024.
7   Jack Watling, *The Arms of the Future: Technology and Close Combat in the Twenty-First Century* (London: Bloomsbury Press, 2024), p.12.
8   Oleh Hukovsky et al., 'Combat Path Sustaining Mental Readiness in Ukrainian Soldiers' in *Parameters*, 54:2 (Summer 2024), pp.23–43.

that continue day and night for weeks and sometimes months. In sum, the Russia-Ukraine War has reaffirmed humanity's central role on the battlefield and checked the *Terminator* school of future war which sees conflict largely a clash between machines.

Extrapolating from a single case study to project into the future is always a dangerous game to play and there are very specific factors that have helped elevate the importance of battle within this war. Of critical importance is the inability of either side to conduct the type of sustained long-range, large-scale attacks into the operational depth of the enemy as demonstrated by the Americans in past wars. However, an important difference between recent and future operations is that control of space, air and the electromagnetic spectrum is likely to be heavily contested in a future war, and this will reduce the effectiveness of deep operations. As such, the tactical battle will become increasingly important and so too will the role of the human on the future battlefield, at least when viewed over a time horizon of 10 to 15 years. This is about as far as prediction can go in terms of extrapolating the present into the future without descending into wishful thinking.[9] There appears to be a consensus that within this timeframe machines, even those driven by AI, will lack the wherewithal to cope with the physical – or indeed the cognitive – complexity of the real world and for now, at least, humans will remain a vital component of war. However, these technologies pose a potent threat both physically and morally, but this is not a new problem and evidence of this can be seen from how armies responded to the impact of the Second Industrial Revolution, which revolutionised the battlefield and war between 1850 and 1945. Re-examination of the past might help us to better understand how we address the new challenges we face on the future battlefield.

Ardant du Picq and His Reflections on Modern War

Before we despair about the plight of humanity on the future battlefield, it is important to remember we have confronted this kind of challenge before. Moreover, the response crafted to address it provides if not a solution, then, a more constructive and methodical way of comprehending the problem and how we might address the impact of technology on the future battlefield. Of relevance here are the writings of *Colonel* Ardant du Picq (1821–1870). Although his thoughts date back to the 1860s, his ideas provide an appropriate starting point in an investigation of the connection between war, technology and humanity because he addressed a similar challenge to that facing soldiers today – the impact of the industrialised battlefield on the morale of the army. A long service soldier in the French military, du Picq witnessed first-hand how the fruits of the First Industrial Revolution changed the character of battle. His observations collected in his book, *Battle Studies*, were inspired by the challenges contemporary European armies faced during the firepower revolution unfolding in the second half of the nineteenth century. He

---

9   Philip Tetlock and Dan Gardener, *Super-forecasting: The Art and Science of Prediction* (London: Random House, 2015).

witnessed the effects of rifled muskets and the Minié ball during the Crimean War and observed how Union and Confederate armies struggled to deal with both rifled muskets and breech-loading rifled artillery.

An interesting addition to this mix was his experience of fighting in Syria against Druze tribal militias, which opened his eyes to the human equation in war. The fundamental question that emerged from his reflections was how to ensure soldiers continued to advance and close with the enemy on a battlefield that created an unprecedented sense of fear. At the heart of his analysis was the recognition of what today is called the 'flight or fight response'. This is an instinctive reaction to a direct threat to life and causes the person to either flee or attack the cause of the danger. Two questions arose in his study. First, why did soldiers ignore the instinct to run, and second, how could their fears be contained on the battlefield of his time? He observed that on the industrialised battlefield, the level of violence was such that each soldier reached a point where the urge to run became too powerful to resist. Within this setting, traditional forms of control, such as coercion and discipline, no longer held those fears in check. The fragility of French soldiers on the battlefield was compounded in du Picq's view by the pernicious effects of broader societal change within France, which he believed was killing the martial spirit of its people. This decline in virtue was attributed to the pernicious effects of what he called democracy, but this might be seen as the symptom of a deeper cause of cultural change triggered by modernity, i.e. industrialisation and urbanisation.[10] Du Picq's observation highlights the wider effects technology can exert beyond the battlefield; a development we are all too familiar with today as we debate how smartphones and social media are changing the values and norms of contemporary society – specifically its supposed lack of resilience.

For du Picq, the answer to the question posed by the dramatic increase in firepower and how soldiers could cope with this challenge was via improved morale. He failed to provide a pithy definition of this concept, but this was largely because, for him, morale was an amalgamation of many different actions and processes, which made it impossible to define. He groups these disparate elements into four broad categories: command, discipline, comradeship and organisation. The amalgamation of these factors generates more than mere courage. As he observed: 'Four brave men who do not know each other would not dare attack a lion. Four less brave men, but who know each other well, with solidarity and mutual support, resolutely attack. There is all the science of the organisation in brief.'[11]

Organisation was the vital force multiplier in du Picq's view, ensuring the less courageous army was victorious in battle. So, for example, when exploring the behaviour of soldiers in warrior armies he observed the more courageous warriors were typically defeated by their less courageous French opponents. He hypothesised the answer to this puzzle lay in the deficient organisation of the warrior army.[12] The French Army took

10   Du Picq, *Battle Studies*, Loc 560.
11   Du Picq, *Battle Studies*, Loc 1877.
12   Du Picq, *Battle Studies*, Loc 2027.

his theory of morale to heart, and it became the foundation of their *offensive à outrance* (offensive to the utmost) doctrine in the lead up to the First World War. This doctrine is mired in controversy and is seen to have played an instrumental role in France's disastrous battles in the first month of the war. It was believed that reliance on morale demonstrated a profound naivety because it assumed willpower could overcome the challenge of firepower and this thinking stymied much-needed change in the tactical organisation of the army.[13] Given du Picq's culpability in the catastrophic performance of the French military it is fair to question his utility in the twenty-first century. I offer two responses to this question. First, there is a view that the French Army literally weaponised du Picq in their efforts to ensure the preservation of a certain kind of army based on an aristocratic officer corps and long service professional soldiers.[14] Second, and connected to the first point, its focus on élan led it to ignore the most significant part of du Picq's analysis, which was the importance of organisation in the generation of morale. This is the part of his theory of war which I believe can be applied most usefully to our study of the changing character of the battlefield today. Two questions arise here. First, to what extent is the organisation of the British Army challenged by anticipated developments on the future battlefield? Second, can we conceive of changes identified by du Picq that might increase its resilience and hence effectiveness in a future battle?

The British Army and du Picq

While there is no evidence showing that anyone in the British Army read or adapted the ideas of du Picq, there is a degree of overlap between elements of his thinking and the British view on how to create and sustain morale. For example, the British Army presumes there is a strong connection between organisational structure and unit cohesion, and between cohesion and combat motivation. The most obvious embodiment of this philosophy lies in the value placed on the regimental system.[15] While the regiment is frequently cited as the creator of morale, studies of combat cohesion assert the actual engine of cohesion lies in the sub-units that make up the regiment. The classic study of this subject remains Shils and Janowitz's study of the performance of the German Army in the Second World War. According to van Creveld, German soldiers were 20 percent more effective than their Western allied counterparts in the battles to liberate Nazi-occupied Western Europe.[16] Shils and Janowitz's analysis concluded that the most important reason why German soldiers were so much more effective lay in what they

---

13   See Robert Doughty, *The Seeds of Disaster: The Development of French Military Doctrine 1919–39* (Hamden, CT: Archon Books, 1985).
14   See Douglas Porch, *The March to the Marne: The French Army 1871–1914* (Cambridge: Cambridge University Press, 1981).
15   See John Baynes, *Morale: A Study of Men and Courage* (London: Cassell, 1967).
16   Martin van Creveld, *Fighting Power: German and U.S. Army Performance, 1939–45* (Westport, CN: Greenwood Publishing, 1982).

called the cohesion created by specific primary groups within the Wehrmacht. What made these primary groups distinctive was the intimacy and strength of the social bonds within the group. In sum, it acted as the principal focus of each member's loyalty to the individuals who made up this unit. In the case of the German Army, Shils and Janowitz concluded that the company (120 soldiers) represented the most important primary group. The need to achieve the respect of the group's members and the close friendships that emerged between soldiers ensured they would fight and sometimes die for each other.[17]

It has been claimed that the organisation of armies and their primary groups – whether it is the company, the platoon or the section – is a manifestation of deep-rooted instincts found within humanity. In the early 1990s, anthropologist Robert Dunbar asserted that the maximum size for any group of primates was determined by brain size – specifically the size of the neocortex. The larger the neocortex, the more individuals with whom you could maintain personal relationships. In the case of humans, the ideal number of relationships was just under 150 people. This number coincided with the size of groups in hunter-gatherer societies, which on average was 150 people. Junger notes how this coincides with the structure of military organisations going back to the Romans; for example, a Roman maniple contained 130 men. A modern infantry company contains broadly the same number. Junger observed that based on his observation of a U.S. infantry company in Afghanistan all the soldiers in the company knew the members of this formation, but, in his view the 'molten core' of the group was the platoon. This formation also coincided with forms of organisation in human prehistory. Dunbar found that the size of hunter-gatherer communities tended to clump around 30 to 50 people, a figure that coincides with the strength of a modern platoon.[18]

However, King challenges this view. He believes the importance of the primary group in the form of the platoon grew exponentially because of the industrialisation of war. Of specific importance was the dramatic increase in lethality soldiers faced on the modern battlefield. This forced armies to disperse which posed a problem – how could commanders get soldiers to advance when confronted by a hail of lead and razor-sharp steel fragments caused by artillery fire and amplified as airpower entered the fray? Faced with such a storm soldiers understandably go to ground.[19] In exploring this issue, the process of innovation and organisational adaptation during the First World War offers an important insight into how subsequent organisational change was introduced to generate and sustain combat effectiveness and morale. So, for example, Stephen Biddle has argued that the modern military that we see today in wars such as in Ukraine, first emerged as a response to the impact of firepower during the First World War. This new system moved away from linear to non-linear tactics and focused on dispersion,

17   Edward A. Shils and Morris Janowitz, 'Cohesion and Disintegration in the Wehrmacht in World War II' in *Public Opinion Quarterly*, 12 (Summer 1948), p.283.
18   Cited in Sebastian Junger, *War* (London: Fourth Estate, 2010), Chapter 4.
19   Anthony King, *The Combat Soldier: Infantry Tactics and Cohesion in the Twentieth and Twenty-First Centuries* (Oxford: Oxford University Press, 2013), p.63.

cover, concealment and combined arms between artillery, infantry and, in the case of the Allies, tanks.[20] Faced by this tactical conundrum King asserts the platoon emerged as an organisational solution to the problem of how to wage modern battle. The platoon existed as an administrative unit for over 200 years prior to the First World War but became a combat formation within modern armies in the second half of this conflict. This change addressed the need for dispersal to dissipate the effects of enemy firepower. In addition, it allowed for the creation of specialist sub-units trained and equipped with the means to fight their way through a modern defence. For King, the significance of the platoon stems from three sources. First, it is 'the tactical unit on which all infantry tactics are built'. Second, it has the task of engaging in extreme violence at close range. Finally, the platoon is the prime location for cohesion in an army. King acknowledges that higher-level formations might claim cohesion resides within their domain, but the important distinction for him is that all members of a platoon know each other, something which is not possible in higher formations. Instead, he believes these other formations display *esprit de corps* – a sense of organisational unity.[21]

The debate over combat cohesion persisted in the Second World War as soldiers struggled to deal with the challenge of modern battle, which increased in intensity, scale and duration. Interestingly, these studies continued to emphasise the key connection between morale and small unit organisation. The negative impact of firepower on cohesion was best illustrated by S. L. A. Marshall in his analysis of the combat performance of American infantry in the Second World War.[22] He claimed that 85 percent of soldiers in small units were seized by fear and failed to use individual weapons when in battle.[23] However, this observation did not result in a radical restructuring of army organisation, but new training methods to instil greater fighting spirit. A more detailed and rigorous analysis of combat during the Second World War carried out by Sammuel Stouffer again reaffirmed the importance of the emotional bonds that formed between soldiers within their units. The link between cohesion and fighting spirit was again identified in the Korean War and Vietnam War.[24]

Interestingly the challenge posed by irregular wars during the Cold War, which produced different psychological and physical challenges, also failed to produce dramatic change in the organisational structure of Western militaries. For example, the British Army fought a succession of small wars through the Cold War and into the

---

20   Stephen Biddle, *Military Power Explaining Victory and Defeat in Modern Battle* (Princeton: Princeton University Press, 2004).

21   King, *The Combat Soldier*, pp.17–18.

22   It is important to note that Marshall's observations caused huge controversy and his sources and methods have been contested.

23   S. L. A. Marshall, *Men Against Fire: The Problem of Battle Command* (Norman, OK: Oxford University Press, 1947).

24   See Roger W. Little, 'Buddy Relations and Combat *Performance*', in Morris Janowitz (ed.), *The New Military: Changing Patterns of Organization* (New York: Russell Sage Foundation, 1964); Charles Moskos, *The American Enlisted Man: The Rank and File in Today's Military* (New York: Russell Sage Foundation, 1964).

post-Cold War era, but the challenges posed by these environments produced little in the way of organisational change as a way of enhancing cohesion and morale. Instead, the British Army somehow muddled through from Palestine to Afghanistan.[25] Studies of social cohesion and combat effectiveness in these wars quibbled over the details of this relationship but its utility was rarely challenged and indeed continues to shape our thinking.

Cohesion and Organisation on the Future Battlefield

The Fourth Industrial Revolution poses a profoundly different challenge to the experience of recent irregular wars. As has been said, the speed and ferocity of the future battlefield is expected to see an exponential leap in lethality.

How then can organisational change improve the resilience and survivability of the soldier on the battlefield? Viewed from the perspective of the human spear of battle, 'the poor bloody infantry', the answer appears to be to create greater dispersal of soldiers across this physical space. However, as in the past, this response challenges the parameters of cohesion because it deprives the soldier of the basic physical and emotional pillars of support deemed vital in preserving fighting spirit, which was precisely the problem du Picq faced. The function of infantry is also going to have to change if soldiers are to survive facing an AI-driven reconnaissance strike complex. Advance to contact and fighting at close quarters will be the exception rather than the rule. According to Robert Scales, future soldiers will function as battlefield sensors in the forward edge of the battlespace. Here, their primary role will be to use surveillance technologies to feed information to the operational commander deployed outside the range of the enemy's weaponry. This vision of future battle implies that such units will be largely isolated and, if attacked, physical reinforcement or extraction will likely be a hazardous exercise, which means they are on their own – even resupply will be a challenge. However, each of these units will be able to draw on the firepower of higher-level formations which also lie outside the range of the enemy's weaponry to defend them if attacked.[26] This network of human sensors will be deployed across the entire battlefront and the information they gather will be used to break the enemy's reconnaissance strike complex and so enable offensive manoeuvre by friendly forces deployed further back. In sum, operational fires, directed from the forward edge battle will be employed to bring about the tactical disintegration of the enemy.

Scales argues that the level of dispersion required by infantry on this battlefield and their new mission cannot be adequately addressed within the existing organisational

---

25   Richard Holmes, *Firing Line* (London: Penguin, 1986); Hugh McManners, *The Scars of War* (London: Harper Collins, 1993).
26   Robert Scales, 'Tactical Art in Future Wars' in *War on the Rocks* (2019) https://warontherocks. com/2019/03/tactical-art-in-future-wars/.

framework of armies. If survival and functionality are to be achieved, a new type of formation which lies somewhere between the platoon and the section needs to be created. Although not prescriptive, Scales argues that a group of perhaps 13 soldiers should be sufficient in this new formation. The size of this grouping will be determined solely by the functions the unit is designed to serve on the future battlefield. The creation of this unit should ensure the sustainment of cohesion, but it will still face significant challenges. The most important of these will be the sense of isolation experienced by these units, hidden and dispersed as they must be.

Shils and Janowitz's note that a factor of great significance in undermining cohesion was precisely the sense of isolation experienced by German soldiers in platoons and companies as they sought to take refuge from the increasingly heavy bombardment from enemy artillery and airpower. Confronted by this constant barrage, soldiers took refuge in cellars, trenches or any place that afforded protection and respite in groups of three or four. Often these elements were trapped for days at a time and as a result the cohesion of the primary group, whether a platoon or company, began to disintegrate. Faced by this situation, the isolated soldier focused increasingly on his own survival. The heavier the attack, the more acute the fear of death or being maimed. The absence of a reliable supply of food and medical assistance also impacted on the morale of soldiers. Reinforcing the power of one's own survival was the increasing competition from his responsibilities and commitment to his civilian primary group – the family. They claimed the 'strong pull of the civilian primary group became stronger as the coherence of the army group weakened'.[27]

Equally important, I presume that physical movement within such a formation will have to be kept to the minimum to avoid detection from enemy optical acoustic or vibration sensors. As a result, the high levels of adrenaline pumped into the body as the fight-flight response kicks in will add to the soldier's stress because adrenaline is typically reduced through physical activity.[28] A direct challenge to the cohesion of the unit lies in its composition in terms of personnel. Given the diverse range of expertise required to ensure it can fulfil its principal role, getting such a heterogeneous group to bond together will require some thought. Command will surely play an important role in the generation of higher morale within this unit. Scales asserts the unit commander will be acting three levels above their normal rank. This is necessary because of the range of tasks assigned to this unit and the level of firepower it will draw on to attack the enemy. However, the demands of this post will impose a severe strain on the person in charge. The creation of this tactical organisation is driven largely by the need to survive and carry out its mission. As such, the cohesion that stems from this 'super squad' is an unintended but beneficial consequence, but will it be enough?

27   Shils and Janowitz, 'Cohesion and Disintegration in the Wehrmacht in World War II', p.290.
28   Other countermeasures are available to limit the impact of this kind of stress.

Do We Need to Adapt the Concept of Cohesion?

Two possible solutions are presented here. The first involves rethinking our under-standing of cohesion as something that is hardwired into the human psyche and draws almost exclusively from social bonds formed within a group. This is not a new idea. In the 1990s, Elizabeth Kier examined the literature on cohesion and concluded 'fifty years of research in several disciplines has failed to uncover persuasive evidence …. that there is a causal relationship leading from primary group cohesion to military effectiveness'.[29] King's exploration of combat cohesion acknowledges the importance of attachments and how they are formed but also claims that the sources of cohesion in today's Western armies stems from a range of other sources, which better explain the connection between cohesion and combat performance. He points out that traditional conceptions of cohesion fail to recognise how this variable can sometimes undermine combat performance as the survival of the group sometimes overshadows its assigned mission.[30] Equally impor-tant, if we look at the realm of sport, we see how teams characterised by low social cohesion still achieve world beating performances. He squares this circle by reminding us that in the Western world, armies today are very different to the generations of soldiers that fought in the Second World War or Vietnam. These were largely conscript forces, but today's armies are composed of volunteers defined by what might be described as a task-driven professionalism. Within this construct, unity is not generated by ideals of nationalism, civic duty, comradeship or personal bonds but rather by a professional ethos. The significance of this concept is that it provides a secular moral framework that governs the internal behaviour of soldiers and their external connections to the society they are dedicated to protect.[31] Thus, 'professionalism may not simply be a series of prac-tical skills for soldiers today, … but also a morality which obligates soldiers to perform their role properly and, indeed, comport themselves generally in a manner which their professional status and colleagues demand'.[32]

This shared value system emerges because of training and working together over a prolonged period. This bond extends across all ranks, officer, non-commissioned officer and other ranks. This blurring and overlap are justified on the grounds that at the level of the battalion and below all soldiers, irrespective of rank, operate in a world they might be called upon to fight. Within this setting officers do not just manage violence they also apply it. Similarly, non-commissioned officers do not merely apply violence but also manage its application. These connections are reinforced by the sense of shared risk.

If viewed in this way, cohesion can be manipulated and adapted to the changing condi-tions facing soldiers on the future battlefield because if we accept the idea that profes-sionalism in the military is task driven then identifying the correct tasks and how best

29   Elizabeth Kier, 'Homosexuals in the U.S. Military: Open Integration and Combat Effectiveness' in *International Security*, 23:2 (Fall 1998), p.18.
30   King, *The Combat Soldier*, pp.31–32.
31   King, *The Combat Soldier*, pp.211–221.
32   King, *The Combat Soldier*, p.342.

to achieve them, drawing on du Picq's construct of morale, which includes command, discipline, camaraderie and organisation, provides a means to address this challenge. Recent calls for a return to a conscript-type army in the UK challenges this conception of a cohesion based on professionalism, but as the Germans demonstrated in the Second World War, conscription and professionalism are not mutually exclusive ideals.

Second, we need to think about the wider impact technology will have on humanity, specifically the social change caused by the Fourth Industrial Revolution. This possibly challenges our existing conceptions of cohesion and how best to sustain this bond in battle. Is it possible that du Picq's concept of the human heart captured in the chapter's opening quote is changing? Contemporary studies of social media and its effects indicate technology is having a profound impact on the human brain of 'Generation Z', particularly in cognitive function, emotional regulation and the kind of social interaction they prefer to undertake. A deeper and more prolonged exposure to the effects of technology will ensure these trends will be amplified in 'Generation Alpha', the demographic group from which armies will draw their recruits in the future. The available evidence presents a mixed picture. On the one hand, physical proximity and face-to-face interaction is less important to young people, which could be a positive on an increasingly isolated battlefield. Within this future setting the soldier might also draw greater comfort from the bond he builds with an emotionally intelligent AI, which it is claimed will become a feature of life in the modern world.[33] In addition, exposure to social media may improve visual spatial reasoning. But, on the other hand, it privileges surface level learning over deeper, reflective thinking and leads to reduced attention span and an inability to focus on complex tasks. Finally, the capacity of working memory is shrinking making it harder to retain information. As humanity becomes increasingly sucked into the 'metaverse' through ever-improved forms of virtual and augmented reality we will need to adjust our understanding of time, space and physical reality to reflect how technology might change consciousness and forms of social interaction. The question, then, is will this mean the future soldier will be more or less comfortable operating on the battlefield – a space described as the loneliest place in the world?

---

33   See Rob Brooks, *Artificial Intimacy: Virtual Friends, Digital Lovers, Algorithmic Matchmakers* (New York: Columbia University Press, 2021).

9

Knowing is Half the Battle: Organising Expertise for All-Domain Operations

J. P. Clark[1]

Artificial intelligence to make sense of vast amounts of data and develop solutions beyond the ability of the human mind; unmanned systems in the air and on the ground that can both seek and kill; attack and defence in cyberspace and the electromagnetic spectrum: there is debate about whether these new capabilities will lead to an entirely new 'character' of warfare or simply modify that which currently exists.

Only time will tell the answer to that question, but in the meantime the unforgiving timelines of personnel management require armies to make practical choices now. The Chief of the General Staff of 2050, after all, is likely already commissioned. What will he or she need to know to be a competent senior leader? How should the army assess and manage a cadre of artificial intelligence experts, and what should these experts know about the larger military profession? Conversely, what must the infantry soldier or tanker know about artificial intelligence?

These are fundamentally questions about expertise, which the army has well established methods for organising – a hierarchy of trades, specialties, roles and corps. Although these divisions of expertise are so ingrained and enduring as to rarely attract much reflection, they reflect deep-set assumptions about boundaries of knowledge and competence. Mechanised- and light-role infantry are similar enough to fall under the same category, but armour is not.

The army also manages expertise through tables of organisation; this management has one obvious and subtler component. The obvious component is the manner by which these tables explicitly dictate the number of experts by trade and seniority that should be in any given unit. But amassing the right number of individual experts no more makes a unit, then placing all of component parts into a bin makes a machine. Military

---

1   The views expressed are those of the author and do not necessarily reflect the official policy or position of the Department of the Army, Department of Defense, or the U.S. Government.

formations also require the expertise to make multiple specialities work together under trying conditions of uncertainty, fatigue and danger. Thus, the subtler component of tables of organisation is their implicit suggestion that the commander and staff possess the requisite expertise to intelligently train and fight all the unit's capabilities.

This chapter explores the challenge of organising expertise for the all-domain battlefield in three parts. The first section examines how individuals with new forms of expertise might be organised within the personnel system of corps and trades. The second section provides a framework of differing levels of expertise to help parse both what knowledge only a few experts must possess and what is essential for everyone to know. The final section builds upon those insights in light of recent battlefield trends to offer some suggestions for how expertise might come together in the form of fielded units.

Organising Individual Expertise: Hobby, Knowledge, Speciality, Corps or Service?

It is obvious that the army will increasingly require experts in fields like artificial intelligence, data science, unmanned aerial systems and cyberspace operations. It is often assumed that new technologies require new organisations, whether a new independent service, corps or command. Sometimes this is the appropriate response. But this reaction also stems from some lazy analogies that assume the aeroplane and tank – and hence their path of incorporation – are the models for military technological adoption. Thus, there is a mixture of good and bad thinking swirling around developments such as, in the United States, the creation first of Space Command, and then later the Space Force. Currently, there are similar debates about whether the same should happen for cyberspace as Congress has recently considered. Similarly, the 2024 annual defence bill passed by the House of Representatives authorised the army to create a 'Drone Corps' that would have not just responsibility for developing doctrine and equipment but also running a central operations centre to oversee drone operations. Technically infeasible and tactically inadvisable, that this astounding suggestion should even make it so far demonstrates the pervasiveness of the paradigm that novel technologies require new organisations.[2]

Yet even in those cases in which the creation of a new organisation is appropriate, it is not as complete and total a solution as some imagine. For instance, despite the creation of Space Force, the U.S. Army (as well as the other services) still retains a space operations career field for officers and several space-related enlisted specialities. This is an example of the general rule that any truly significant technology will have so many applications as to require more than a single organisational solution to fully realise its potential.

---

2   Angus King and Mike Gallagher, *Cyberspace Solarium Commission: Final Report*, March 2020, https://www.solarium.gov/report, accessed 21 October 2024; U.S. Congress, House of Representatives. *Servicemember Quality of Life Improvement and National Defense Authorization Act for Fiscal Year 2025*. H.R. 8070, 118th Congress, introduced in House 18 April 2024, Sec 924.

Aviation provides a more familiar example. The creation of an independent air force did not mean that the army was not profoundly affected. Aside from the obvious examples of airborne infantry, air defence and helicopters, the practice of fires, intelligence and logistics are all also intimately intertwined with the employment of aviation.

To gain a more nuanced perspective into how expertise in rapidly developing technologies can evolve over time, it is useful to look back to the early twentieth century, when the army faced similar challenges with the incorporation of aviation, the internal combustion engine and electricity for battlefield use.

The Royal Air Force is one model for the creation of a separate organisation to foster new expertise. It has the honour of becoming the first independent air force in the world, less than 15 years from the Wright brothers' first flight and just six years after the conversion of the Air Battalion of the Royal Engineers to the Royal Flying Corps. With over a century of intervening history, it is easy to overlook just how rapidly that organisational development occurred. But if we apply that same timeline and model to the present, then the creation of the Royal Space, Cyberspace or Unmanned Aerial Vehicle Forces are already years behind schedule, and depending upon when one fixes the 'Kitty Hawk moment' for artificial intelligence and machine learning there is only about a decade remaining to create the Royal Artificial Intelligence Force on schedule. These tongue-in-cheek examples raise some serious questions. Is it wise to so quickly determine an organisational solution for an emerging technology? Even if we thought the answer was 'yes', would such a radical solution be feasible outside of the rather extraordinary context of national mobilisation for a world war?

The evolution of the U.S. Air Force, therefore, is thus likely both more prudent and realistic. Although Congress considered establishing an independent air force as early as 1914, it did not actually do so until 1947; significantly, this was after another enormous wartime expansion had already created the full apparatus of aviation-facing administrative, personnel, supply and acquisition organisations necessary to support an independent service. Prior to that, aviation had progressed through several stages of growth within the Signal Corps before becoming an air corps equivalent to other branches like the artillery, and then later on to an Army air force equivalent to all of the ground forces combined. Although airmen chafed under these arrangements, this gradual organisational growth was a practical necessity that also allowed time for the implications of the new technology to emerge.

Rather than wish for an incredible leap forward, it is better to ask, how might we determine which 'cradle' is best to nurture a developing field of expertise that has not yet reached organisational maturity? There is nothing inevitable about these choices. The British Army initially chose to place aviation within the Royal Engineers, while the U.S. Army chose the Signal Corps. Historian David Johnson has brilliantly shown that interwar developments in American aviation and armour were conceptually anchored in the parent organisations from which they developed.[3] There are choices to be made, and

---

3   David E. Johnson, *Fast Tanks and Heavy Bombers: Innovation in the U.S. Army, 1917–1945* (Ithaca, NY: Cornell University Press, 1998).

we should be deliberate in thinking through possible paths of organisational development for today's nascent technologies.

Most new areas of expertise, however, are more likely to follow patterns of adoption similar to those of the internal combustion engine and electricity. Those cases suggest that any significant new technology will require multiple kinds of adaptation. These technologies did lead to the creation of new organisations such as the Royal Electrical and Mechanical Engineers, Royal Tank Regiment and Royal Corps of Signals. But they also necessitated other changes at a lower level. For instance, within enduring functions like logistics, veterinarians and farriers gave way to turret mechanics and petroleum specialists. Finally, even for positions that seemingly remained unchanged, the knowledge required to perform the same function has been transformed. Whereas a nineteenth century commander of a recce unit had to understand the care, limitations and capabilities of horses, today an understanding of vehicle maintenance and logistics and the characteristics of the electromagnetic spectrum are essential requirements, even though the core expertise of reconnaissance remains.

We should expect artificial intelligence, data science, cyberspace operations, unmanned systems (air, ground and subsurface) and the exploitation of proliferated sensors through open source intelligence to have similar effects. They, too, will produce some combination of new units, new trades and new knowledge for generalists. For instance, division intelligence officers, in addition to much of what they currently are required to know, will need a working knowledge of the mechanics of artificial intelligence, data science, unmanned systems and open source intelligence. Within the division intelligence cell there will be new positions dedicated to those functions, and new units – such as an unmanned aerial system unit – to gather the information.

What then, in practical terms, should the British Army do to prepare for a future in which new forms of expertise are emerging and growing in importance while others change or are even rendered obsolete? Although it is impossible to predict the exact course that adaptation will take for a specific technology, it is possible to create a general framework for how the Army would like to foster emerging fields of expertise. One potential organising principle for such a framework would be to establish several different archetypes of technological adaptation, similar to the distinction between the tank and electricity previously described. The framework would then establish some basic principles for how the Army would foster expertise for each of the different archetypes. The organisational progression would be quite different for a technology that might eventually become a specialised corps than for one that will be broadly diffused across functions. Some of the practical problems to work through would be to determine when to establish new trades or corps and how to foster expertise in the interim before that point is reach; the role of outside experts and organisations, such as civilian professional credentialing organisations or higher education; and how to determine when some kinds of expertise would be better accomplished by government civilians or even contractors. The answers to these and similar questions might vary for a given technology as it matures; in the case of aviation, for instance, what was necessary in the early days – to literally get the enterprise off the ground – was quite different than what was required a decade or two later. Thinking through such progressions will help the Army make better decisions, hopefully avoiding problems created by early decisions made purely on immediate considerations that must then be painfully corrected later on. In addition to the benefits to the institution, such a framework would also provide clarity and manage expectations for individuals considering going into new areas of expertise. Additionally, it would make clear to those in traditional roles that they too will be affected by new fields of expertise and will be expected to adapt. In short, such a framework would speak both to the individual who fancies themselves the J. F. C. Fuller of artificial intelligence and the equivalent of the interwar cavalrymen who refused to give up the horse.

Organising Levels of Expertise: Executor, Planner and Commander

It is well understood that everyone in the army, regardless of rank, requires some combination of specialist trade and generalist professional expertise. The U.S. Marine Corps ideal of 'every marine a rifleman' is grounded in hard-won experience, appeals to the martial instinct and fosters a powerful institutional mind-set. But such ideas can be taken to an extreme and preclude sensible institutional choices. In the case of the Marine Corps, one reason why it can take such a hard position on emphasising generalist expertise is that it relies on both the Navy and Army for technical, administrative and logistical support. Just how much general military knowledge should a medic or aircraft mechanic, much less a data scientist, possess when gaining and maintaining that expertise comes at the cost of time otherwise devoted to honing specialised skills? The limiting factor of time available in any individual's career makes the balance between the two a zero-sum game.

These are hard questions that defy easy answers. A framework differentiating among three levels of breadth and depth of expertise – executor, planner and commander – provides a useful line of departure for thinking through these issues.

Executors

Executors possess the detailed knowledge necessary for the employment of a specific function or system. This includes some working knowledge of other intersecting functions and systems as well. For instance, a tank commander must have some knowledge of how mechanised infantry are employed. Due to the exacting requirements of transforming a recruit into a competent soldier in a short period of time, the army has well-honed systems for classifying executor knowledge at junior ranks into defined trades (e.g., radio operator, machine gunner) and then imparting the necessary expertise. The same is true for officers in corps built around a technical function, such as pilots, doctors and engineers. These fields have explicit qualifications for expertise. In the case of pilots, these standards were developed largely within military institutions. In the case of doctors and engineers, the basis is often civilian professional standards, although often with additional requirements for supplementary skills specific to military applications. Whether a private carrying a machine gun or a pilot flying an Apache, the commonality is that the military is often adept at defining expertise for individual performance. The matter becomes more difficult when it comes to what this essay will refer to as 'supervisory executor expertise'. Commanders of artillery and aviation regiments are perhaps the clearest examples of such expertise. It would be unthinkable to place any officer, no matter how talented, who was not a gunner or aviator in command of one of these units. The commander of these units must have deep technical and tactical expertise to train and employ the unit. As with howitzers and helicopters, so it is true with other systems and functions as well; each has some inherent requirement for supervisory executor expertise. The proper level of supervisory executor expertise will vary – it might be a corporal or it might be a brigadier – but it is there and the army should have a sense for what it is. One nuance in this determination is that what is required for training might be higher for employment; this will be addressed in greater depth later, but for now it is sufficient to note that it is often the case that a more senior supervisory expertise is necessary to train units. But once they are trained, sub-units, detachments or teams can then be sent out under more junior supervisory executors to actually operate as combined arms teams.

Planners

Planner expertise is the ability to integrate multiple functions in execution. Typically, planners are several years into their career, and so also have executor expertise in their own speciality as well. Nonetheless, in contrast to executors, planners are characterised by the breadth of their knowledge. The year-long curriculum of theory, history, simulations and staff rides at the U.S. Army's School of Advanced Military Studies to train planners for work at division and corps is indicative of the expertise required by higher echelon planners. At lower echelons, an example of planner expertise is the fire support officer able to integrate whatever mixture of mortars, howitzers, rockets and missiles, attack helicopters, unmanned aerial systems, and ground-attack aircraft in a way that makes best use of the different characteristics of whatever resources are available. Fire support officers do not have to be able to fly an Apache, but they do need to know many of the technical and tactical factors that govern its employment. This is the expertise of a planner. In practice, planner experience is applied in a collective manner in teams within a staff. Thus, there is no need for an individual planner to have mastered the integration details of every capability within a division. This is fortunate as it is impossible for a mid-career officer to amass such expertise. Nonetheless, there is a requirement for a cadre of individuals distinguished by their ability to see the bigger picture and how various functions all come together. A recent initiative within the U.S. Air Force underscores the value of such planners, as well as the limits of what might be expected of them. By the mid-2010s, it had become apparent that simply assembling teams of air, space and cyberspace executors was not producing sufficiently integrated operations. There was the need for planners who had familiarity in all three. To meet this need, the service created the Multi-Domain Warfare speciality – 13O within the service's personnel nomenclature – for mid-career officers. Select individuals attend a transition school to build planning expertise in the integration of air, space and cyberspace capabilities, which then becomes their speciality for the remainder of their careers.[4] Shortly after the creation of the 13O designator, a U.S. Army War College study team examining the larger issue of joint all-domain command and control for the Joint Staff spoke with some of those responsible for establishing the course and training the early cohorts. One of the major objectives of the Army War College study was to identify the major non-technical barriers to achieving all-domain operations. Among the chief concerns was whether existing headquarters staffs had the competence to integrate all of the domain capabilities envisioned in operational concepts. More specifically, what are the practical limits of how much technical and tactical detail a mid-career officer can be expected to master? The overwhelming consensus to this question among the 13O trainers was that the air-space-cyberspace troika was about the limits. When asked if it was possible to build an 'all-domain planner' who would also be able to integrate ground and naval operations, the trainers thought that was too much. Their opinion was that even the 13O programme was already straining the limits of individual expertise.[5] If true, this has two implications. The first is that developing tools to supplement planner expertise might be a priority for artificial intelligence applications. The second is that developing the right mixture of different 'flavours' of expertise (e.g. ground-space-electronic warfare or air-space-cyberspace) in planning cells and operations centres will be critical.

Commanders

Commanders must possess the expertise necessary to give general direction, provide intelligent oversight, and, most of all, make hard operational decisions grounded in a fundamental understanding of all the functions inherent within their organisations. Put simply, commanders must have enough knowledge of all of the capabilities they employ to be able to apply a commander's fundamental skill: judgement. One implication of all-domain operations is that the sphere of commanders' expertise must expand to incorporate ever more novel capabilities. The commander does not require the mastery of the executor or even the technical familiarity of the planner. But while commanders do not need to have the same level of depth of expertise, they must be absolutely confident in what they are required to know because the responsibility of decision rests upon their shoulders. One of the U.S. Army's generals leading the development of the multi-domain operations concept – who was also a seasoned combat leader – neatly illustrated this point in an observation to the author. He noted that a current division commander who, for instance, might have been commissioned as an armour officer would still be confident when closely questioning or providing firm guidance to a senior artilleryman or aviator. Our general officers commanding have accumulated sufficient command

---

4   '505th Command and Control Wing graduates first-ever class of multi-domain warfare officers', *Air Force News*, 18 October 2019, https://www.505ccw.acc.af.mil/News/Article-Display/Article/1992177/505th-command-and-control-wing-graduates-first-ever-class-of-multi-domain-warfa/.

5   J. P. Clark, Joe Broome, Derrick Franck Jr, and Michael Loftus, *Command in Joint All-Domain Operations: Some Considerations* (U.S. Army War College, 2020).

expertise in relation to traditional capabilities. But, he noted, 'when the "weirdos" from the [special technical operations] vault come out with some piece of paper, my peers do not know what to ask; they are uncomfortable and hastily sign the authorisation, hoping that the weirdos go back to the vault as quickly as possible.'[6] Though perhaps overdrawn, the vignette nicely illustrates the fundamental challenge of adding new domains. At whatever level a capability is integrated into a larger combined arms team, commanders must have the basic expertise (and be supported by staffs with the appropriate planners) to competently orchestrate its employment.

Organising Collective Expertise: Echelons on the All-Domain Battlefield

Once the British Army generates individuals proficient in employing, integrating and commanding new technologies as described in the first two sections, how does it take the next, most critical step, of organising them into units for actual employment? In practical terms, the problem is to determine how many different functions should be integrated into each echelon from company to division. How 'all-domain' can and must our units be at each of these different echelons? Unfortunately, various contemporary trends and considerations pull us in different directions.

The executor/planner/commander framework presented above suggests that the competence of staffs and commanders is one important constraint. More complex units – measured by how many different functions they encompass – require larger staffs and more broadly experienced commanders and staff principals. Yet the need for survivable commands posts in the face of the modern 'reconnaissance strike complex' limits how large staffs can be, particularly for battle groups and brigades. A capable enemy will punish units with headquarters that are immobile or have conspicuous physical or virtual signatures. As noted earlier, artificial intelligence will undoubtedly become a valuable aide to commanders and planners, effectively increasing the productivity and expertise of individuals. Yet as Jack Watling of RUSI notes in his observations of 'unmanned' systems in Ukraine, there are irreducible minimums of staffing that are impossible to escape. Extended around-the-clock operations, casualties and requirements for occasional rotation off the line mean that any critical position will have to be several individuals deep, even if the task could notionally be done by a single person augmented by artificial intelligence.[7]

---

6   Conversation with the author in late 2017.
7   Jack Watling, 'Automation Does Not Lead to Leaner Land Forces', *War on the Rocks*, 7 February 2024, https://warontherocks.com/2024/02/automation-does-not-lead-to-leaner-land-forces/. This topic is also addressed by Major General Patrick Ellis, the director of the U.S. Army Network Cross Functional Team in 'Establishing and Maintaining Command & Control on the Battlefields of Tomorrow', *The Crucible – The JRTC Experience Podcast*, 26 September 2024, https://www.youtube.com/watch?v=GLgPdj7_qCg.

Similarly, the requirement for broadly experienced commanders and staff principals pinches hardest at the battle group and brigade levels. With the first two decades or so of a career largely consumed in acquiring deep executor expertise – and perhaps some planner expertise, as well – when and how do commanders and operations officers gain the knowledge of functions like electronic warfare or the full suite of air-ground littoral operations?[8] Again, artificial intelligence is likely to be of some use, but it will not solve all problems. Indeed, it is likely to be more helpful to planners – those doing the 'science' of integration – than to commanders who are having to make decisions of leadership 'art' that incorporate such intangibles as morale and the responsibility of accepting potentially lethal risk.

Thus, the factors of command post survivability and limitations of mid-career commanders and staff principals suggest the division as the best echelon for full integration of all the army's functions. Yet this solution has its own problems. One obvious pitfall is that delaying the point in a career when commanders are required to integrate more functions only makes the cliff of expertise that must be scaled that much steeper when it arrives. If battle groups and even brigades remain largely as they have been in the past, then how do we get past the situation of the general officer unable to give intelligent direction described in the previous section? Furthermore, general officer rank, unfortunately, does not convey powers beyond normal human limits. In his study of division command, Anthony King has suggested that the scope of expertise of today's battlefield exceeds what one individual can competently manage, and so therefore some system of communal command might be necessary.[9] As King notes, this suggestion tends to draw fierce resistance from military officers, even from those who he gives as exemplars of what he suggests. If the army wants to prove King wrong and maintain the traditional mode of command, it must think deliberately about how to impart all-domain expertise – at all echelons – to commanders.

Another objection to pushing much of the integration of different functions and domains to the division level is that the modern battlefield will simply not allow it. The great revolution in military organisation that occurred during the First World War was to push the integration to far lower levels. That war saw the shift from infantry regiments organised into pure rifle companies with smaller detachments of machine guns or other special weapons held at the regimental level to squads and platoons containing

8   Presumably the use of unmanned aerial systems for straightforward tasks like 'beyond the next rise' reconnaissance or strike in direct support of manoeuvre will be fairly straightforward. Yet as these systems develop, full air-ground littoral integration, however, will require a much more complex range of tasks, not unlike a traditional air campaign to include offensive and defensive counter air, electronic and kinetic suppression of air defences, and deception. Integrating this effort with ground operations will be a significant challenge. For a sense of these new missions, see Justin Bronk and Jack Watling, *Mass Precision Strike: Designing UAV Complexes for Land Forces* (London: RUSI, 2024), pp.22–44.

9   Anthony King, *Command: The Twenty-First-Century General* (Cambridge: Cambridge University Press, 2019).

multiple types of weapons at the end of the war. Today in Ukraine, we see a similar push of capabilities, like first-person view drones down to the lowest levels. This seemingly clear example, however, does come with a caveat. While both sides have pushed integration to low levels, they have also demonstrated an inability to conduct operations at the pace and scale desired by Western armies. They have conducted operations largely at the company-, platoon- or even squad-level. Thus, the constraints facing the battle group and brigade outlined at the beginning of this section have not been overcome. Instead, the war in Ukraine has adopted a pattern of small-scale tactical actions within an attritional campaign. Such a pattern would likely not be politically acceptable for the British Army; therefore, it must find some way of integrating multiple functions and domains at pace and scale.

In trying to determine a solution to that problem, it should be noted that force generation and force employment will likely have to be considered as two distinct elements that must be reconciled into a single solution. To an extent, this is already done. For training and administrative purposes, the army tends towards functional organisation, often regiments, to ensure that there is sufficient supervisory executor expertise to enable professional development and ensure quality training. There are good reasons for this, as the U.S. Army learned with its shift towards brigade combat teams in the 2000s. One consequence of that shift was a loss of proficiency when artillery battalions were under infantry or armour brigades rather than a division artillery, or military intelligence companies under a brigade engineer battalion rather than a military intelligence battalion. These problems have prompted a shift back towards more functional organisations, at least in garrison, under the theory that for force employment in operations these trained units can be broken into smaller detachments for use in combined arms formations. In short, a gunner colonel trains a battalion to a level of proficiency so that it can then be employed in operations by a tanker colonel. But does this theory hold?

A sobering trend of modern warfare is the extent to which tactical success, if not simple survival, requires the competent integration of all battlefield functions into cohesive teams. Even in the simple 'old days' this was hard. Decades of after-action reports from the U.S. Army's combat training centres testify to the difficulty of integrating the familiar functions of manoeuvre, fires, mobility/counter-mobility and logistics. Successful units have well-developed standard operating procedures refined and practised through multiple iterations of rigorous training.[10] But the task has become even harder because there are now the additional requirements of both using and guarding against the enemy in the electromagnetic spectrum and the air-ground littoral. A weakness in any one of these areas can be exploited by a competent adversary. As analyst Stephen Biddle notes, the trend of failed offensives in Ukraine somewhat obscures the

---

10   These lessons run throughout the excellent podcast 'The Crucible' series produced by the Joint Readiness Training Centre available at https://www.youtube.com/@TheCrucible–The RTCExperience or on most podcast catchers. See particularly Series 2, 'If I Would Have Only Known'.

larger lesson that the offensive is still possible, but success requires an even greater degree of all-domain proficiency than before.[11] It, therefore, cannot be taken for granted that the functional organisation for training and combined arms organisation for operations model is sufficient. At the least, it will require careful attention to ensuring that both sides of the equation, as well as the transition, receive proper attention.

In the face of these competing, perhaps irreconcilable, demands, the temptation is to give up and hope that the current organisation – grounded as it is in centuries of accumulated practice – is fit for purpose. Indeed, the purpose of this chapter is not to argue for radical change based on clean-sheet, first principles reasoning, as such experiments are likely to lead to even greater grief.[12] Instead, the army should develop some means to ensure that executors, planners and commanders all have sufficient expertise in relation to whatever different functions are entrusted to them. Such a system could take many forms. It also has risks; a poorly designed system for gauging expertise might easily become unwieldy, unhelpful, or both. Nonetheless, the army should be able to say with confidence that an operator, staff officer or commander has the expertise to be competent. If the current career progression does not provide this expertise, then such a framework would indicate what changes to education and training experiences are required to produce this competence. And if it is found that there simply is no way to prepare an officer to be competent in integrating so many different functions by a given point in their career, then it is then incumbent on the army to develop organisational, doctrinal or technological solutions that compensate for those limits. It is not tenable to simply ignore the problem and hope that somehow leaders have all the expertise required without a deliberate, explicit method of ensuring that is the case.

11   Stephen Biddle, 'Back in the Trenches', *Foreign Affairs*, 102:5 (September/October 2023), https://www.foreignaffairs.com/ukraine/back-trenches-technology-warfare.
12   The U.S. Army Pentomic Army experiment of the 1950s was an extreme example of such institutional adventurism, Andrew J. Bacevich, *The Pentomic Era: The U.S. Army Between Korea and Vietnam* (Washington DC: National Defense University Press, 1986); Brian M. Linn, *Elvis's Army: Cold War GIs and the Atomic Battlefield* (Cambridge, MA: Harvard University Press, 2016), pp.73–98, 126–128.

10

Untangling the Sociology of Post-Human War

Thomas Crosbie

War, as the late British political philosopher Christopher Coker argued, is 'the human thing'.[1] Coker took that formulation from Thucydides (who needs no introduction to readers of the present volume). What Coker, Thucydides and generations of like-minded philosophers of war had in mind is perhaps best laid at the feet of Aristotle. Aristotle thought of species as defined in fundamental ways by their most characteristic behaviour. From Aristotle's perspective, war is not our *telos* (our destiny), but merely our *entelechy* (the purest expression of our sociality). War is then the most characteristically human thing, but this cuts in two directions. On one hand, we find humans engaging in war, warlike behaviour, or attempts to prevent or mitigate war across time and space. On the other hand, war (as we currently understand it) is shaped by our humanness. War is *our* thing, bearing the traces of our way of being. Just as two rams will inevitably butt heads, any two groups of people are, in this way of thinking, bound to relate to one another through war – if not through the violence of war, then through the pains taken to avoid, mitigate or resolve such violence.

Coker was not simply reheating a classic debate, but rather enquiring as to whether war was still *just* ours. Have we already lost our monopoly over the direction of human violence, and violence derived from human means? War, born of humanity, might be leaving humanity behind, a baton passed to the lifeless hands of artificial intelligence (AI), machine learning and other forms of automation. The 'human thing' no longer, war enters its post-human era.

An idle thought, perhaps, but there is a disconcerting degree of truth in it. 'Post-human war' is the very thing of science fiction, yet there is good reason to dwell on the potential for something like it to emerge (if it has not already). Indeed, eight years after Coker wrote his article, many of his concerns have already drifted from

---

1   Christopher Coker, 'Still "the Human Thing"? Technology, Human Agency and the Future of War', *International Relations*, 32:1 (March 2018), p.24.

the realm of speculation into mundane reality. 'China's military shows off rifle-toting robot dogs', reads a bizarre headline on CNN.[2] Yet the future jostles uncomfortably with the past. The battlefields of Ukraine boast hypersonic missiles and trench warfare.[3] Slowly, once-exotic technologies are filtering to the forefront. Autonomous unmanned vehicles, nanotechnology, directed energy weapons, upward falling payloads, a weaponised space domain: once hallmarks of science fiction, now the arsenals of great powers.[4]

NATO's key concept development communities have begun to speak of the need for information to move at 'the speed of relevance'.[5] Humans, unfortunately, can only think and act so fast: often, it is presumed, slower than the speed of relevance. And so, while the exotic technologies just listed free us from certain long-standing spatio-temporal limitations, in doing so they may well shackle us to new ones. At any rate, they herald a striking change: one fundamentally human feature of war, namely human decision-making, is muted, if not entirely silenced when decision points become unobservable (whether due to speed, location or virtuality).

Understandably, debates over the future of war are generally focused on sophisticated new technologies, quickly demanding a degree of technical understanding that few actually possess. This chapter takes the opposite approach, shunning the technologies of the future in order to look back at the persisting social dynamics of the past. To that end, it explores two related ideas, each sparking off from the idle thought that there is or could be such a thing as 'post-human war'. The first concerns war's enduring nature and

2   Brad Lendon Gan Nectar, 'China's Military Shows off Rifle-Toting Robot Dogs', *CNN*, 28 May 2024, https://www.cnn.com/2024/05/28/china/china-military-rifle-toting-robot-dogs-intl-hnk-ml/index.html.

3   Cedric Pietralunga, 'Trench Warfare Makes a Comeback in Ukraine's Fight against Russia', *Le Monde.Fr*, 30 September 2023, https://www.lemonde.fr/en/international/article/2023/09/30/trench-warfare-makes-a-comeback-in-ukraine-s-fight-against-russia_6142009_4.html; Lyle Goldstein and Nathan Waechter, 'China Evaluates Russia's Use of Hypersonic "Daggers" in the Ukraine War', *RAND*, 12 January 2024, https://www.rand.org/pubs/commentary/2024/01/china-evaluates-russias-use-of-hypersonic-daggers-in.html.

4   U. S. Government Accountability Office, 'Science & Tech Spotlight: Directed Energy Weapons | U.S. GAO', accessed 28 June 2024, https://www.gao.gov/products/gao-23-106717; Joe Saballa, 'China Developing Biological, Cyber Weapons for Covert Warfare: Study', *The Defense Post*, 28 August 2023, https://www.thedefensepost.com/2023/08/28/china-biological-cyber-weapons/; ESD Editorial Team, 'The State of Autonomy, AI & Robotics for Russia's Ground Vehicles', 26 June 2023, https://euro-sd.com/2023/06/articles/31798/the-state-of-autonomy-ai-robotics-for-russias-ground-vehicles/; Betty Wehtje, 'Increased Militarisation of Space – A New Realm of Security | Beyond the Horizon ISSG', 6 June 2023, https://behorizon.org/increased-militarisation-of-space-a-new-realm-of-security/; 'Upward Falling Payloads', accessed 28 June 2024, https://www.darpa.mil/program/upward-falling-payloads.

5   Ann Marie Dailey, 'NATO Needs a Plan for Military and Nonmilitary Instruments of Power to Work Together', *Atlantic Council* (blog), 2 November 2023, https://www.atlanticcouncil.org/blogs/new-atlanticist/nato-needs-a-plan-for-military-and-nonmilitary-instruments-of-power-to-work-together/.

changing character, a concept we inherit from Carl von Clausewitz.[6] If war is a human thing, then post-human war is war of a different nature, surely, bearing a meaningfully different character. To that end, the chapter looks backward to sketch 10 fundamentally human features of war. The second idea is simply to look with post-human eyes at how these features might transform or disappear in a future conflict arena where humans are no longer the primary actors.

The Nature of Human War

Clausewitz's understanding of war is a useful starting point in thinking through the humanness of war. For Clausewitz, as is widely known among military practitioners, war's nature is enduring, while its character is ever-changing. Its nature is, in a sense, an inconvenience. War occurs (in this understanding) when a group of people uses force or the threat of force to advance their interests (the politics part of Clausewitz's thought), but in doing so discovers that reason (including, critically, expert military advice) is joined by emotion and chance, and actions are modulated by friction and fog.

Defining war in this way allows Clausewitz to separate it from other forms of contest or struggle. War and wrestling, for example, are similar in some respects, but by no means all respects. Indeed, war is a unique form of conflict, distinguished by the fact that in its very nature it reflects the messiness of human relations and the limitations of human senses. There is no form of war (which is to say, human war) that escapes emotion, chance, friction and fog.

War's character is a different matter. For Clausewitz, 'the character of war' refers to the specific ways instruments of national power are wielded across domains and operating environments in the attempt to use force or the threat of force to achieve political interests.[7] Countering insurgencies or conducting large-scale conventional operations are very different things, and those tasked with doing so will fight very different types of wars, but in either case they are indeed waging war.[8]

We take from Clausewitz five features of war, derived directly from his definition, but reflecting the collective wisdom of those generations of soldiers and scholars who

---

6   Carl von Clausewitz (Michael Howard and Peter Paret, trans.), *On War* (Princeton: Princeton University Press, 1984).

7   'Instruments of national power', 'domains' and 'operating environments' are all, of course, anachronisms, but the terms are introduced here to draw the reader's attention to how Clausewitz's understanding fits well within the current NATO understanding.

8   Those struggling with the nature-character debate are directed to Bollman and Sjøgren's recent analysis of this long-standing debate. See Anders Theis Bollman and Søren Sjøgren, 'Rethinking Clausewitz's Chameleon: Is It Time for Western Militaries to Abandon the Idea of War's Immutable Nature?', in Thomas Crosbie (ed.) *Military Politics: New Perspectives* (New York: Berghahn Books, 2023), pp.48–69.

found in this definition something powerfully true about the world.[9] The first five human features of war are, simply enough: its political character; the role of emotion in shaping behaviour; the role of chance in shaping outcomes; the role of friction in modulating actions; and the presence of 'fog' in limiting comprehension and understanding.

Soldiers and scholars continue to find much of value in Clausewitz's formulation, and indeed there is much there that speaks to us today. Nevertheless, Clausewitz had a minimal conception of the social world. Drawing ecumenically from primatology, aetiology, classical social theory and empirical military studies, five more features can be added to give a richer sense of what makes war 'the human thing'.

We can consider, for example, how we compare with our closest relatives. Harvard primatologist Richard W. Wrangham helpfully untangles the mystery of human aggression by comparing observational data on simple human societies with that from primatology studies of chimpanzees and bonobos, finding that rates of violent 'reactive' aggression among our relatives are orders of magnitude higher than we experience in our own communities.[10] Humans are, comparatively, averse to violence, something our extreme sensitivity to violence (evident in our susceptibility to psychological trauma) makes plain.[11] And yet, unlike bonobos (but like chimpanzees), human societies globally are characterised by 'proactive' aggression.

Humans and chimpanzees share a form of violent aggression, referred to by primatologists and anthropologists alike as 'raiding'. Humans, however, have a second form: ritualised combat, where parties to a conflict agree upon certain rules and limitations (the origin of what we today refer to as the Laws of Armed Conflict or International Humanitarian Law). Why did humans invent this second form of conflict? The benefit of ritualised conflict is that it establishes a means of limiting the spread of violence (which, after all, we find especially intolerable).

Still, chimpanzees have failed to achieve this level of organisation, and so there must be more to the story. The mystery unravels when we compare our skeletal muscle with that of chimpanzees, our fellow raiders. Humans have much lower rates of 'fast fibre', which, present at high rates among chimpanzees, imparts what appears to us to be their 'super strength'.[12] Unlike chimpanzees, whose muscles are strong enough to rend skin from the bone of other members of their species, we humans need weapons to easily inflict fatal wounds upon one another. Ironically, our weapons make raiding far more

9   For example, Gerhard Wheeler, 'Ukraine's Fascinating Trinity', *CHACR* (blog), 6 June 2023, https://chacr.org.uk/2023/06/06/ukraines-fascinating-trinity/; Brian Cole, 'Clausewitz's Wondrous Yet Paradoxical Trinity: The Nature of War as a Complex Adaptive System', *Joint Force Quarterly*, 96:1 (2020), pp.42–49.
10   Richard W. Wrangham, 'Two Types of Aggression in Human Evolution', *Proceedings of the National Academy of Sciences*, 115:2 (January 9, 2018), pp.245–253.
11   Cort A. Pedersen, 'Biological Aspects of Social Bonding and the Roots of Human Violence', *Annals of the New York Academy of Sciences*, 1036:1 (2004), pp.106–127.
12   Matthew C. O'Neill et al., 'Chimpanzee Super Strength and Human Skeletal Muscle Evolution', *PNAS*, 114:28 (2017), pp.7343–7348.

fatal than is the case among chimpanzees, since human raiding cultures strike when their adversaries are unarmed.

Having invented weapons, we thereby created an extreme asymmetric vulnerability whenever we lay our weapons down (as we must do when we sleep). Thus, human raiding could lead to an endless cycle of violence if there were no alternative. Ritualised conflict provides that alternative, and together these two forms of violent aggression constitute what Clausewitz recognised as war. Still, deception and surprise remain essential to success, even in rule-bound conflict.[13] Although in modern states, belligerents do not physically lay down their weapons when they sleep, the asymmetric advantage that occurs when an attacker is armed and ready, while the defender is taken unaware and unprepared, are enormous, and military doctrine encourages exploiting such opportunities.

Our image of human war is coming more into focus. Humans are proactive aggressors, preferring to take adversaries by surprise when possible, but also wary of triggering cycles of violence, and hence equally predisposed towards ritualised (rule-bound) violence. Regardless of whether belligerents share a system of rules, both will inevitably seek to exploit surprise and deception when possible.

One final point, essential to the sociology of conflict but often overlooked in other disciplines, is the dual valence of violence, first noted in a systematic way by German sociologist Georg Simmel.[14] Simmel's interest in conflict at all scales revealed to him the socially-adaptive character of conflict, even violent conflict. While we routinely recognise the centrifugal quality of violence (which, again, humans find especially damaging), we often downplay its centripetal quality. It is evident, however, that conflict does not merely tear at the social fabric linking belligerents, it also reinforces the ties binding those fighting together.

This lightning-quick review of human social conflict provides five more features that we would do well to keep in mind as essentially human aspects of war. In addition to the five features we drew from Clausewitz (political interest, emotion, chance, friction and fog), we can add the following. Human war is typically proactive, not reactive. Human war includes raiding behaviour, but also includes ritualised conflict. Human war foregrounds the role of deception and surprise. And human war is both centrifugal and centripetal, giving rise to powerful solidary bonds within fighting groups.

That, then, provides a reasonably comprehensive overview of war as humans practice it. Would technologies that displace human agency also undermine these 10 features of human war?

---

13   Barton Whaley, *Stratagem: Deception and Surprise in War* (Cambridge, MA: Center for International Studies, Massachusetts Institute of Technology, 1969); Robert M. Clark and William L. Mitchell, *Deception: Counterdeception and Counterintelligence* (Washington DC: CQ Press, 2018).

14   George Simmel, *Conflict And The Web Of Group Affiliations* (New York: Simon and Schuster, 2010).

Post-Human War: What Would Be Different?

Wars of the future will remain recognisably 'our thing' so long as they are defined by those qualities that have always defined the human way of war. They will become something new and different if they cease to be so defined. Let us then briefly consider each of our 10 features in turn, to see how AI-dominated decision-making processes may depart from human approaches. Table 1 summarises the key differences between the two forms of war.

Table 1: Ten Features of Human and Post-Human War

Feature	Human War	Post-Human War
(1) Aims	Aims are defined by political interest.	Aims are defined by human political interest, 'on' or 'in' the loop.
(2) Emotion	Mediated perceptions of emotion shape political interest.	Emotions are targeted as primary influence node.
(3) Chance	Linear decision-making models aim to minimise role of chance while allows for inevitable margin of error.	Quantum estimates aim to model stochastic systems to achieve precision despite uncertainty.
(4) Friction	Friction serves as a holistic 'reality tax'.	Human-created friction is minimised, but information overload causes new forms of friction.
(5) Fog	Fog created by few sensors, limited or vulnerable communications networks, interoperability problems, and unwillingness to share information.	Fog created by spoofing, misinformation, information degradation.
(6) Form of Aggression	Wars are proactive forms of aggression.	Wars may become reactive, driven by automatic response.
(7) Raiding	Humans raid when asymmetric advantage is greater than benefit of remaining within system of rules.	Potential risk of setting responses to levels of asymmetric advantage.
(8) Ritualised Conflict	Humans abide by rules of conduct in war to minimise spread of violence.	Weapon systems may work on slightly different interpretations of rules of conduct, increasing risk of violence.
(9) Deception/ Surprise	Deception and surprise are important for achieving favourable outcomes.	Deception and surprise remain essential, but target of deception may switch to automated systems or AI.
(10) Centripetal/ Centrifugal	Conflicts have both centripetal and centrifugal social effects.	Automated systems may identify benefits of centripetal effects.

Will Post-Human War Be Politics By Other Means?

The greatest danger posed by off-loading decision-making lies in freeing the logics of violence from the yoke of political interest. Sociologist Lewis A. Coser describes conflict scenarios lacking a defined goal as 'non-realist conflicts'.[15] Wars with poorly-defined or rapidly changing goals are often accompanied by an increasing cycle of violence. These dangers are self-evident and would likely only arise if humans were well and truly 'off the loop' of decision-making entirely.

Will Post-Human War Be Shaped by Emotion?

A more likely area where post-human war dynamics emerge is in the role of emotion shaping behaviour in war, but perhaps not in the direction we tend to think. For Clausewitz (writing before the rise of modern media, let alone social media), emotion affected political decision-making, which interacted with military leadership decisions. Today, our post-truth democracies are shaped more by the flow of emotion than ever before.[16] AI systems may lack innate emotion but attempts to shape populations' emotions are essential to modern warfighting, whether viewed from the perspective of NATO's Comprehensive Approach, or Russia's Reflexive Control, and any other leading theory of war. War dominated by algorithmic decision-making will likely focus on human factors to an even greater degree than is currently the case.

Will Post-Human War Be Shaped by Chance?

Our understanding of chance has changed dramatically in our post-quantum era.[17] Indeed, quantum computing begins by replacing classical, deterministic probability with probability amplitudes set in non-causal models of reality. In other words, managing 'chance' (probability) would be at the very centre of AI-driven forms of war, although in a completely different way than it has been in the long history of human war.

Will Post-Human War Be Limited by Friction?

Friction in the Clausewitzian sense refers to the inevitability that doing things on the battlefield will be more difficult than expected, a notion that serves as a sort of reality tax on military planning. While this concept may seem anecdotal, it has surprising predictive power and reflects the enormous complexity inherent in war.[18] The strategy scholar Nikolas Gardner argues that while AI systems may 'reduce friction resulting from human limitations, they will likely increase informational uncertainty, and unintended escalation'.[19]

15   Lewis A. Coser, *Functions of Social Conflict* (New York: Simon and Schuster, 1964).
16   Lee McIntyre, *Post-Truth* (Cambridge, MA: Massachusetts Institute of Technology Press, 2018).
17   Luigi Accardi, 'Quantum Probability: New Perspectives for the Laws of Chance' in *Milan Journal of Mathematics*, 78:2 (December 2010), pp.481–502.
18   Barry D. Watts, *Clausewitzian Friction and Future War* (Washington DC: Institute for National Strategic Studies, National Defense University, 2004).
19   Nikolas Gardner, 'Clausewitzian Friction and Autonomous Weapon Systems', *Comparative Strategy*, 40:1 (January 2021), pp.86–98.

Will Post-Human War Be Limited by Fog?

For Clausewitz, the 'fog' of war is closely linked to the friction of war but refers particularly to matters of perception and understanding. The proliferation of sensors, standardisation of operating systems, use of resilient and backup systems, and so on are all designed to help modern militaries overcome the fog of war. In doing so, there is a human danger that too much information becomes overwhelming to human analysts. In a post-human war, the same problems would likely arise through a different set of means: spoofing signals, feeding misinformation into adversary algorithms, and similar attempts to degrade the quality of information in order to mislead sensors and AI systems.

Will Post-Human War Be Proactive Rather than Reactive?

Human war typically expresses proactive aggression, rather than reactive aggression, but AI could easily reverse this pattern. This may or may not be in our interest. Cold War nuclear brinkmanship theorists conceived of a wide range of more or less desirable forms of automating responses to threats. One particularly undesirable scenario revolved around a three-actor model: two established nuclear powers with predictable response patterns, whose relations are disrupted by the appearance of a new nuclear power who may intentionally or accidentally trigger an event that is misattributed to one of the original powers. This is the spectre of 'catalytic nuclear war', and it is representative of an escalation dynamic that is even more troubling today than when it was first conceptualised.[20] The fundamental concern is that states (or non-state actors) may automate strikes to exploit brief windows of opportunity. This accords with contemporary thinking about deterring AI-driven attacks across environments and domains, which aim to leverage scarce resources to achieve brief periods of dominance within bounded spaces. While this thinking is intended to describe multi-domain operations *during* wartime (i.e. once belligerents have passed the legal threshold separating confrontation from armed conflict), these systems are intended to be in place already during the cooperation, rivalry and confrontation periods (according to NATO doctrine).[21] Inadvertently, our attempts to create systems that are highly responsive to our adversaries' attempts to exploit temporary weaknesses may encourage the use of sensors that trigger reactions that bypass the existing political level decision-making process. We all benefit when reactive aggression is kept to a minimum, in part because we are biologically (including psychologically) exceptionally vulnerable to violent attack, but also because the greater role rationality plays in moderating proactive, relative to reactive, aggression. Violent reactions, in other words, are both damaging in themselves, and carry the secondary damage of undermining confidence in 'cooler heads' (rationality) prevailing in the future. Post-human conflicts may involve more reactive aggression if we automate response systems, which

---

20 James Johnson, '"Catalytic nuclear war" in the age of artificial intelligence and autonomy: Emerging military technology and escalation risk between nuclear-armed states' in *Journal of Strategic Studies*, 45:1 (2020), pp.439–477.

21 See Figure 1.4, 'The continuum of competition', in NATO Standard, AJP-01, *Allied Joint Doctrine* (Edition F, Version 1) (December 2022).

we are very likely to do if our adversaries do so as well. Spoofing, deep fakes, growing cultures of paranoia and distrust, and weakening international and institutional norms all contribute to increasing the 'slipperiness' of this metaphorical slope towards an increasing propensity towards reactive aggression.

Will Post-Human War Be Characterised by Raiding?

Humans conduct raids when they become convinced that exploiting an asymmetric offensive advantage outweighs the benefit of remaining within the existing system of rules. For simple societies, this was largely about attacking when your enemies were sleeping or otherwise unprepared. For contemporary, complex societies, the cost-benefit analysis of leaving the system of states and transgressing international law only rarely favours launching an unprovoked attack, and so 'raiding' in our world is largely about exploiting military notions of surprise and deception during times of war. In a post-human conflict scenario, the cost-benefit calculation associated with breaking international laws and norms may once again change to favour the use of raiding. In automated systems, decision makers may set automated responses to levels of asymmetric advantage, as discussed above in relation to reactive aggression, although in this case due to a principled decision to actively exploit an adversary's fleeting moments of vulnerability.

Will Post-Human War Be Characterised by Ritualised Conflict?

he alternative to raiding is ritualised conflict. Post-human conflict scenarios will undoubtedly also feature ritualised conflict, in the sense of conflict bounded by powerful norms and limits. Most significantly, laws and regulatory regimes (organisational, national and international) will not be swept aside simply because weapon systems or military decision-making become automated.[22] Nevertheless, legal scholars are highly sensitised to the differences that machine-driven rather than human-driven decision-making processes post with respect to the rule of law, with concomitant impact on military operations.[23] Ritualised conflict is predicated on clear and effective communication, with belligerents recognising shared norms and agreeing to act within agreed bounds. The uncertainty of attribution looms especially large as a potential spoiler, both due to technological capabilities and their attendant psychological effects. Even more significant is the possibility that adversarial systems will be aligned in principle but not in practice: automated systems may be set to respond to mutually agreed limits, but since they use different algorithms based on different processes of learning, they may respond at diverging points, contributing to rapid escalation without corresponding political intent.

---

22 Thomas Crosbie and Meredith Kleykamp, 'Military Systems of Justice: A Sociological Overview', *Journal of Political & Military Sociology*, 47:1 (April 2021), pp.37–59.
23 Bérénice Boutin, 'State Responsibility in Relation to Military Applications of Artificial Intelligence', *Leiden Journal of International Law*, 36:1 (March 2023), pp.133–150; Forrest E Morgan et al., *Military Applications of Artificial Intelligence: Ethical Concerns in an Uncertain World* (Santa Monica: RAND Corporation, 2020).

Will Post-Human War Be Characterised by Deception and Surprise?

In the collection book of wisdom we attribute to Sun Tzu, the reader is told that 'all warfare is based on deception', and that 'to mystify, mislead, and surprise the enemy' is one of war's first principles.[24] Barton Whaley's qualitative study of 122 historical cases confirmed this wisdom for modern war, finding the combination of both surprise and deception to be highly predictive of success; the absence of one or the other much less predictive of success; and the absence of both to be strongly predictive of failure.[25] Despite a temporary decline in usage in some military doctrine during the expeditionary warfare era, military thinkers predict both deception and surprise will be increasingly significant in future large-scale conventional operations, as high-tech forms of deception – e.g. spoofing, misinformation and data corruption – are expected to achieve the psychological effect of surprise in human operators on the multi-domain battlefield.[26] But what of non-human operators? While deception concepts can be applied on a near one-to-one scale when switching from a human to post-human vantage point, the same does not apply to surprise. Automated forms of conflict are not likely to feature non-human actors experiencing the psychological states of confusion, emotional exhaustion or similar debilitating effects of surprise. Nevertheless, an equivalent state of disruption may be achieved by overwhelming sensors or finding unexpected exploits in seemingly stable systems. In this sense, a 'surprised' AI is still conceivable, although its characteristics would differ from the human experience of surprise.

Will Post-Human War Have Both Centrifugal and Centripetal Effect?

This question asks us to think about war from two diametrically opposed perspectives. The persistence of centrifugal effects seems obvious, until we consider that wars fought between automated systems might be sanitised to a very great degree. Doing so would require an exceptionally robust form of ritualised conflict. On the other hand, perhaps the most alarming possible implication of a post-human form of war concerns the centripetal effects of conflict. Wars often produce benefits for societies, and especially for elite groups within societies (particularly so groups who can avoid paying the costs of war). This truth is expressed in human cultures through various forms of militarism, a widely studied phenomenon.[27] Contrary cultural forces routinely challenge militarism, emphasising the ethical and moral costs of war. Post-human forms of conflict might weigh these factors in profoundly non-human ways and arrive at conclusions that may act against our species' interests.

---

24   Sun Tzu (Lionel Giles trans.), *The Art of War* (Standard Ebooks, 2024), p.53, https://standardebooks.org/ebooks/sun-tzu/the-art-of-war/lionel-giles.

25   Whaley, *Stratagem*; Clark and Mitchell, *Deception*; William L. Mitchell, 'The Art of Deception and the Role of Intelligence Education', *Royal Danish Defence College*, 19 March 2016.

26   John E. Luckie, 'Surprise: Past, Present, Future', (Master's Thesis, Fort Leavenworth, KS, School of Advanced Military Studies, U.S. Army Command and General Staff, 2021), p.34.

27   Paul Higate and John Hopton, 'War, Militarism, and Masculinities', in Michael S. Kimmel, Jeff Hearn, and Raewyn Connell (eds), *Handbook of Studies on Men and Masculinities* (Thousand Oaks, Calif: Sage Publications, 2005), pp.432–447.

Conclusion

As noted at the beginning of this chapter, war is the human thing. It shapes us, and we shape it. While its hold over us is by no means slackening, the reverse may not be true: indeed, our control over war is failing, in certain distinctive ways. The human approach to war has been marked by our vulnerabilities and limitations, as well as our most positive traits: our preference for security, our desire for social bonds, and our capacity for rule-following. We excel at increasing the lethality of war, but we also excel at containing its lethality, mitigating its harms, and resolving disputes without recourse to violence.

What has changed is the rise of automated systems capable of adopting decision-making roles in the projection of violent force. Since these systems are becoming available to human communities around the world, they trigger anxieties about our adversaries' automating time-consuming decision-making processes, granting them an assumed advantage. To forestall such an outcome, we are tempted to take such actions ourselves (whomever the 'we' may be). This all-too-human response to threat is troubling because with it comes the dim spectre of post-human war, something we have never yet experienced, and which we can barely imagine.

Nevertheless, it is possible to make a first foray into this exotic topic. As an initial orientation, we can think through the humanness of war: here, we started by exploring the sociology implicit in the thinking of the greater philosopher of war, Carl von Clausewitz. This provided five features of human war: the role of politics; the role of emotion; the role of chance; the role of friction; and the role of what he referred to as 'fog'. A sequence of reflections about the science of social life gave rise to five more features: the role of proactive aggression; the role of raiding; the role of ritual; the role of deception and surprise; and the simultaneously centrifugal and centripetal characteristics of war.

War as a social act likely precedes our origin as a species. Warring has been observed in virtually all human social groups, sharing distinctive traits that differ from the organised violent conflict of other primates. For over a hundred years, social theorists have tried to define common features of war as a human social act. Increasingly, however, truly unprecedented changes in the human-technology interface of military organisation seem to herald an era of warring which is no longer simply human. This chapter sketched a first look at what social theorists consider the essence of war as a human social act, considering how predicted changes in military organisation align with and sometimes depart from what has made war a typical human act.

By reflecting on how 10 essential features of human war might evolve, transform or disappear entirely, this chapter has aimed at untangling what a sociology of post-human war might look like. Post-human war will certainly feature deception and surprise and play out as proactive aggression in both ritualised and raiding forms. It may be characterised by a decreasing role played by chance, friction and Clausewitz's fog. It will differ from human war in critical respects, including potentially an increasing distance between war and politics and an increasing potential for raiding (both very troubling possibilities). Other differences will be evident in how automated systems target the emotions of mass publics; how surprise manifests among non-human actors; and how war itself is viewed as a more appealing prospect due to the valorisation of its centripetal effects. Only with great caution, then, should we let the humanness of war slip from our grasp.

11

British Generalship in the First World War

Spencer Jones

British generalship in the First World War has been a contentious topic for over a century. The terrible cost of the conflict aroused the ire of politicians, none more so than the Prime Minister, David Lloyd George, who cursed the generals for their 'futile' and 'criminal' offensives.[1] His polemical *War Memoirs*, published in the 1930s and widely serialised in British newspapers, were pivotal in cementing the public image of blundering generals squandering the lives of brave men. This theme was picked up in the 1960s and given a new lease of life by Alan Clarke's entertaining but unreliable polemic *The Donkeys*, a best-selling book which popularised the term 'lions led by donkeys'.[2] The media amplified the concept in the stage play and film *Oh! What a Lovely War!*, and most famously in the popular BBC television series *Blackadder Goes Forth*.

Yet this view has been challenged by a range of historians. The author of the British Army's *Official History*, Brigadier General James Edmonds, emphasised the unprecedented challenges the army faced as it evolved from a small, highly trained expeditionary force to a mass citizen army engaged in intense warfare.[3] Edmonds stressed that while mistakes were undoubtedly made, the army developed into a formidable force and emerged triumphant by 1918. This theme has been adopted by subsequent generations of historians, notably John Terraine, Peter Simkins and Gary Sheffield.[4] These authors have advanced the idea that the British Army experienced a brutal learning curve as it adapted to modern warfare on the Western Front. This process would eventually produce a well-equipped and battle-hardened army that served as the spearhead of

---

1   David Lloyd George, *War Memoirs, Volume I* (London: Ivor Nicholson and Warts, 1936), p.534.
2   Alan Clarke, *The Donkeys* (London: Mayflower, 1964).
3   J. E. Edmonds, *Military Operations, France and Belgium,* 14 volumes (London: HMSO, 1923–1949).
4   John Terraine, *White Heat: The New Warfare 1914–18* (London: Sedgwick & Jackson, 1982); Gary Sheffield, *Forgotten Victory* (London: Abacus, 2001); Peter Simkins, *From the Somme to Victory* (Barnsley: Pen & Sword, 2014).

the Allied armies as they advanced to victory in the Hundred Days' offensive (8 August to 11 November 1918). The concept of the learning curve is widely accepted in academic circles and is a useful framework, although the suggestion that the process was smooth and consistent can be misleading.

British generalship experienced its own learning curve during the conflict. The roots of the British approach to command lay in the pre-war army. This was a unique force. It was the smallest army of any major European power and the only one which relied solely on voluntary enlistment. The regular army numbered 249,000 men but the majority were in garrisons scattered around the Empire, with only 120,000 soldiers retained in Britain to serve as an Expeditionary Force in the event of a crisis. By comparison, France and Germany both anticipated deploying well over one million soldiers at the outbreak of war, and even the underfunded Belgian army boasted a strength of 150,000 men.

Nevertheless, the pre-war army had several advantages. As the only major European army that relied solely on voluntary enlistment, the army benefited from longer and more intense training. Man for man, the British Army was the best trained force in Europe.[5] Furthermore, its officer corps had more combat experience than any other army in Western Europe. Of 157 battalion colonels in 1914, 138 had seen action somewhere in the Empire.[6]

The army's doctrine reflected this level of experience. Embodied in *Field Service Regulations*, it emphasised initiative and the authority of 'the man on the spot' to make battlefield decisions. This combination of high training standards and combat experience made the army a small but formidable fighting force. But its ability to conduct large-scale operations was considered a weaker aspect. The small size of the army and its parsimonious budget limited the scale of training exercises.[7] This led the army to focus on training at battalion and brigade level while work at divisional level was often limited to map exercises and the annual army manoeuvres.

This was a problem for generalship. The designated commander-in-chief of the British Expeditionary Force (BEF), Sir John French, had commanded a 9,000-man cavalry division in the Boer War (1899–1902) but had had little opportunity to direct an army-sized force in exercise prior to 1914. There was a casual assumption that he would rise to the challenge and impose his will upon the army in wartime.[8] But French was always unlikely to achieve this lofty ambition. A fiery character with a scandalous personal life, his greatest assets were his physical courage and his popularity with the common soldier. But all his command experience had been gained in a small force where action was often emphasised at the expense of coordination.

---

5   For more on tactics and training, see Spencer Jones, *From Boer War to World War: Tactical Reform in the British Army 1902–1914* (Norman: University of Oklahoma Press, 2013).

6   Peter Hodgkinson, 'The Infantry Battalion Commanding Officers of the BEF', in Spencer Jones (ed.), *Stemming the Tide: Officers and Leadership in the British Expeditionary Force 1914* (Solihull: Helion & Co., 2013), pp.293–314.

7   Simon Batten, *Futile Exercise? The British Army's Preparations for War 1902–1914* (Solihull: Helion & Co., 2018).

8   Jones, *From Boer War to World War*, pp.51–54.

This lack of experience was also felt at staff level. Budget restrictions meant that there was no standing staff for five of the BEF's seven divisions, meaning that officers were hastily assembled to fill the roles on the outbreak of war.[9] French added to the confusion by insisting that he went to war with two chiefs of staff.[10] The problems with this approach soon emerged when the army was thrust into a high-intensity campaign in 1914 which saw it undertake the longest fighting retreat in its history (only exceeded by the retreat through Burma in 1942) as German forces tore through Belgium and drove the Allies back to the gates of Paris.[11]

Command and control broke down in the campaign. French failed to coordinate his forces and his primary Chief of Staff, Brigadier General Archibald Murray, suffered a breakdown that necessitated revival with an unknown stimulant that may have been cocaine.[12] The chiefs of staff for 3rd Division and 4th Division broke under the strain of war and became casualties.[13] The most effective commander in this period proved to be General Horace Smith-Dorrien of II Corps, who made the key decision to stand and fight at the Battle of Le Cateau on 26 August 1914. Notably, Smith-Dorrien chose to disobey orders to continue the retreat on the grounds that the pursuing Germans were too close to withdraw safely. This act of independence epitomised the essence of *Field Service Regulations* but would further poison his already hostile relationship with John French.

The BEF would survive the gruelling 'great retreat', but command and control remained uncertain throughout the remainder of 1914. Most of the army's engagements in this period became 'soldier's battles'. The British assault at the Battle of the Aisne in September exemplified this tendency. Smaller units of the BEF distinguished themselves by seizing bridgeheads across the river, but the subsequent advance was hampered by lack of coordination between divisions. This led to brave but piecemeal assaults against strong German positions that overlooked the Aisne, all of which were defeated. Similar problems emerged at First Ypres in October and November. Higher command had largely broken down by the middle stages of the battle, and the key battlefield decisions were made by brigadier generals.[14] The British line held at Ypres, but only at a tremendous cost.

9   Only 1st and 2nd Divisions retained a peacetime staff. The remaining infantry divisions and the sole Cavalry Division had to appoint their staff at the outbreak of war.

10 Stephen Badey, 'Sir John French and Command of the BEF' in Jones (ed.), *Stemming the Tide*, pp.37–40.

11 For more on this campaign, see Richard Holmes, *Riding the Retreat: Mons to the Marne Revisited* (London: Pimlico, 2007) and Spencer Jones, *The Great Retreat of 1914: From Mons to the Marne* (London: Sharpe Books, 2014).

12 John Bourne, 'Major General Sir Archibald Murray', in Jones (ed.), *Stemming the Tide*, pp.63–64.

13 F. Boileau, 3rd Division, suffered a catastrophic mental breakdown and committed suicide; J. E. Edmonds, 4th Division, suffered a physical and mental collapse that necessitated his evacuation to hospital.

14 On this see Michael LoCicero, 'A Tower of Strength: Brigadier-General Edward Bulfin' and Spencer Jones 'The Demon: Brigadier-General Charles FitzClarence VC', in Jones (ed.),

The 1914 campaign shaped the BEF for the remainder of the war. It showed many of the strengths of the pre-war army: excellent leadership from junior and middle ranking officers, high standards of individual training and impressive tactical skills. Yet it also revealed weaknesses. Coordination between divisions was often lacking and its overall command performance was uncertain.

Although the BEF had fought admirably in 1914 that had come at a terrible price. The army had suffered 89,000 casualties by the end of November and its distinctive character was lost forever. Its place would be taken by Territorials and volunteer New Army formations from Britain and the wider Empire. These forces were ill-trained and lacked equipment, and it was clear that they could not be expected to perform at the same tactical standards of the pre-war army. Furthermore, they now faced a heavily entrenched German Army that had occupied strong defensive positions along the Western Front. Defeating this force would prove exceptionally difficult.

British generalship was also shaped by 1914. Many of the senior officers who survived the campaign (except Smith-Dorrien who was unfairly sacked by John French in May 1915 in the continuation of their feud) guided the British army for the rest of the war. John French was replaced as commander-in-chief in France in late 1915 but became commander-in-chief of the Home Army and exerted substantial political influence. Douglas Haig would take his place on the Western Front and would lead the army through the intense fighting of 1916–1918. His army generals were all pre-war regular officers, as were the majority of the BEF's corps commanders. This provided homogeneity and an understanding of the doctrine embodied in *Field Service Regulations* but may have also contributed to a certain rigidity of thinking.

The extent to which British generalship adopted a consistent and recognisable model of thought has been the subject of much debate. Tim Travers argued that the army possessed a structured vision of battle as occurring in three distinct phases: preparation, which included a 'wearing down' fight and the drawing in of the enemy's reserves, followed by a rapid and decisive offensive which would then lead to an exploitation phase.[15] Travers criticised this model for its rigidity and noted that there was a tendency to rush the attritional first phase in pursuit of a rapid breakthrough. To Travers, British generalship was rigid and inflexible, with a top-down approach that left little room for innovation or exchange of ideas.

Martin Samuels built on this concept and argued that the BEF operated a system which he termed 'umpiring'.[16] Under this approach British commanders set broad objectives and then left their subordinates to fight the battle with minimal intervention aside from the occasional piece of advice. This deliberate abnegation of command was maintained even when it was evident the battle was not going according to plan. In this

Stemming the Tide.
15   Tim Travers, *The Killing Ground* (London: Unwin & Allen, 1987).
16   Martin Samuels, *Command or Control? Command, Training and Tactics in the British and German Armies, 1888–1918* (London: Routledge, 1996).

sense, Samuels argued that British generalship operated a warped and ineffective form of mission command.

Yet these interpretations have been rejected by other historians who emphasise that British command remained rooted in its flexible pre-war vision of war.[17] The pre-1914 British Army was as concerned with imperial security as it was with a potential European war. The almost bewildering array of geographies and opponents that might be faced in imperial expeditions necessitated an adaptable, problem-solving approach rather than adhering to rigid principles. The problem lay not in a flawed conception of generalship, but instead was a matter of scale. The army underwent the largest expansion in its history and was pitted against a German force considered the finest in the world, in conditions where technology favoured the defender. Setbacks were almost inevitable, but the army's culture of adaptability ultimately allowed it to develop an effective model of command.[18]

There is no doubt that the rapid transition from a small professional force to a mass citizen army created serious difficulties. Existing regular officers were swiftly promoted to take command of new divisions but were given little time to acclimatise to their new responsibilities. This problem was compounded by a critical shortage of trained staff officers that was not completely resolved until early 1917. In 1915 demand for staff officers completely outstripped Britain's ability to supply them. In desperation, the army offered new staff officers a truncated training course in Britain before deploying them to France to shadow a more experienced man and learn on the job.[19]

This created a dangerous combination of problems. Inexperienced generals and novice staffs found themselves leading brave but poorly trained citizen soldiers against a first-class enemy. The situation was worsened by a tendency to devise unrealistic objectives and overly complex manoeuvres, both of which were a common feature of many British plans in 1915 and 1916, while poor coordination between infantry and supporting arms was the norm. There were fleeting moments of success such as the British attack at Neuve Chappelle in March 1915, which achieved local surprise and came close to capturing the crucial ground of Aubers Ridge. But an attempt to renew the engagement at the Battle of Aubers Ridge in May 1915 was an utter disaster and proportionately one of the worst single days of the war for the army, with some 11,500 casualties suffered for no significant ground gained.[20]

17   Key work on this aspect includes Andrew Duncan, 'The Military Education of Junior Officers in the Edwardian Army', Unpublished PhD thesis, University of Birmingham 2016; Aimée Fox, *Learning to Fight: Military Innovation and Change in the British Army 1914–1918* (Cambridge: Cambridge University Press, 2016); Jones, *From Boer War to World War.*

18   For the strongest expression of this argument, see Fox, *Learning to Fight*, pp.240–250.

19   On the evolution of British staff systems, see Paul Martin Harris, 'The Men Who Planned the War: A Study of the Staff of the British Army on the Western Front 1914–1918', PhD thesis, King's College London, 2016.

20   Adrian Bristow, *A Serious Disappointment: The Battle of Aubers Ridge 1915 and the Munitions Scandal* (Barnsley: Pen and Sword, 1995).

The major offensive at Loos (September–October 1915), the largest battle fought by Britain up to that point in the war, exemplified many of the army's weaknesses at the time. British command hoped that a prolonged preparatory bombardment and a release of chlorine gas would suppress the German defenders and allow the attackers to seize their position. In places the gas attack had the desired effect, and British troops captured their objectives. But attempts to exploit this success proved disastrous, with inexperienced divisions rushed to the battlefield and thrown headlong against entrenched, unshaken German defenders. The defeat at the Battle of the Loos cost the British Army some 60,000 casualties, representing approximately 25 percent of all the casualties that the army suffered on the Western Front in 1915. The setback was so severe that it shook the government's confidence in army command and led to a major reshuffle.

The biggest change was the removal of Sir John French from his role as commander-in-chief. Although his poor handling of reserve forces was given as the reason for his dismissal, the reality was that he had been living on borrowed time for much of the year. French's failures in 1914 have already been noted, and his approach to command in 1915 was equally unimpressive. He was overwhelmed by the scale of the war, dispirited at its terrible toll and hampered by frequent bouts of illnesses. His relationship with the British government became increasingly fractious as the year wore on, which added to his woes. Perhaps the greatest complaint against French was his lack of direction for his forces. He has been accused of practising a 'hands off' style of command, leaving battlefield generalship to his favoured subordinate and eventual replacement Douglas Haig, the commander of First Army.

Haig was an obvious replacement for French due to being the most experienced British battlefield commander in France, although it must be noted that he further promoted his cause through a carefully coordinated whispering campaign that undermined political confidence in Sir John French. Haig had commanded the British offensives at Neuve Chapelle in March 1915, Aubers Ridge and Festubert in May 1915, and Loos in September–October 1915.

Haig's experiences as the commander of First Army would shape his tenure as commander-in-chief and are worth considering. His method was largely in line with pre-war expectations. Battle planning would be delegated to corps, who in turn asked their divisional commanders for proposals. These proposals were then considered by the corps commander and drawn into a formal plan, which would then be returned to Haig for assessment. Yet Haig's temperament created tensions in this process. One of his great weaknesses was his excessive optimism, which tended to grow as the day of the battle drew nearer. As a result, he frequently tinkered with the plans of his subordinates to include additional objectives and plans for cavalry exploitation. The bloody defeats of 1915 did nothing to dent Haig's optimism.[21]

---

21 For a critical examination of Haig in this period, see J. P. Harris, *Douglas Haig and the First World War* (Cambridge: Cambridge University Press, 2008). For a counterpoint, which argues

As commander-in-chief from 1916 Haig continued to advocate for ambitious plans that did not match the army's capabilities. This would be one of the most frustrating aspects of Haig's command. He recognised the limitations of his army in 1916, noting that the newly raised formations were poorly trained and lacked experience in major operations.[22] Yet his optimism overcame any doubts about the strength of his forces. Indeed, Haig had grounds for some confidence in this year. A coordinated series of Allied attacks termed the 'General Offensive' were putting German forces under severe pressure, while the vicious attritional struggle at Verdun was draining German manpower at a prodigious rate. Yet his optimism also owed something to his weak staff at GHQ. His Chief of Intelligence, John Charteris, had a troubling tendency to tell Haig what he wanted to hear.[23] Haig's Chief of Staff was a pre-war protégé, Launcelot Kiggell, who was a competent administrator but who was in awe of his chief and provided little, if any, independent advice. These factors tended to amplify Haig's optimism and convinced him that a decisive victory was within reach.

Haig's subordinates also had a challenging relationship with their chief. All but one of Haig's army commanders were his own appointments and some of them owed their careers to their chief. Henry Rawlinson of Fourth Army was a particularly important figure in this regard. Rawlinson had disgraced himself in 1915 when he made a botched attempt to scapegoat a subordinate for his own errors. Haig intervened to save Rawlinson's career, and Rawlinson had a sense of obligation to him for the remainder of the war.

Perhaps overawed by Haig's reputation and power, subordinates rarely challenged him even when they disagreed with his decisions. The most dangerous example of this tendency would be found at the Battle of the Somme, when Rawlinson's methodical 'bite and hold' plan of attack was rejected by Haig in favour of an ambitious assault designed to achieve a decisive breakthrough. Rawlinson never believed in this concept but acquiesced without argument.[24] This alteration played a key role in the tragedy of 1 July 1916. The British preparatory bombardment was fatally diluted by the need to engage multiple lines of German defences to allow the entire position to be pierced, rather than focussing on the front line and ensuring it was thoroughly suppressed to support the infantry in a limited advance. The result was a disaster of unprecedented proportions. The first day of the Somme remains the single bloodiest day in the history of the British Army.

Despite a staggering setback on its opening day, the British Army would continue the offensive until November 1916. The battle would serve as a crucible that slowly turned the army from a large but inexperienced citizen force into a veteran army that

that Haig was experiencing his own learning curve, see Gary Sheffield, *The Chief: Douglas Haig and the British Army* (London: Aurum, 2011).

22   John Bourne and Gary Sheffield, *Douglas Haig: War Diaries and Letters 1914–1918* (London: Aurum, 2006), pp.177–180.

23   Jim Beech, *Haig's Intelligence* (Cambridge: Cambridge University Press, 2013).

24   On this, see Robin Prior and Trevor Wilson, *Command on the Western Front: The Military Career of Sir Henry Rawlinson 1914–1918* (Barnsley: Leo Cooper, 1994), pp.137–153.

was capable of inflicting heavy damage upon its opponents. By the end of the battle in November the army was attacking using tanks, creeping barrages and close air support in a manner that was simply impossible in July.

Command arrangements also improved. Although bedevilled by the limitations of First World War communications, a combination of growing experience, improved staff work and superior coordination between arms could produce notable local success. Yet challenges remained. Integrating technology was challenging, and Haig's decision to commit Britain's nascent tank force in September 1916 would remain controversial for decades after the war. Haig's optimism continued to influence the battle, as he insisted attacks continued through October and November even as the deteriorating weather made advances ever more difficult. Above all, the German Army fought ferociously to hold its ground and counter-attacked whenever positions were lost. The result was a relentless attritional battle notable for its bloodshed. By the time the battle drew to close in mid-November the British Army had advanced approximately five miles at its furthest point for the cost of 420,000 casualties.

Haig, and indeed other Allied commanders, saw the results of 1916 as largely positive. At a strategic level the signs were promising. In early 1917, the German Army was forced to make its first large-scale voluntary withdrawal since trench warfare began as it fell back to the newly prepared Hindenburg Line. Furthermore, the British Army had emerged from the Somme as a battle-hardened force that had improved at all levels. It was now better trained and equipped than ever before, and was commanded by men who had, for the most part, proven themselves in battle.

The superior fighting power of the British Army was evident in the early part of the Battle of Arras (April–May 1917). In contrast to the disaster of the first day of the Somme, the first day of the Battle of Arras was a striking success that represented the deepest British advance since trench warfare had begun. Although partially explained by errors in German deployment, superior British planning and preparation were the key element in this triumph.

Yet the difficulties of First World War fighting would soon become apparent. The commander of the offensive, Edmund Allenby of Third Army, misread the situation and assumed that the German Army on his front had collapsed. He gave orders to pursue a broken enemy, only to find that the Germans had recovered from their opening setback and were now in strong positions. Allenby, under pressure from the ever-optimistic Haig and conscious of the need to support the mutinous French Army, hurried his forces into a string of poorly prepared assaults that suffered appalling losses.[25] The failure was severe enough that it prompted a protest from Allenby's corps commanders and led to him being removed from command, although he would find redemption commanding the Egyptian Expeditionary Force in the Middle East.

---

25   Harry Sanderson, 'The Black Day of the British Army: The Third Battle of the Scarpe, 3 May 1917', in Spencer Jones (ed.), *The Darkest Year: The British Army on the Western Front 1917* (Solihull: Helion & Co., 2022).

Haig himself was not discouraged by the latter stages of the Battle of Arras and, true to his personality, focused on the positives. His optimism was enhanced by the success of the meticulously prepared British offensive at Messines Ridge in June 1917, which captured a strategically important position at a comparatively low cost.

But Arras and Messines Ridge highlighted an intellectual division that was becoming apparent at the highest levels of the British Army. Haig's vision of a breakthrough attack that would achieve major strategic results has been noted, but since 1915 there had been an informal school of thought within the army that believed the key to breaking the Western Front was through a series of carefully prepared 'bite and hold' attacks that inflicted attrition on German forces.[26] The early phase of the Battle of Arras and the capture of Messines Ridge seemed to confirm the validity of the concept. By the summer of 1917 the Chief of the Imperial General Staff William Robertson was in favour of using such methods in the future. But Robertson's advice to Haig to pursue this approach was hampered by troubled British civil-military relations and had little effect on the commander-in-chief.[27] Indeed, Haig's next offensive, the Third Battle of Ypres, would be his most ambitious of the war.[28]

Third Ypres would be the most controversial of all of Haig's battles. There is still no academic consensus on whether his generalship here was worthy of praise or condemnation. His defenders have placed much of the blame on the commander of Fifth Army, Hubert Gough, for failing to understand Haig's intentions.[29] But other historians have challenged this interpretation, with the most recent study of the battle concluding that the blame lay largely with Haig.[30] The lack of consensus is reflective of the complexity of the battle. Facing an innovative German defence and conducting most of the battle in appalling weather conditions, it is impressive that the British Army achieved all that it did. By the time the battle officially ended in November the Passchendaele Ridge had been reached, albeit not secured, and Haig perhaps planned for a renewal of the battle in early 1918.[31] But the cost had been heavy. There had been over 250,000 British casualties and, uniquely, the army's morale had been severely shaken amidst the waterlogged devastation of Ypres.

The controversies of the battle caused lasting damage to British civil-military relations, exacerbated by the false dawn at the Battle of Cambrai (November–December

---

26   Spencer Jones, '"To Make War as we must and not as we should like": The British Army and the Problem of the Western Front 1915', in Spencer Jones (ed.), *Courage without Glory: The British Army on the Western Front 1915* (Solihull, Helion & Co., 2015).

27   Spencer Jones, 'David Lloyd George and British Strategy on the Western Front 1917', in Jones (ed.) *The Darkest Year*, pp.38, 44.

28   Jones, 'British Strategy', pp.40–43.

29   Sheffield, *The Chief*, pp.227–228.

30   Nicholas Ridley, *Far from Suitable? Haig, Gough and Passchendaele: A Reappraisal* (Solihull: Helion & Co., 2024), pp.251–271.

31   The final act of the battle took place in December. On this, see Michael Locicero, *A Moonlight Massacre: The Night Operation on the Passchendaele Ridge, 2 December 1917* (Solihull: Helion & Co., 2014).

1917), and by the end of the year the government's frustration with the armed forces was boiling over into fiery exchanges in Parliament. Although he did not say so in public, the Prime Minister, David Lloyd George, had lost faith with Haig and wanted to prevent any further bloody offensives in 1918. Lloyd George planned to refocus the British war effort to the Middle East where casualties were lower and prospects of success brighter. To this end, the government withheld reinforcements from the Western Front and insisted that the BEF must maintain a defensive posture for the year. The government also reordered Haig's GHQ, removing the supine Charteris and Kiggell, and replacing them with more independently minded officers.

There is a certain contrast between the government's disillusionment with Haig's generalship and the state of the army in 1918. Although its declining manpower was a cause for concern, the development of the BEF from 1916 was stark. Its combat capability had improved dramatically. It was now better trained, better equipped and capable of mounting sophisticated operations with a high degree of confidence. Indeed, although 1917 had ended with the disappointments of Third Ypres and Cambrai, a notable feature of the year was the BEF's growing ability to break into German positions. Combined arms, including large numbers of tanks by the end of the year, and coordination between divisions and corps, had all shown marked improvement over the course of the year. These improvements, the result of hard-won experience, were also reflected in superior planning, generalship and staff work.

The BEF would need all these advantages in 1918 as it was plunged into the most dangerous year of the war since 1914. In March, Germany launched its *Kaiserschlacht*, a series of huge offensives designed to crush Britain and France before reinforcements from America arrived in sufficient strength to turn the tide of war. Operation Michael struck the overstretched British Fifth Army on the Somme front in March and came close to breaking the force entirely. That Fifth Army was able to mount a fighting retreat owed much to the improved quality of the army, and key decisions made by officers on the ground. Fifth Army was driven back to Amiens with heavy losses but was able to hold the line at the gates of this vital logistics hub.

The next major German offensive, Operation Georgette, was aimed towards Hazebrouck near Ypres. The fighting here was desperately hard, prompting Haig to issue a famous order of the day which announced, 'with our backs to the wall and believing in the justice of our cause each one of us must fight on to the end'.[32] The Germans gained almost nine miles of ground at the limit of their advance, but British resistance was fierce and the attackers' losses were heavy. Crucially, Hazebrouck remained in British hands.

Frustrated on the British front, Germany would undertake major offensives against the French in May and June 1918. This gave the BEF some precious respite and allowed the army to make good its losses. Replacement equipment and fresh drafts arrived to

---

32   A discussion of this order and its effects can be found at 'With our Backs to the Wall…' Sir Douglas Haig's Special Order 1918', https://blogs.bl.uk/untoldlives/2018/04/with-our-backs-to-the-wall-sir-douglas-haigs-special-order-1918-.html, accessed 1 November 2024.

swell the ranks, and by July 1918 the army was ready to resume aggressive operations. Offensive operations began in July, including the impressive Australian-led victory at the Battle of Hamel, but it would not be until August that the full weight of the BEF was ready to begin its attack.

The blow would fall at the Battle of Amiens on 8 August. The architect of the battle was Henry Rawlinson, once again commanding Fourth Army, who had learned many valuable lessons from the Battle of the Somme. He had assembled an impressive assault force which included nearly 600 tanks and a tremendous concentration of artillery. Careful staff work had assembled the army with a degree of secrecy and the scale of the attack would be a surprise to the Germans. The results were, from a British perspective, spectacular. Within five days, the BEF advanced 13 miles and captured some 50,000 German prisoners. The scale of the success must surely have tempted Haig to push his forces further, but he demonstrated that he had learned from past mistakes in 1917 and brought the battle to a close on the advice of his subordinates.

The Battle of Amiens would raise the curtain on a series of Allied attacks that are collectively known as the Hundred Days' Campaign. The German Army was beginning to crumble by this stage of the war, having suffered enormous losses of men and material in their doomed spring offensives, but were still capable of fierce resistance. German command pinned their hopes on reoccupying the formidable Hindenburg Line position and holding out until winter brought the campaigning season to a close. Yet this once formidable obstacle was broken in a matter of days at the Battle of the St Quentin Canal in September. The speed with which the BEF could now organise and deliver powerful offensives imposed an operational tempo on the German Army which it could not match. Although the fighting remained fierce and casualties could often be high, the BEF would win an unbroken string of victories from Amiens in August until the armistice in November.

By 1918 the BEF had reached the pinnacle of its learning curve. It is tempting to argue that the army won its victories in spite of its generals, but this is an overly narrow viewpoint. A strong case can be made that by the final year of the war the British officer corps represented a meritocracy with honours earned in battle. This was apparent at all levels of command, whether it was Haig's moderation of his runaway optimism and willingness to close offensives rather than pushing on ambitiously, or in the ability of corps commanders to organise fearsome attacks on German positions with just a few days' notice.

The tantalising question remains as to whether this level of effectiveness could have been achieved without such bloodshed. There is no doubt that the price of learning on the Western Front was appallingly high, and some of the command decisions between 1914–1917 are difficult to explain or excuse. It is this aspect that continues to inform modern debate. What is certain is that by 1918 the furnace of war had forged a new generation of British generals. These men commanded forces of unimaginable size and complexity compared to pre-war standards. Yet the cost to reach this point had been immense and would become a source of contention after the war. Nevertheless, to dismiss the British Army as 'lions led by donkeys' is simplistic and ignores the pivotal role both commanders and soldiers would play in achieving Allied victory.

12

The Very (AI) Model of a Modern Major General

Michael S. Neiberg[1]

Generative AI and Strategic Thinking

The disruptive and revolutionary advent of artificial intelligence is upon us, offering strategic leaders unprecedented tools to navigate the complexities of twenty-first-century warfare. While AI is not a substitute for human judgement or a magic bullet to eliminate uncertainty, its potential to augment decision-making, enhance situational awareness, overcome cognitive bias and challenge assumptions is now undeniable. This chapter explores ways that AI, when properly employed, can serve as a cognitive force multiplier for senior leaders. It delves into some practical applications of AI, from generating historical analogies to red-teaming ideas, and highlights the importance of human-AI collaboration in enhancing the cognitive skills needed to achieve strategic success.[2]

If used with creativity and a healthy dose of scepticism, even the current off-the-shelf AI tools can help senior leaders and their staffs to see problems more clearly and eliminate faulty assumptions more quickly. AI, when properly understood and utilised, can behave as a team member that can help senior leaders tackle some of the most fundamental and challenging cognitive tasks they face. If improperly used, AI brings with it the risk of increasing confusion, information overload and a blind acceptance of conclusions reached via flawed algorithms or bad data. Consequently, in our rapidly changing strategic environment, mastery of this new technology will be a critical asset for senior leaders.

---

1   The views expressed are those of the author and do not necessarily reflect the official policy or position of the Department of the Army, Department of Defense, or the U.S. Government. My thanks to Jonathan Boff and Thomas Spahr for their thoughtful comments.
2   For purposes of this chapter, I used the models Perplexity, Claude, and Gemini but my choice of these models should not be read as an endorsement of any single model or the companies that produce them.

Although there are myriad applications for AI, this chapter focuses on generative artificial intelligence, a branch of artificial intelligence and machine learning that 'generates'
new information from a pre-trained dataset. Put simply, it translates user inputs written
in plain English (called prompts, about which more below) into numeric codes called
tokens. It then uses highly sophisticated algorithms to plot those tokens in multidimensional grids to find words, concepts and names that are found most often in combination
with those from the prompt. Through repeated calculations, these models can 'learn'
which answers are most effective; they can also learn which methods best generate them.
AI can therefore rapidly become more 'intelligent' by improving its performance without
human intervention.

As a basic introduction, it may be helpful to think in terms of the common acronym
GPT. The 'G' stands for generative, meaning that the point of an AI model is, simply,
to generate something. A user's prompt may ask for text ('write me a two-paragraph
summary of this chapter'), a picture ('make me an image of a bored reader suffering
through this chapter'), a poem ('write me a haiku about a rug that really ties the room
together') or a process ('explain to me the steps for setting the correct ignition timing
on a 1955 Chevy Bel Air'). Recently, AI has begun to produce videos, transcripts of lip
reading from surveillance cameras, narrations of text based on a pre-recorded human
voice, and even complete podcasts with human-sounding voices.[3]

The 'P' stands for pre-trained. Without getting into too much detail, every AI model
(sometimes called an LLM or large language model) is 'trained' to do some set of tasks on
a given set of data. At their most basic, a model can be trained on data from the internet
to perform generative tasks like the ones noted above.[4] More sophisticated systems can
be 'fine-tuned' to perform more specific tasks from a smaller or 'closed' dataset. In short,
before relying on AI to solve a problem, be sure that you know what data it was trained
on and what it was trained to do. Although most of the major AI models are now capable
of performing a wide variety of tasks, AI trained to translate text from Arabic to Farsi
may do a poor job of, say, playing checkers, even though the latter is a much less complex
skill than the former.

---

3   This last capability generated controversy when an AI company trained a model on actress
     Scarlett Johansson's voice. Less controversially, Carnegie Mellon University trains AI with
     faculty voices (with the faculty member's permission) to produce lectures for distance
     education courses. The process saves time (such lectures can be made in one-sixth the time)
     and any edits a professor wants to make can be done as easily as editing the script. There is
     no need to rerecord the entire lecture. For the Johansson controversy, see Alex Werpin, 'Sam
     Altman Dodges Scarlett Johansson AI Voice Controversy', *Hollywood Reporter*, 30 May 2024,
     https://www.hollywoodreporter.com/business/business-news/sam-altman-comments-
     scarlett-johansson-ai-voice-controversy-1235911854/, accessed 13 September 2024.
4   Many models are trained on a data set with a hard stop data. For example, a model may be
     trained on data before 1 July 2024. To access data on the internet after that date, it may use
     a technique called RAG (Retrieval Augmented Generation) that searches the internet for
     germane data to add to its response.

The 'T' stands for transformer, the incredibly sophisticated hardware and software that helps machines 'learn'. Two features are important for our purposes. The first is that transformers work on probability. As a result, they do not return the same answers to the same prompt every time. Second, although the models are getting better all the time, because they operate on probabilities there is a chance that they can return wildly incorrect answers. If I ask it to design an itinerary for a day trip to Versailles, for example, there is a slim chance that it will design an itinerary for a day in North Versailles, Pennsylvania. In AI terms, these false answers are called 'hallucinations'. An answer built from a previous hallucination, of course, will also be a hallucination. Just because an answer comes from an AI model does not make it infallible or beyond questioning; if anything, the opposite is true, and you may have a very disappointing day trip indeed.

Prompt Engineering

The key to working with AI lies in prompt engineering, a fancy term for making sure that you ask the AI good questions. With apologies to my non-American friends, an example from the world of American sports will hopefully illuminate the issue. In April 2024, a prominent American sports magazine gave my hometown baseball team a 22.7 percent chance of making the playoffs. Aside from being oddly specific, the number struck me as wildly optimistic given how bad the team had been recently and how little it had done in the off season to get better. I prompted AI to give me reasons to be hopeful. It returned the usual meaningless sports chatter about talented young players, the ability of sports to surprise us and the possibility of existing players maturing. To put it mildly, these answers were unsatisfying. A few similar queries got me nowhere, so rather than assume that AI was useless to solve my problem, I reengineered the prompt. I asked AI what algorithm or mathematical theorem might give my team a 22.7 percent chance of making the playoffs. With just a little nudging, AI pointed me to a theorem called Laplace's law of succession, which, when using my team's data over the previous five seasons, produced an exact 22.7 percent chance of making the playoffs. When I ran the same data with three other teams, I also got the magazine's precise estimated chance of making the playoffs. With a few minutes of time and a crucial change in my prompt engineering, I learned that the magazine had not made its prediction based on any specific knowledge of my team but merely by inputting modern-day baseball data into a theorem from an eighteenth-century French mathematician. I left this short exercise even more pessimistic about my team's chances. More importantly, however, I learned valuable lessons about prompt engineering and the need to challenge answers that seem flawed.[5] Just because the magazine gave a number that seemed precise and

---

5   For those who might want to know more about Laplace's law, see https://ericneyman. wordpress.com/2020/11/29/an-elegant-proof-of-laplaces-rule-of-succession/, accessed 14 September 2024.

accurate did not mean that the conclusion it reached was sound.[6] Finally, I learned that I could use AI to help me identify the logical processes used by others, and, crucially, analyse their weaknesses.

Good prompts are specific and set conditions. Instead of prompting 'how can history help officers understand the current war in Ukraine?' we can write a prompt like: 'Assume you were a historically trained NATO staff officer when Russia invaded Ukraine in 2022. What five lessons from the First World War would you have given to your team as a guide for understanding how the current war might develop?' I ran that prompt as a test with a small but reliable First World War dataset that I was building, and the AI model returned the following five lessons in less than three seconds:

1. Expect rapid movements over vast spaces: Unlike the static trench warfare of the Western Front, the Eastern Front in the First World War was characterised by comparatively quick movements over large areas. This suggests NATO should prepare for a potentially fluid and dynamic conflict zone in Ukraine.
2. Recognise the importance of logistics and supply lines: The vast distances involved in Eastern European warfare make logistics and supply lines critical. In the First World War, armies often outran their supply lines, leading to operational pauses. NATO should focus on maintaining robust and flexible supply chains to support Ukrainian forces.
3. Be prepared for shifting alliances and complex political dynamics: The Russian Revolution and ethnic conflicts in the imperial periphery led to a series of shifting alliances during the First World War. NATO should anticipate potential political instability and changing allegiances among various factions within Ukraine and the broader region.
4. Understand the significance of key terrain and strategic points: In the First World War, control of critical locations like railways, river crossings, and fortresses played a crucial role. NATO should identify and prioritise key strategic points in Ukraine for defence or as objectives.
5. Anticipate the use of cavalry and mobile forces: Cavalry remained more important on the Eastern Front than in the West during WWI. While modern warfare has evolved, the principle of mobile forces for rapid manoeuvre remains relevant. NATO should consider how to counter Russian mobile units and support Ukrainian mobility.[7]

Whether you are dismissive of this technology or excited by it, something that can produce results like these in seconds is important for military leaders to understand. Changing the prompt by asking the AI model to act as a British staff officer or a naval

---

6   As I write this in the middle of September 2024 my team is, as I predicted, very far away from a playoff spot and has been for several sad months.
7   The data set I used was a small sample of relevant articles from the peer-reviewed https://encyclopedia.1914-1918-online.net.

officer will change the response because the prompt has given the model more information to tokenise and plot. Experimenting with a case as silly as a baseball team's chances of making the playoffs can help users better understand prompt engineering so that they can get the most out of AI when trying to shape answers to more important questions. It should also help senior leaders become better at questioning the answers that people proudly present as fact because they were generated by AI.

As many data scientists like to say, AI is as bad now as it will ever be. Major improvements are happening constantly, in part because the AI models can teach themselves at great speed and scale. They do not sleep and they can make thousands of calculations per second. In short, between the time I write this and the time you read it, AI may have made several leaps forward that render some of the arguments here less relevant. Some people are predicting that we will soon see AI models that will not require prompt engineering at all. They will be able to learn from your past inputs to design prompts for you. AI technology is moving that quickly.

AI is therefore a clearly disruptive, potentially revolutionary technology that is not coming over the horizon but is here now. It brings with it a host of massive problems including the enormous amount of energy that AI needs to store and train data, the possibilities of its use for nefarious ends like misinformation and 'deep fakes', and the risks of what can happen if human beings use it without proper training and guidance.[8] Leaders at all levels will have to wrestle with this new technology. When used properly, it can help leaders solve a surprising array of cognitive problems, including checking this chapter for logical flaws, poor sentence syntax, and key points that I may have missed. It also wrote the first draft of the abstract above.[9]

For all that AI can do, it is still subject to hallucinations and the GIGO problem: garbage in, garbage out. Some AI experts have grown concerned that the power and seeming wizardry of AI make this problem even larger, as people may assume that any answer that AI produces is automatically objective, infallible or superior to one produced by humans. Some have redefined GIGO to mean 'garbage in, gospel out' because of the aura that surrounds AI and, I suspect, our need in the current information environment to find unbiased 'truths', however they are produced.[10] Leaders will therefore have to approach AI with some basic understanding of how it works and a healthy dose of cynicism, but as I hope to show, when used ethically, responsibly and creatively, it can help leaders solve a surprising array of complex problems, a few of which I outline below.

---

8   See, among many others: Brian Calvert, 'AI Already Uses as Much Energy as a Small Country. It's Only the Beginning,' *Vox*, 28 March 2024, https://www.vox.com/climate/2024/3/28/24111721/ climate-ai-tech-energy-demand-rising; Vincent Boulanin, Netta Goussac, and Laura Bruun, and Luke Richards, 'Responsible Military Use of Artificial Intelligence', *Stockholm International Peace Research Institute*, https://www.sipri.org/sites/default/files/2020-11/responsible_military_use_of_ artificial_intelligence.pdf, accessed on 2 September 2024.

9   I used Gemini to check this article, prompting it to act like an editor of a scholarly book. It provided five specific recommended changes, three of which I accepted.

10   Credit to Simon Albert at the AI firm Adarga for the garbage in, gospel out phrase.

Searching for and Testing Historical Analogies

When the unexpected happens, our brains naturally search for analogies.[11] Doing so helps us to make the unfamiliar seem more familiar. If current event (A) feels to us like something in the past (B), then we can begin to think about how to approach (A) as people once approached (B). But our search for analogies faces cognitive hurdles that can lead us down unhelpful paths. These hurdles include the tendency to rely on historical analogies with which we are most familiar (called the availability bias), the ones that seem to suggest our own preferences most strongly (called the confirmation bias), and the limits in our own historical knowledge. Moreover, once we mentally anchor onto an analogy, it can be difficult for us to move away from it.[12]

AI can, when properly prompted, help senior leaders to refine and test the analogies that they and the people around them use. When asked for historical analogies to the war in Gaza after 7 October 2023, my Army War College students naturally thought most often of their own experiences of urban warfare in Iraq. On the surface this analogy seemed appropriate enough, but it was skewed by their own recent experiences (called, naturally enough, recency bias). We prompted an AI model to suggest analogies at the strategic level to the war in Gaza that might help senior military officers gain insight into the conflict. The model then added to our set of possible analogies the Irish Troubles, the Combined Bomber Offensive of the Second World War, and the Battle of Manila in 1945. The latter two represent cases of heavy civilian casualties, while the first offers a case with some important strategic similarities.

The point of the exercise was not to settle on a single 'right' analogy, but to help us think more deeply beyond our initial responses. AI helped us to test the strengths and weaknesses of each of our analogies. We prompted it to explain why it suggested the Irish Troubles analogy, one that none of us had considered. It highlighted factors such as: the interplay of ideology, religion and contested territorial claims; the challenges of fighting asymmetrically; the importance of the United States as a player in a long-term peace process; and the difficulties of finding points of compromise between protagonists with divergent worldviews and historical narratives. By using AI, we widened the terms of our discussion and thought through case studies we had not considered. The result was a much richer and deeper discussion. The cost was less than 15 additional minutes of time to design the prompts.

---

11   See Yuen Foong Khong, *Analogies at War: Korea, Munich, Dien Bien Phu, and the Vietnam Decisions of 1965* (Princeton: Princeton University Press, 1992); Daniel Kahneman, *Thinking Fast and Slow* (New York: Farrar, Strauss, and Giroux, 2013).

12   For more on cognitive bias, see Daniel Kahneman, Daniel Lovallo, and Oliver Sibony, 'Before You Make That Big Decision', *Harvard Business Review*, 89:6 (2011), pp.50–60.

Red-Teaming and Challenging Groupthink

Most AI models default to being conversational, complimentary and even flattering. After all, the companies that own them want users to feel comfortable interacting with them. But users can prompt AI models to become good critics or to act as a demanding boss or to find flaws in any argument, no matter how solid. Users can give AI models policy suggestions and ask them to provide criticisms from a variety of lenses. When we asked an AI model to critique a student's idea of the United States giving more advanced weapons to Saudi Arabia to fight the Houthis, it returned seven possible implications for consideration: repairing the strained bilateral relations between the United States and Saudi Arabia; increasing the tensions between the United States and Iran; the possibility of increased Houthi operations in response; the need to combine weapons transfers with greater maritime security operations; the risk of civilian casualties among the Yemeni people; the chance that Saudi Arabia might use the weapons for other purposes; and the risk of the conflict spilling over to other parts of the Middle East. It also, when prompted, helped us think through the possible consequences of inaction. In short, it became a team member willing to challenge ideas, albeit one we still had to question.

Teams sometimes prioritise a group's social cohesion over the need for constructive disagreement.[13] AI, however, has no incentive to keep the tone of the group friendly (unless one prompts it to do so) nor does it have an innate bias either to like or dislike an idea because of its relationship to the person who advanced it. This capability can help to control the sometimes-unhealthy amount of influence of a superior's ideas on younger staff officers eager to please their boss. AI will critique ideas in the same way regardless of the rank of the person who advanced them. Strategists can thus benefit from uploading their policy ideas to AI models and letting the model provide criticism that they may not get from their peers or their subordinates. With the right prompting, a user can fine tune the criticism, asking the model to be more critical or to focus on a specific part of an argument. Users can also prompt AI to behave like a tough boss, a peer from a partner nation, a sceptical journalist or an infinite number of other personas. AI is a great editor; I used it to critique this chapter from multiple perspectives.

Perspective Analysis

We tend to dismiss behaviours we do not understand as irrational. From a strategic perspective, this tendency is dangerous because it removes our capacity to engage in strategic empathy. Belittling an adversary as irrational, moreover, can lead to the false assumption that it will not be receptive to diplomacy or economic incentives; the only option is to prepare to fight it. AI can help mitigate this problem through a technique

13   Sean Wise, 'Can a Team Have Too Much Cohesion? The Dark Side to Network Density', *European Management Journal*, 32:5 (October 2014), pp.703–711.

known as perspective analysis. A user can ask AI why North Korea insists on spending its limited resources on nuclear weapons instead of food or why the Russians see their war in Ukraine as existential when it seems to us such an irrational and perfidious war of conquest.

We may not agree with the answers we get because they may not conform to our own understandings of the past and present. They may also not conform to our understandings of rationality. But AI will help us avoid blind spots by generating narratives to help explain adversary behaviour. When prompted, AI explained Iran's proxy strategy as a function of its relative military weakness, its geopolitical position, the revolutionary ideology and historical perspective of its leadership, its fear of encirclement by rivals, its desire to create a deterrent against invasion, and its quest to find allies in a rapidly changing and generally hostile region. We may still disapprove of Iran's behaviour, but such an analysis allows us to quickly develop a better understanding of Iran's worldview that in turn allows us to build strategic empathy and look for ways to either counter an adversary's narrative or exploit a weakness in their worldview.[14]

Strategic Forecasting

While AI excels at analysing existing data, its ability to predict the future remains poor. Still, as a rule, humans also tend to forecast badly.[15] It might, however, soon be possible to build AI systems that, with a thoughtful human 'in the loop,' can improve strategic forecasts by building human-machine teams that use the best abilities of both. AI can handle enormous amounts of information at scale and speed. It is therefore ideally suited to find connections between data points, even in documents written in different languages.

My colleague Thomas Spahr and his team designed just such a system in Afghanistan as the American withdrawal began to diminish the number of human analysts and sources on the ground. They built a system called Raven Sentry that used AI to analyse nearly two decades of open source intelligence from weather patterns, calendar events, and even from news of market and mosques closing at unusual hours to build a model that predicted future Taliban attacks on Afghan provincial and district centres.[16] In this

14   Remember, we are talking about empathy (trying to obtain a deeper understanding of a situation from someone else's viewpoint) not sympathy (agreeing with or adopting that viewpoint). See, for example, Matt Waldman, 'Strategic Empathy: The Afghanistan Intervention Shows Why the U.S. Must Empathize with Its Adversaries', *Journal of Strategic Studies*, 33:6 (2010), available at: https://www.belfercenter.org/publication/strategic-empathy-afghanistan-intervention-shows-why-us-must-empathize-its-adversaries, accessed 31 March 2024.
15   Research does, however, suggest that it is possible to get better at this skill. See Philip E. Tetlock and Dan Gardner, *Superforecasting: The Art and Science of Prediction* (Crown Publishers, 2015).
16   Thomas W. Spahr, '*Raven Sentry*: Employing AI for Indications and Warnings in Afghanistan', *Parameters*, 54:2 (2024).

case, the team leveraged the ability of AI to compile and analyse information at scale and speed to provide actionable intelligence quickly enough to prevent attacks.

If it is true that intelligence analysis is about looking for connections between 'smudges' of data, then AI can help analysts by looking for correlations and causations between those smudges. Just as Raven Sentry did at the tactical level, it should now be possible to build accurate AI models that can at least warn strategists of changes (even subtle ones) in the strategic environment that can make it less stable. Had such a system existed, it might, for example, have found linkages among the multiple strands of 'fuzzy' data leading up to the terrorist attacks of 11 September 2001 in time to help leaders direct resources towards prevention. AI might soon be able to work like a warning light in an aeroplane, alerting the human pilot of a potentially dangerous situation that needs attention. Of course, such a system will depend on humans learning to understand and, when appropriate, trust it.

Data and the Strategic Use of History

Data is the key. Without it, AI models have nothing to analyse. Right now, most of the major AI models use large databases 'scraped' from the internet. If the data includes conspiracy theory websites or wildly inaccurate data from a poorly done study, then the results from AI will be less reliable. Fortunately, we do have mountains of highly relevant data just waiting to be processed sitting in archives around the world. As more and more of these archives become digitised, AI models can take advantage of case studies and data from the entirety of the human experience. AI models could comb through custom-ised datasets comprised of hundreds of thousands of documents throughout the centuries to find useful analogies, test hypotheses, look for patterns and help with forecasting.

Creating such datasets will be time-consuming; they face numerous technical, bureau-cratic and even legal challenges. But it should be possible, especially as more archives digitise their material. Just as Raven Sentry used high-quality data to improve decision-making, AI should be able to analyse data from the world's archives. The strategic appli-cations of such a process could be limitless: AI could use Lord Alanbrooke's papers to provide 'his' insights on contemporary problems; it could combine data from various archives on a single event like Operation Overlord; or it could analyse data on a problem like military recruitment over the centuries to look for common patterns and solutions. Such a use of AI might not give perfect clarity to today's problems, but it should help to strengthen the thinking and test the hypotheses of the people wrestling with them.

A Model for Using genAI

We can think of a five-stage process for using AI to solve problems, only one stage of which is performed by computers. First, a team should define the problem it is facing and decide whether it is appropriate to use AI to help solve it. Second, the team should design the prompts and choose the models and data best suited to give good answers. Only then should the team bring AI into the discussion for the third part of the process, producing output. In the fourth stage, subject matter experts decide on the meaning of the AI output and assess its utility. Fifth and finally, the team uses this process to effect some kind of decision or change.[17]

Below is a fictitious example that I used at my home institution to show this process in action. The case study is fictitious, but the prompts and responses are real:

First: Define the Problem. Let us imagine that my dean came to me to ask if we could create a module for students using the Korean War as an historical analogy for the war in Ukraine. He knows that although I have no special expertise in either Korea or Ukraine, I am an historian trained to think in terms of analogies. I could therefore assess the response that an AI model might return and judge the utility of his idea. He also knows that I have access to a dataset of official histories of the Korean War and some digitised archival material that an AI model could use to solve the problem.[18]

Second: Design the Prompts. I spent most of my time in this exercise deciding how best to prompt an AI model to answer the dean's question. I experimented with several prompts and finally decided on the following: 'Write me two paragraphs evaluating the strengths and weaknesses of using the Korean War of 1950–1953 as an historical analogy to the war in Ukraine today. The audience is senior military leaders studying at a professional military school. Use the documents in the dataset that I built.' This prompt told the AI what I wanted it to do, who I wanted it to consider in its answer, and what data to use.

Third: Receive the Output. The AI model returned the following two paragraphs: The Korean War of 1950–1953 offers valuable insights as an historical analogy for the current war in Ukraine, but it also has significant limitations that senior military leaders must consider. The strengths of the comparison lie in the similarities of great power involvement, the potential for escalation, and the challenges of limited war. Like Korea, the Ukraine war has drawn in major powers, with Russia invading and NATO countries supporting Ukraine, raising the risks of a broader conflict and even nuclear threats. The Korean War also illustrates the difficulties of fighting

---

17 With some experience, one can actually use AI in all stages of this process. AI can, for example, be an excellent resource for brainstorming.

18 In this case I used the U.S. Army's official histories of the Korean War as a dataset. They can be found here: https://history.army.mil/html/bookshelves/resmat/korea/intro/commemorative-products.html. I also uploaded descriptions of a few of our lesson objectives to give the AI model data about our course. Obviously, all of this material is unclassified and open source. Never upload classified or controlled material into an AI model that is not specifically designed to handle it as it may be 'scraped' by another AI model.

a limited war with restraint to avoid direct confrontation between major powers while still achieving objectives, which parallels the U.S. and NATO's efforts to support Ukraine without triggering a wider war with Russia.

However, the historical and geopolitical contexts differ significantly, with the Korean War occurring during the bipolar Cold War era and the Ukraine war in a more multipolar world. Advances in military technology, differences in geography and terrain, and the nature of the regimes involved also limit the applicability of the Korean War analogy. Therefore, while the Korean War offers some relevant lessons, military leaders must carefully analyse both the similarities and differences and avoid over-relying on this or any single historical analogy when formulating strategies for the unique challenges of the war in Ukraine.

In a matter of mere seconds, the AI model returned a response that is as good as something I could have produced if given several days.[19] The point, of course, is not whether the answer is perfect but whether it gives me a solid basis in a short time frame to address the dean's question. Although I am not an expert in Korea, I do know enough military history to judge the AI answer as highly reliable. The more important the impact of an AI-informed decision, the greater the level of scrutiny we must apply, but this answer, combined with my own expertise, gave me the confidence to answer the dean.

Fourth: Assign Meaning to the Output. In this case, I told the dean that I thought we could indeed do what he asked. We could design a module for students using the Korean War as an historical analogy, focussing on the strengths and weaknesses that the AI model returned. Knowing my own institution and its educational needs better than the AI does (at least for now), I also told him that the exercise would have the additional benefit of teaching our students about the history of Korea, itself a region of strategic importance for them to study.

Fifth: Decide on Impact. Armed with my answer, the dean could go ahead with his plan. He could implement a new curriculum module focused on the Korea-Ukraine analogy, determine lesson objectives, develop materials to train faculty to teach the module, and determine the amount of time he wishes to dedicate to it. The process, crucially, involved a teaming of human subject matter expertise with the speed and processing power of AI. In this case, the cost was negligible in terms of money and perfectly reasonable in terms of faculty time.

The most productive and most useful applications of artificial intelligence require interdisciplinary teams with diverse ranges of talents. The more intellectually and culturally diverse the team, the better the prompts and the interpretation of the outputs will be. AI

19   As a reminder, the sample use case is fictitious, but the AI responses are real.

is, therefore, not the exclusive preserve of the computer scientists, although they must be a crucial part of the team. There is a place for people of all backgrounds in this emerging world of artificial intelligence. We need all skill sets if we are to maximise the potential benefits of this revolutionary technology.

Senior leaders should treat AI as a team of eager young staff officers. It will work hard, try to make you happy, and sometimes make mistakes.[20] AI is a special kind of teammate, one that comes with an alluring sense of technological wizardry. Senior leaders need to take great care not to put too much faith in it, a cognitive bias known as automation bias. This teammate, just like a human one, needs leaders to train it, understand its strengths and weaknesses, and question the answers it produces. But when used thoughtfully, AI can be an asset unlike any other in human history. Its utility is only limited by our creativity and the data we give it.

20   My thanks to my dean, Edward Kaplan, for introducing me to that useful metaphor.

13

Generals and Generalship: What Defines Them?

Jonathon Riley

If we are to answer the question posed in the title of this chapter we must start at the beginning – to establish what is meant by a general, and by generalship – good or bad. It is a subject upon which many eminent authorities have already written, among them such names as Sun Tzu, Carl von Clausewitz, Anton Jomini, John Ruskin, J. F. C. Fuller, Martin van Creveld, John Keegan and Richard Holmes. In the presence of this august company, all judgements may be inadequate.[1]

At the outset, we must be clear that this is not a discussion about the peacetime role of general officers, where they will be judged by standards of administrative competence, or according to the prevailing political culture, or against passing social norms. No, this is a discussion about generalship in war, where generals are judged by results just as those of Russia, Ukraine and Israel are being judged during the current struggle. Those who have failed, or have been perceived to have failed, have paid dearly; President Putin has sacked at least 11 general officers since the invasion of Ukraine, for example.[2] No general can stand the consequences of failure in war at any time, especially when weapons of mass destruction may be employed with truly devastating effects; and routinely where the glare of the legal and media spotlights illuminate military operations today as never before.

Considerable care is needed when discussing generalship in an historical context. The responsibilities and required competencies of a general have changed over the centuries and one must be careful not to judge Napoleon or Wellington, for example, by modern standards. Our understanding of strategy, the operational art and battlefield tactics are

---

1   For a full discussion on the subject in an historical context, see Jonathon Riley, *Napoleon as a General. Command from the Battlefield to Grand Strategy* (London and New York: Continuum Books, 2007), Chapter 1.
2   Isabel van Brugen, 'Full List of Russian Commanders Dismissed by Putin in Ukraine War', *Newsweek*, 18 July 2003 available at newsweek.com/full-list-russian-commanders-dismissed-putin-ukraine-war-1813706, accessed 3 April 2024.

different from theirs: complex, modern war – sometimes referred to as '4th Generation War' or 'Three-Block War' – was far in the future in 1815. Technology too has advanced in the intervening period: the full effects of the Industrial Revolution had hardly begun to be felt by 1815, and technology then was little different from what it had been 100 years before. Looking to more modern times, a battalion commander today, at least in the U.S. Army, has more firepower, over greater ranges, and can see more of the battle-field, by day and night, than his counterpart at corps level during the Vietnam War.

Nor do our cultural norms make any sense in the context of the world of, say, 1815 – when slavery was still widely practised, women had no role in statecraft and democracy was considered a dangerous and Jacobinical idea. Our norms make no sense to that period any more than theirs do to us. Thus, it is not right to judge a field commander with the benefit of hindsight, because he made his decisions based on the informa-tion available at the time: our lives and experience go forward, following what Steven Hawking calls 'the arrow of time';[3] we are able to review those experiences by looking back, but we cannot change them.

Later in this chapter I will address the increasingly rapid advances in military science that dictate the employment of forces under a general's command in modern multi-domain operations. But I contend even so, because war is adversarial, it remains an art, rather than a science, and that therefore generalship too remains an art, although tempered by science, rather than a straightforward exercise in professional competency. War 'is the foundation of all the arts', wrote John Ruskin, 'it is the foundation of all the high virtues and faculties of men.'[4]

'For what art can surpass that of the general? – an art which deals not with dead matter but with living beings, who are subject to every impression of the moment, such as fear, precipitation, exhaustion – in short, to every human passion and excitement. The general has not only to reckon with… time, weather, accidents of all kinds, but he has before him one who seeks to disturb and frustrate his plans and labours in every way.'[5]

There are, therefore, no simple criteria for assessing good generals, or at least what makes a good general.

A common dictionary definition of the general speaks of one who holds 'extended command': not helpful in itself. Moreover, generals come in different sizes. A briga-dier general commands a brigade group or task force engaged in the close or deep or rear operations within the context of a higher formation. A major general commands a division which is, however configured, the lowest level of command that plans and conducts operations simultaneously, and carries on the close, deep and rear fight. A lieutenant general commands a corps, which today is more an operational than tactical

3   Stephen Hawking, *A Brief History of Time. From the Big Bang to Black Holes* (London: Bantam Dell Ltd, 1998), Chapter One.
4   John Ruskin, 'Lecture III, "War", to the R.M.A. Woolwich', in *The Crown of Wild Olives* (New York: A.L. Burt, 1900), p.66.
5   Albrecht von Boguslawski (Lumley Graham, trans.), *Tactical Deductions from the War of 1870–71* (London: Henry S. King & Co and Creswell's, 1872), p.68.

level formation with responsibility for a theatre of operations, its lines of communication and its interaction with the air, space, maritime, nuclear, virtual or cyber, media and legal components of a force. Thus, the first defined aspect of generalship is command of a fighting formation, of combined arms, services and components, engaged in war.

Above this, at the highest level, a general will be responsible for managing the military aspects of his country's policy and strategy, and the spending of its blood and treasure in war to achieve the goals of policy and strategy: policy being about the objectives or ends sought by a government or a coalition and, in reality too, the means provided to generals by governments, strategy being about the ways this will be achieved. At the strategic and operational levels there is, for generals at that level, a circular aspect to the relationship of ends, ways and means. Generalship will determine the ways to achieve the given ends but, since the decision by any state to make war is a political one, no government – we hope – will take such a course without having the means to do so: the dramatic and it seems unfinished reductions in the defence capability of our country ought therefore to be giving rather more cause for concern than they seem to be doing faced with the power – and willingness to use it – of Russia, China, Iran, North Korea and various non-state actors like Hezbollah, Hamas and the Houthis. It is true that strategic objectives are achieved through means as diverse as diplomacy, economic power and information as well as military power; but in the end, the threat or use of military power is often the decisive factor. Professor Sir Hew Strachan in his book *The Direction of War* contends that strategy is an attempt to make concrete a set of objectives through the application of military force to a particular case;[6] it deals not with policy in the first instance, but with the nature of war – not a bad summary but implicit in it is the idea that strategy is first and last about military force, which is questionable. Even if it is only partly true, however, it means that senior military commanders and staff officers have a duty to help shape both strategy and policy by being clear about the means required and the deficiencies therein. Given the parlous state of British defence, the willingness of the current government to lock horns with Russia is, to use a well-worn word, incredible.[7] No general should ever engage in a war that he knows he cannot win.

If the connection between the setting of objectives and priorities and the allocation of resources to achieve those objectives is not properly addressed, then the result may be under-resourcing, which is what British governments of all political parties did in both Iraq and Afghanistan – but especially Iraq. Under-resourcing means failure in the worst case; a downward revision of objectives in most cases; the inability for the general in command of the theatre to carry out certain tasks; or in the best case, a considerably extended timetable to achieve success. Did the Russians perhaps fall into this trap in Ukraine? Designating the war as a 'special military operation' and engaging only about

6   Hew Strachan, *The Direction of War* (Cambridge: Cambridge University Press, 2014), p.64 et seq.
7   See, for example, the Defence Secretary's oral statement on the war in Ukraine on 10 September 2024, which went well beyond condemnation of Russia's actions and support for Ukraine; www.gov.uk/government/ accessed 17 September 2024.

190,000 troops including local levies and Interior Ministry troops, they were always outnumbered, if not outgunned, by their opponents.

The late Professor Sir Michael Howard rightly said that armed forces are an indispensable aspect of nationhood and no proper state can do without them. They define how other countries, whether allies, adversaries or neutrals, view you. The views of other countries will be shaped by both the size and capabilities of those forces, and their record of success. War, he continued, may be an evil but those who renounce its use find themselves at the mercy of those who do not. The purpose of the use, or threat of use, of armed force and armed forces, is designed to coerce other states into a particular course of action, or else dissuade them from one. Here again, generalship is woven into this essential attribute of statehood both in the design of the armed forces and in how they are used. Strategy involves the use of force and *that* is what generals do.[8]

What yardsticks, therefore, can be employed to judge how good a general is, or is not? The first may be performance against those unchanging principles of war. There is some variance between different nations as to how many of these there are, but those which are generally agreed on are listed in British military doctrine and do not need to be rehearsed here.[9] The measurement that can be made is the degree to which the general understands and applies those principles and in doing so achieves victory in the realm of that great judge and teacher – war. Sun Tzu set this out many centuries ago: 'In war, then, let your great object be victory…. Thus, it may be known that the leader of armies is the arbiter of the people's fate, the man on whom it depends whether the nation shall be in peace or peril.'[10] General Rupert Smith tellingly said in this context that the general has to be the man – or nowadays, the woman – who in a military organisation can recognise any problem or issue, in its entirety; define those things which are likely to be decisive (and very rarely is that one event or action only); and having done this, change the situation to advantage in order to *win*.[11] Put yet another way, he must balance his ends, ways and means while preventing the other side from doing so. It is government policy which defines the ends required in a war. Governments will also allocate the means to conduct a war, unless they have neglected defence (as they so often do). Strategy and the operational art describe the ways: it is the general who, having been given the ends and the means, must determine the ways; and to make war without having done so is to court disaster. But at the highest level, the general must give politically aware military advice on the available capabilities and attainable objectives, since no government

8   Michael Howard, *Studies in War and Peace* (London: Temple Smith, 1970), pp.17, 154, 193, 196; Michael Howard, *The Causes of Wars and Other Essays* (London: Temple Smith, 1983), pp.36 & 131.
9   *Joint Doctrine Publication 0-01, British Defence Doctrine* (Ministry of Defence: DCDC, 2008), pp.2–3 – 2–5.
10   Sun Tzu (James Clavell, ed.), *The Art of War* (New York: Barnes & Noble, 1983), p.14.
11   Lecture to the Higher Command and Staff Course, Joint Services Command and Staff College, 2002. See also the discussion in Rupert Smith, *The Utility of Force* (London: Penguin, 2005).

should be allowed to go to war without having provided its generals with the means to do so. In Britain, this is the business of the Chief of Defence Staff, supported by the Service Chiefs and the Chief of Joint Operations; in the United States, it is the business of the Joint Chiefs. In our own country, there is a dissonance between the stated aims of government and the military means provided to achieve them – a dissonance that has steadily grown since the end of the Cold War under all governments and which has accelerated rapidly in the last decade. Can Britain seriously aspire to be a prominent nation in NATO, holding in perpetuity the post of Deputy Supreme Allied Commander Europe, for example, with an army of only 70,000 and commensurately small naval and air forces? Going back to the point about not engaging in wars that cannot be won, then surely generals still have a duty and a right to object when means do not match ends.

The second yardstick is by reference to the human condition, for at any level, the general is *the* central figure. As J. F. C. Fuller noted: 'The Gauls were not conquered by the Roman legions, but by Caesar.... It was not the French Army which reached the Weser and the Inn, it was Turenne.'[12] The human condition in the art of war remains central, until perhaps artificial intelligence (AI) replaces it – more of which later in this chapter. It remains central because of the moral component of war and of the exercise of command, especially decision-making. The general must apply judgement and have the courage – both moral and physical – to make his decisions stick within the constraints of the laws of armed conflict even though the cost in life and limb may be heavy.[13]

The exercise of command by a general is not, therefore, to be confused with simple leadership, or information processing. Command encompasses the three essential functions of leadership, control and management (of men and resources) and decision-making. These functions vary according to the size and complexity of an armed force but must always be exercised. Command is like sovereignty: it is indivisible. Napoleon remarked on this at an early stage in his career as a general when faced with a division of command of the Army of Italy between himself and Kellermann. Writing to the Directory in Paris in May 1796 he said that: 'I am certain that one bad General is better than two good ones.'[14] And if command is indivisible between commanders, it is also not possible to separate a commander's responsibilities from his authority over resources, and his accountability for the consequences of actions undertaken in his name. As General John Kiszely always rightly pointed out when commanding the 1st Armoured Division, experience shows that if these are separated, trouble always follows. Troops, resources and tasks may be delegated to subordinates, but always in pursuit of one end – the ultimate responsibility for achieving that end cannot be delegated, nor divided. Kiszely has also pointed out that much of the decision-making required by generals is aimed, at all levels, at seizing and maintaining the initiative – making the enemy dance to your tune

12   J. F. C. Fuller, *Generalship. Its Diseases and Their Cure. A Study of the Personal Factor in Command* (Harrisburg, PA: Military Service Publishing Co., 1936), p.30.
13   See the discussion in Carl von Clausewitz (Michael Howard and Peter Paret, trans. & eds), *On War* (Princeton: U.S.A., Princeton University Press, 1976) pp.100 et seq.
14   David Chandler, *The Campaigns of Napoleon* (London: George Allen & Unwin, 1967), p.158.

– through seeing or creating opportunities, using the offensive in the physical and virtual realms, taking calculated risks, achieving superior tempo and sustaining one's forces.[15]

At low levels, command and leadership are often synonymous, so what distinguishes the sort of leadership required by a general, who is perhaps best thought of as a leader of leaders? The first thing is physical and moral courage, usually more of the latter than the former for a modern general – another distinction with historical times when a general was expected to be in the forefront of battle. Moral courage for a general usually hinges on those hard decisions alluded to earlier, which incur the probability, not just the possibility, of death and injury to combatants and civilians on both sides. It is worthy of note that modern assessments of moral courage and character are frequently bound up with views of morality. In this context, there is a distinct connection between professional competence or fitness to command, and social (frequently sexual) behaviour. This connection is fuelled by the activities of the modern media. No such connection existed before very recent times and any attempt to draw it would have been regarded as insane: *mores*, or customary standards of behaviour, are historically and culturally specific. One can say that if such standards had been applied, say, 200 years ago, then neither Napoleon nor Wellington, cited earlier in another context, would have got very far.

On the other hand, there have been many cases over the last century where generals have conspicuously ignored the laws of armed conflict: from the Japanese and the S.S. in the Second World War; through the North Koreans and the Vietnamese – North and South – in their wars as well as, at times, the Americans in the latter case; to all three of the factions in the Balkan Wars of the 1990s; and most recently the Russians in Ukraine. This has produced short-term successes of a kind but in the long term it is always counterproductive. World opinion may not matter much to those who behave in this way, but justice has a long arm, as the generals hanged by the war crimes courts of Nuremberg and Tokyo, and more recently Ratko Mladić and others, can testify. Professor Sir Lawrence Freedman explores this topic in the context of a number of civilian officials and senior officers who have been in positions of authority in war and peace across Africa, Asia, South America and Europe. What should generals do when civilian leaders require action that is either illegal, or which is in conflict with moral or professional values, or which exceeds the capabilities of the armed forces? Or where politics and egos are the compelling drivers of strategy, rather than national or alliance goals? And how should those civilian leaders respond if generals refuse to obey their orders?[16]

Perhaps the most important thing that any general does in war is to make decisions. He may make decisions intuitively or through process – but even when relying on intuition, the wise general will use his staff to assess those decisions using a formal process such as the estimate, in the light of the enduring factors of time, space, the environment and

---

15   Major General J. P. Kiszely MC, 'Seizing the Advantage, Seizing the Initiative – New Opportunities, New Challenges' in *RUSI Journal* (August 2000), pp.1–4.

16   For the detailed discussion, see Lawrence Freedman, *Command: The Politics of Military Operations from Korea to Ukraine* (London: Allen Lane, 2022).

the available resources. Process also allows those decisions to be tested against the object of any general's problem – the enemy – using wargaming. But intuition, the product of intelligence and experience, can be trusted and one noteworthy aspect of those generals with well-developed intuition, like George Patton, Bill Slim and Erwin Rommel, is that their timing was excellent – as was their ability to recognise a change in the situation.[17]

Decision-making can be severely impeded at the operational and strategic levels by the demands of a coalition or alliance. For British generals, operating in an entirely national context has been rare over the last two centuries or more. Leaving aside internal security and counterinsurgency operations, one can cite perhaps only the Anglo-Zulu and Anglo-Boer Wars of the late nineteenth century; the campaign in Madagascar in the Second World War; the Falklands War and the intervention in Sierra Leone as having been undertaken by solely British forces. It is scarcely conceivable that Britain could or would fight any war today without allies. Command in this context will generally go to the biggest contributor. But whatever the mission, the general must understand what his coalition partners will and will not do, what are their caveats and red lines. In respect of the NATO mission to Afghanistan and the International Security Assistance Force, for example, there were a number of nations who would not permit their soldiers to move outside the base perimeter wire at one end of the spectrum, while at the other end, there were nations who professed no caveats at all. In the context of coalitions and alliances – the two are not the same but here is not the place to expand on that. Where tempo is low and risk is low, such as in a humanitarian operation, the frictions of multi-nationality – national objectives and red cards, language, culture, different procedures and so on – can be disentangled gradually over a period of weeks and months. They are thus tolerable, and tolerable to a very low level in the force structure; multinational battlegroups, for example, operated in Bosnia and in southern Iraq.

Where tempo is higher, and risk is greater, in an all-out war against a single enemy, the rules are different. Consider the likes of Napoleon, Hitler, Milosevic or Saddam who all were able to demand instant and complete obedience and controlled the strategic communications messaging; they consulted no clients or allies, called no councils of war, heeded no red cards. Putin today is such a figure, as is President Xi of China, and Kim Jong Un in North Korea. Such an opponent will always operate at a higher tempo in making and implementing decisions than an alliance, or even a coalition. It is the general who must ensure that the ways and means to deal with this mismatch in tempo are addressed where they should be, at the strategic level, allowing the operational commander as much freedom of action as possible.

The sort of decision-making in changing circumstances, and the flow of information required to support it, raises the question of the position of the general in battle, in order to do the essential three things that a general must do to properly exercise his command. General Julian Thompson has described these as being first, to find out what is going on, secondly to communicate his intentions to his subordinates (and by implication his

17 Clausewitz, *On War*, p.102.

superiors) and third, to keep in contact with the staff so that they can solve problems and adjust resources.[18] Command and control for a general in a war are about *communications* in relation to *time*, so that decisions can be made that will control the course of events.

But to return to the legal and media aspects of the modern battlefield, a fourth essential function must be added to Thompson's list: the general must be able to explain himself and his actions – to his superiors, to his own people and to the uncommitted. This is one area in which the role of the commander has changed greatly in recent times. For many years we were all schooled in the belief that whoever makes and implements a decision faster than his opponent gains a tremendous, decisive, advantage – we had to go round the OODA [Observe, Orient, Decide and Act] loop, or the Boyd Cycle, like a hamster in a wheel.[19] Seeking vainly for certainty in the uncertain field of combat, we all learned, would result only in being made to react to a more agile enemy with a superior tempo of making and implementing decisions. This logic leads to the view that in any contest between two opponents, one of whom relies heavily on process and technology, and one who relies on intuition, the latter is more likely to triumph if all other things are equal. Nothing in current force-on-force conflicts suggests that this has changed; but in Iraq, and later Afghanistan, it was necessary to modify that view. Because, in insurgencies, the enemy will manufacture incidents that appear to make government forces responsible for severe civilian casualties; or because mistakes are made; or because the media is usually happy to condemn legitimate forces unheard; but most importantly because legitimate armed forces need to be sure that they are operating within the laws of armed conflict, they are now *obliged* to quest for certainty. In part, this is because of the increasing nexus between violence, whether intra or inter-state, corruption and organised criminality. Opponents can currently hide behind criminality because in law, criminals are civilians and armed force cannot be used directly against civilians.[20]

Where destructive force is applied, it must be applied on the basis of excellent, multi-source intelligence and every general must be his own intelligence chief to a greater degree perhaps than ever before. Such force must be applied appropriately to its target to achieve the desired effect, and only the desired effect. Any general must also have his strategic communications staff and legal adviser very close at hand. The Israelis are aware of this in their current campaign in Gaza, even though, because their survival as a people is, in their view, at risk, they care less than we may do about world opinion.[21] However, there are cases in recent times of generals who have come dangerously close to

18   Lecture to the Higher Command and Staff Course, 2002.
19   Thomas Hughes, 'The Cult of the Quick', *Aerospace Power Journal*, 15:4 (Winter 2001), pp.57–68.
20   Jonathon Riley, 'The Nexus: War, Insurgency and Criminality. Operational Experience from Bosnia to Iraq', speech at the RUSI, June 2009; available at www.generalship.org/articles, accessed 27 September 2024.
21   See, for example, Alan M. Dershowitz, 'Civilian Deaths in Gaza: Relatively Low', 28 January 2024, https://www.gatestoneinstitute.org/20343/gaza-civilian-deaths, accessed 18 September 2024.

prioritising a media presence and public image, over serious issues of command. The laws of libel being what they are, we can name no names.

Throughout the execution of an operation, therefore, the general must be in a position constantly to receive the best available information, review the situation, making fresh estimates in the light of events, and changing the plan as required – since as any soldier knows, no plan survives contact with the enemy intact. Clarity of thought, decision and action are essential; and in war, so is speed. Only thus will risks be calculated and the initiative be maintained. The general's intuitive process will be continuous, and the experienced general will in a sense feed it by positioning himself at the right place – and thereby develop an intuitive sense of where to be, at what point in the battle, so completing a circle. This must be balanced by the need to quest for certainty, discussed earlier, where targeting is concerned to avoid disproportionate collateral damage.

There are those who say that that because of the sort of complexity encountered in modern conflict, intuitive decision-making is no longer possible: that the general is faced with so many facets of a campaign, that he will be forced to rely on some formal process of evaluation in order to be able to make every decision. I offer the view, however, that the converse is true, especially if one accepts the contention that war and conflict are not wholly rational pursuits. The general who surrenders himself to process, or who allows himself to be deluged by the massive amounts of data available from modern command systems, and who abandons intuition, becomes the prisoner of that process and therefore of predictability. Defeating an agile opponent in conventional or unconventional war or dealing with a complex dispute in a peace support operation, or even addressing the priorities and risks in humanitarian interventions, requires a clear head and the ability to see the essentials.

Does the advance of technology change any of this? Technology provides new opportunities and challenges but does not alter the human condition. But as technology changes, so the employment of military forces must adapt to it. This is a relationship that is constant and always in need of attention since if it is ignored, disasters follow. The full effects of the Industrial Revolution during the nineteenth century were not, for example, matched by changes in tactics with the resulting carnage of the American Civil War, Franco-Prussian War and the first years of the Great War.[22] During the latter part of the twentieth and the early part of the twenty-first centuries, the rate and pace of technological change has increased ever more rapidly, making this relationship more than ever pivotal for a general. The notion of cyber warfare was certainly evident during the Cold War, as both sides strove to control the electromagnetic spectrum as it was then exploited. It was the Russian Admiral Sergei Gorshkov who in 1973 stated that success in the next war would go the side which best exploited the electromagnetic spectrum.[23] The Russians' ability to jam modern precision-guided munitions, such as

22   See the discussion in John Terraine, *The Western Front: 1914–1918* (London: Hutchinson & Co. Ltd, 1964).
23   Cited in, among many others, Abdul Karim Baram, *Technology in Warfare: The Electronic Dimension* (Abu Dhabi: Emirates Centre for Strategic Studies and Research, 2009).

joint direct attack munitions, Excalibur 155mm shells and high mobility artillery rocket system missiles is simply part of that continuum, albeit one that has accelerated and is accelerating.

In that context, the acceleration of the rate and pace of technological change and with it the widening of the battlespace to include space – especially in the light of Chinese adventures in the direction of the moon,[24] the digital realm of information and offensive cyber capabilities. Cyberspace is ungoverned space outside the military sphere, never mind within it. This expansion will be likely to confine a general more closely to his main headquarters. It will be here that the means will be found to manage this massive flow of information and here it will be analysed, focused on and channelled. It is from here that the complexities of a coalition will be managed. It is here that technologies with rapidly evolving capabilities, such as hypersonic missiles, drone swarms and glide bombs, must be controlled. It is here that analysis will best be made on what means should be applied to required objectives – and objectives may now range from physical territory to capturing the imaginations of peoples; or to secure or deny vital resources such as minerals, fossil fuels, rare earths or water supplies. Anthony King explores this migration of command, suggesting that a more collective style of command and control is more suited to the needs of networking and decentralisation.[25] It is an opinion, but it fails to recognise the vital issue of the general's ultimate responsibility, which cannot be delegated. Books on generalship by academics are all well and good – but even the most brilliant has never carried that heavy rucksack of responsibility when in command – especially on operations.

What is not at issue, however, is that the boundaries between the tactical, operational and strategic levels of war are becoming blurred and the general's expertise, and that of his staff, must range more widely. Tactical brilliance and personal physical courage are no longer enough. The risks of miscalculation, therefore, are increasing and the possibilities of mitigation are diminishing. A foretaste of this came in Iraq, where there was not just an imbalance in strategic ends, ways and means facing the generals in the theatre of operations, but a vacuum in strategy created by the lack of forward planning at government level which they and their staffs had to fill. The presentation of strategic objectives and the operational ways and means to achieve them was presented and reviewed by General John Abizaid in U.S. Central Command, General George Casey in Baghdad, and even national contingent commanders when needed, at the higher tactical level.[26]

24   See, for example, Simone McCarthy, 'China's Chang'e-6 moon mission returns to Earth with historic far side samples', *CNN*, 25 June 2024, https://edition.cnn.com/2024/06/25/china/china-change-6-moon-mission-return-scn-intl-hnk/index.html; accessed 18 September 2024.

25   Anthony King, *Command: The Twenty-First-century General* (Cambridge: Cambridge University Press, 2019).

26   See, for example, Jonathan Bailey, Richard Iron and Hew Strachan (eds), *British Generals in Blair's Wars* (Farnham: Ashgate Publishing Ltd., 2013), Chapters 1, 5, 6.

Being more closely tied to the main headquarters will inevitably give the general less opportunity for human contact through visits to subordinate commanders and troops on the ground. Technology will therefore have to provide the means of building that essential mutual trust, understanding and confidence between commanders through online contact rather than face-to-face meetings: assuming that the enemy's technology does not take down these capabilities. The human factor remains, in spite of where technology goes.

However, AI may be the biggest game-changer in that equation even though technology rarely delivers what it promises, at least in the near term. If used as a staff tool, its powers of mathematical and logical calculus could greatly increase the powers of the staff, so long as it is not allowed to become a substitute for intelligent judgement and analysis – especially, for example, in determining what is a deception, engineered deliberately to attract AI-driven algorithms. AI programmes and algorithms are often highly aggressive, the result of being designed for business, and they may be difficult to restrain when restraint is needed. In effects-based warfare, there are always two sorts of effects: those that are intended and those that are not. Nor can AI be trusted with making moral or legal judgements, it could not, for example, carry out a proportionality test since such a test is highly subjective and based as much on art as on science. Any general who allowed that responsibility to pass from his hands would still be accountable for the consequences of any actions taken, in that blinding glare of the legal and media environment. If AI were to be allowed to replace the human factor in command then the logical conclusion is war between opposing AI-led forces, in ungoverned space. If, in such a situation, AI were to harness control of the means of war in space, the cyber and nuclear domains and combine them with nanotechnologies and biotechnologies, then the results can only be guessed at – but such a proposition marks the end of generalship as we have understood it.

14

Artificial Intelligence and Human Intuition

Andrew Sharpe

The lists of books that explore what makes a good general (or, come to that, a bad general) are endless and varied. The lists of qualities that such books generate, however, have a degree of repetition in them. First off, soldiers tend to like generals that have a habit of succeeding. Even those with a reputation for harshness were almost always forgiven for their severity by the troops they commanded, as long as they showed competence at generalship. In short, if a leader could be trusted to win on the battlefield their soldiers would forgive them much off the battlefield. At the heart of the military leader/led relationship sits the soldiers' belief that their general will be responsible for delivering them into situations in which they will most likely win. Close second to that comes their belief that this competence will mean that their lives will not be lost (or, at least not lost needlessly) through the decisions of their general. Some of this is through an obvious desire for self-preservation, some of it is for reasons of 'glory', some for reasons of belief in a moral rightness, and much is simply for a pragmatic desire to be able to reap the rewards of victory rather than the penalties of defeat.

From Frederick the Great to George Patton, the harsh eccentric has had the trust of his troops; and from Genghis Khan to Frank Kitson, the ruthless and focused professional may have earned the hatred of his enemies but, again, has had the trust of his own troops. Examples abound: General 'Black Bob' Craufurd, so called because of his combination of dark moods and strict disciplinarian approach, was a trusted leader of the Light Division in the Peninsular War, until his mortal wounding in the breach of the walls of Ciudad Rodrigo in 1812; trusted not just by his men, but also by his commander, Wellington, because of his competence and focused determination. Or Thomas 'Stonewall' Jackson, the Confederate general known for the uncompromising rigour with which he trained his men, and his stubbornness in combat, who, nevertheless, held the respect and affection of the men that he led through three campaigns (losing only one single engagement, after receiving and believing erroneous intelligence, at Kernstown in the Valley Campaign of 1862). Bernard Montgomery, awkward, terse, arrogant, thin-skinned and quite unable to get on with his peers and superiors, nevertheless had successes, arguably, as much through the trust and confidence that those fighting under him had in his ability to deliver results as for any other reason. Montgomery's turning of the tide in the North African desert, his ruthless training regime for those under his command, and his track record of bravery from the First World War, gave him credibility with his troops – and he capitalised on that initial credibility by repeatedly assuring his soldiers that he would continue to deliver glittering successes (even when he did not). Wellington, probably undeservedly, had a reputation for coldness and dispassion concerning his men, but his troops would follow 'Old Nosey' wherever he took them. And Napoleon Bonaparte, despite his belief in stirring the passion of his fighting troops, was capable of incredible callousness when it came to the spending of their lives – yet, with impassioned cries of *Vive l'Empereur* his cannon-fodder would march, cheering, wherever he sent them. In short, soldiers are prepared to put their faith in generals who win, or, at least, have a reputation for winning, and not in those who do not.

So, at the heart of good generalship sits professional competence in the battlespace. In this respect, in force development circles in the UK and, widely, elsewhere, it is often argued that professional competence, both in the generals themselves and in their staffs, will be enhanced by the obvious benefits of well-designed, well-programmed, well-directed and well-used artificial intelligence (AI). Perhaps a general's intuition alone needs no longer be the deciding factor? The delivery of faster, better filtered and sorted, relevant data can change the OODA [Observe, Orient, Decide and Act]-loop turning-circles very much in favour of those who hold the AI upper hand. Thus, human *coup d'oeil* can be hugely enhanced by machine *coup d'AI*. But, in the discussion of the relative merits of artificial intelligence and the human factors involved in military command and decision-making, a distinction needs to be drawn, from the outset, concerning the differences between information and intelligence, instinct and intuition.

In the sense explored in this chapter, information and intelligence concern the gathering, from and through multiple sources, of facts, insights, opinions, evidence, indicators, verifications, analysis and any other source of that agglomeration of data that helps commanders and staff officers to develop a better picture of their own and their opponents' circumstances, options, intents and contexts. In amongst all of that noise, if they are lucky, or their sources and processes are good enough, they may even have their attention drawn to those so-called 'faint signals' in the clutter that, so often missed with foresight, are seized upon by the historians and analysts, armed with hindsight, who reflect upon what the decision makers 'should have known or understood'. The provision of all of the above can be delivered by a mix of human and artificial sources and processes. Once delivered and absorbed, the well-informed commander is then able to make (better) decisions.

Instinct can be defined as an inborn and natural, often fixed, pattern of behaviour in animals (and thus also humans) in response to certain stimuli. This implies a way of behaving that is not learned in a formal way, nor measured and considered, but concerns instead a natural desire, often overwhelming of logic or other emotions or considerations, that generates a tendency to make one want to act in a particular manner. Instinct is thus not an intellectual process at all and requires little or no conscious thought or analysis. This is not a machine or artificial trait, but a very animal one. Instinctive decisions can be made and acted upon without reference to the sort of information or intelligence described in the paragraph above. Actions born of instinct are the product of how people feel, not of what people think.

Intuition, on the other hand, combines that inborn instinct with experience, learning, the accumulation of knowledge and understanding, and an ability to listen wisely to information, intelligence and advice. Intuitive decisions can look and feel very much like instinct, but they come with much more than animal reaction. Intuition is, at base, a combination of how people feel, tempered by what people think. It is often said that the acme of military command in war sits with a leader's ability to 'decide what is decisive'. Within this ability to spot the significant opportunity comes not spur-of-the-moment thinking (which is closer to instinct), but a nurtured talent that enables one to spot the moment to act for decisive effect. Whether it is Alfred's decision to leave the Somerset Levels in May 878 and sally out to unpick the Viking armies piecemeal at Edington and Chippenham, or Wellington's cry of 'By God, that will do nicely!' as he threw a half-eaten chicken leg over his shoulder and mounted up to order his army to cease their route march and to turn to and engage the French Army at Salamanca in 1812, the great military commanders throughout history have had the ability to recognise the tipping points and exploit them for advantage. Intuition, therefore, sits at the very heart of good generalship. And intuition, although it can be supported by machines and AI, remains (so far), like instinct, a very human trait.

There are, of course, other essential capabilities that mark out the great generals from the pedestrian ones. Beyond merely earning soldiers' trust through a consistent demonstration of professional competence, soldiers expect their generals to be courageous. Sometimes (although only rarely) it is enough to have demonstrated physical courage in a more junior appointment. Under most circumstances, though, this sort of demonstration of early courage is merely the groundwork for later trust and recognition. Soldiers trust those who share their hardships and risks. And soldiers trust those who, demonstrably or quietly (they will find out anyway), take risks on their behalf that they are not in a position to take for themselves: taking career and personal risks, for example, by standing up to the powerful and being unafraid to confront awkward truths. Soldiers will give their loyalty to those above them who, they perceive, are loyal to them. Those, on the other hand, who place themselves and their own interests ahead of those that they lead (regardless of how they are perceived by their military or political superiors) will be quickly found out and held in contempt by their subordinates. In short, those two very different traits of moral and physical courage are vital tools in the general's knapsack.

Finally, good generals need to possess the mental and physical fitness and health that provides them with stamina. Patience, concentration, levelheadedness, professional curiosity and the ability to be comfortable with chaos (and work out a path through it, rather than try to resolve it) all need to be layered upon a bedrock of studied professional knowledge and understanding. A well-trained mind, a mind that has done its mental press-ups, a well-informed mind that can focus, and stay focused, is likely to be able to stay the mental course when the going gets tough. And, as the Royal Army Physical Training

Corps would have it, that *mens sana* has to sit within a *corpore sano* if it is to work to best effect. That is not to say that generals should still all be beating their young officers and junior non-commissioned officers on a run, or out-performing them in the gym. Good for them if they can, but that is not the point; their health and fitness is no longer about their PT prowess, but rather it comes into play when long hours and exhaustion, especially when exacerbated by danger and privation, do not interfere with their ability to think straight and to act decisively. The ability to manage stress calmly not only maintains a healthier body, but also helps to manage the unfolding of complex and often unforeseen events with insight and decisiveness. Thus, for a general, learning breathing exercises while sitting still is as important, or, perhaps, more important, than being able to breathe freely while running. The point, at this stage in their careers, is that their physical state must not be allowed to interfere with the workings of their mental state.

These qualities explored above (professional competence along with moral and physical courage, supported by loyalty, and mental and physical stamina) when combined, appear and reappear in any assessment of good generalship – including by Jonathan Riley elsewhere in this book. And, importantly, the right combination of these qualities in a person also delivers that vital element of war – an ability to inspire other people. If Clausewitz was right when he stated that war is, at its first and its last, the most human of businesses, then the very human ability to inspire others is also likely to remain important.

So, generals need to be inspirational individuals, professionally competent, brave, loyal, intuitive and enabled by physical and mental endurance. It is not the place of this chapter to investigate the question, but it would be interesting to spend some time exploring the notion of an AI-powered machine's ability to inspire humans in adverse circumstances by generating in itself all of those qualities listed. It is not a question with an obvious answer; after all, machines could easily generate a habit of delivering winning outcomes, could be programmed to prioritise the safety and survivability of their own people, could probably learn to spot 'what is decisive', could surely be taught a moral code of 'rightness and wrongness' that would allow them selflessly (they have no concept of self) to stand up to superiors, and, with that same lack of idea of self, machines can certainly be programmed to be 'physically courageous' and put the safety of others before their own. And machines certainly have the stamina (mental and physical) to flog on when humans drop with exhaustion. Relentless *coup d'AI* indeed. But we also know that machines are now perfectly capable of flying passenger aeroplanes from departure to destination without any human being present, yet human passengers continue to feel the need for a team of humans in the cockpit. Humans still do not trust machines to deliver them safely to their destinations. AI can write and play music that pulls upon the full range of human emotions, but AI does not understand why or how it does that. So, it seems that machines may have a growing part to play in that very human business of leadership in war, but we are still a long way from inspirational generalship by AI. Interesting – but perhaps a discussion for another time.

For now, then, this chapter will focus on a couple of examples of the human aspect of generalship, before concluding to ask how AI might have been able to enhance the decisions of the past with a view to informing the future. While discussing the human aspect of generalship, however, it is also worth exploring the human aspect of providing support to generals. Generals, for most of history, have been supported by their staff. It is the staff that, if they are doing their jobs well, free up the general to practice generalship: to 'decide what is decisive'. Typically, a general's staff will provide administrative support; intelligence collection, analysis and processing; the management of battle and the passage of orders; logistics insight and support; planning; communications; liaison; and many other functions besides. AI may, perhaps, be able to enhance, support or even replace many of those staff functions. Often ignored, and of vital importance, however, is also the staff's ability to provide (often in the form of the right chief of staff) a balance for the character of the general: caution in the face of impetuosity, for example, or attention to detail to balance grandiose visions. Or approachability to balance aloofness.

Perhaps best known of the British generals of the Second World War was Bernard Montgomery. Less well known (other, perhaps, than by military historians with an interest in the period) is Freddie de Guingand. Montgomery, through his victory in the Second Battle of El Alamein in October 1942, is often considered the British general who turned the course of the war from repeated Allied failures to a growing, and eventually unstoppable, tide of Allied successes. (He certainly saw himself, and promoted himself, in that light.) There is no doubt that Montgomery was a successful general – he had his tactical and operational failures too, but, on balance, his battle theory of administering what he called 'colossal cracks' upon the enemy worked.[1] Montgomery's critics, of which there are many, argue that there was nothing particularly new about this thinking, he simply used it at the time when the Allies' ability to generate combat power (industrially, and in terms of equipment and manpower numbers) began to overtake the Germans'. After 'turning the tide' in North Africa, historians are divided, to say the least, about the competence and successfulness of Montgomery's tactics. There is much less division of opinion among historians about Montgomery's ability to get on with his fellow generals. There is little doubt that, without the protection and support of General Sir Alan Brooke, the Chief of the Imperial General Staff, Montgomery's several setbacks and his obnoxious character would have ensured that his moment in the limelight was short-lived.

Montgomery was not a likeable or a liked person. His experience during the First World War (decorated for gallantry, severely wounded, and later serving on the staff) gave him contempt for senior officers (which persisted even when he became one) and a sense of responsibility for his soldiers. It was his early successes in North Africa, a regular interaction with his soldiers and this sense of communicated responsibility that inspired such confidence in the men he led. A mixture of necessary national propaganda

---

1   'Colossal cracks', which is to say, in broad terms: avoid any decisive action until you have built up very favourable force ratios; meanwhile, put your troops through a ruthless training regime to prepare; look for enemy vulnerabilities; distract the enemy; then hit the enemy hard with overwhelming force at their vulnerable points.

and shameless self-promotion by Montgomery also sustained him as a lionised figure in the public imagination in wartime Britain. But there was no such inspiration or confidence with his peers and superiors, with whom relationships were almost always fraught with tension and difficulty.

Montgomery's blunt, egotistical, self-promoting, arrogant rudeness alienated him from almost all of his British contemporaries, including Churchill. From Operation Husky and the invasion of Sicily onwards, the same repellent attitude proved to be equally irritating to American generals, including Paton, Bradley, Clark and Eisenhower.[2] In short, regardless of whether he was any good as a tactician, operator or strategist, or not, Montgomery was unable to form or maintain a cordial working relationship with any of his peer or superior commanders. For this he needed a chief of staff who could not only harness the power of his staff and make sure that his self-possessed boss listened to the product of their work and advice, but also could ensure that whatever talent Montgomery did possess could be put usefully to work by counter-acting the ill-feeling among those senior officers with whom he interacted.

Enter Major General Francis 'Freddie' de Guingand. A colleague (and protégé) of, and friendly with, Montgomery before the war, by chance de Guingand was the Brigadier General Staff at HQ 8th Army when Montgomery was appointed to its command. This made it easy for Montgomery to promote him and move him across swiftly to be his chief of staff. Montgomery had enough wisdom to understand that he needed support from someone who he knew, who he could trust to be good at his job, and who would act as a foil for his own awkwardness (and who would be unfailingly loyal out of a combination of friendship and personal debt of gratitude). De Guingand was both an experienced infantry soldier and an accomplished staff officer. He was also tactful, cheerful, modest, empathetic, persuasive and charming: qualities that Montgomery lacked.

Throughout the desert campaign, the planning and, indeed, the direction of the operations of the 8th Army lay as much with de Guingand as they did with Montgomery. De Guingand was a meticulous staff officer, with both a good eye for detail and for ground. He was an accomplished intelligence officer. He was also a positive and persuasive leader of the weary staff officers of the 8th Army. This combination, along with plenty of operational experience, allowed him to complement Montgomery's coldness, stubborn single-mindedness, and more grandiose 'big-hand/small-map' planning approach, and his insistence on the generation of overwhelming force ratios. As a combination they were highly effective. For all of his personal failings, and despite regularly belittling and

---

2   Eisenhower was at great pains, both during and after the war, not to publicly criticise anyone alongside whom he had fought, but in private he made little secret of his contempt for Montgomery. In a private letter sent to General Hastings 'Pug' Ismay he says '...I think that, regardless of how he might have conducted and expressed himself during the post-war years, he would scarcely stand much chance of going down in History as one of the great British captains. Alexander was much abler. And he was modest.' See Appendix D, John Kiszely, *General Hastings 'Pug' Ismay: Soldier, Statesman, Diplomat – A New Biography* (London: Hurst Publishers, 2024).

disparaging de Guingand, Montgomery had enough self-perception to know that he relied upon him heavily. Indeed, despite repeated bouts of illness, Montgomery intervened several times to have de Guingand returned to duties and retained at his side.

In his 1951 autobiography *A Soldier's Story*, General Omar Bradley summed this situation up succinctly as:

> …a brilliant staff officer, dedicated to anonymity and his job, de Guingand went one step further by complementing the personality of his chief. In Freddy [*sic*], as de Guingand was affectionately known to the American Command, we found a ready intermediary and peacemaker. For whenever the distant attitude of Montgomery ruffled a U.S. staff, it was good old cheerful Freddy who came down to smooth things over.[3]

So what? Well, in the context of this chapter this example of the relationship between a commander and a principal staff officer illustrates an important point. AI, machines, may very well be able to enhance, or even replace, a range of staff functions, but there are many functions that remain distinctly human. A machine could never have compensated for Montgomery's abrasive manner – indeed, arguably, the cold logic of a machine would have been likely to exacerbate its effects rather than counterbalance them. For every 'Monty' in military history (and there have been plenty of them) their effectiveness (and longevity) in command has often hinged upon the human characteristics of a 'Freddie' – their key supporters, advisers and advocates. Faster, better data has no role here.

As another mini-case-study we could take the contrasting characters and styles of Napoleon and Wellington, who fought successful campaigns against each other's armies, but met only once in combat. Much is made in the history books of the supposedly different styles of these two men: one an expert in the headlong onslaught, the other the master of the reverse slope and the measured defence. One is often labelled as headstrong and belligerent, the other as prudent and cautious. These perceived differences, however, do not bear much scrutiny. Indeed, it is the similarities between the two men that we may find more instructive.

Both took their profession intellectually seriously. Every account of both men paints a picture of studious individuals who read, exhaustively, the history of war and warfare and the accounts of the great captains of the past. Both had an eye for detail, military and administrative (although both also had the wisdom to delegate the management of that detail to others). In short, from an early point in both men's careers they began a professionally relevant mental exercise programme to ensure that they understood the breadth of their profession. Napoleon, for example, could easily have focused his learning on simply being good at doing his job (as an artilleryman), rather than being professional at his profession (as a warfighter). He chose to do both. The point here is that both individuals were not just a store of information for information's sake, but that

---

3   Omar Bradley; *A Soldier's Story* (New York: Henry Holt and Company, 1951), p.209.

they had built up, over years of conscious effort, a body of understanding that allowed their own instincts to be tempered, before they then absorbed the information and intelligence specific to each problem that confronted them. They were entitled to use their intuitive skills because they had worked on them.

Both men repeatedly demonstrated moral and physical courage. Napoleon's rise to power saw multiple instances of almost reckless courage, none more famous perhaps than his storming of the bridge at Lodi in May 1796, alongside the then Colonel of Grenadiers Lannes and several other senior officers (the no-doubt-embellished legend had Napoleon crossing the bridge, fighting off cuirassiers, seizing a killed officer's horse and single-mindedly turning the tide of battle). Then the same thing again, a few months later at the Battle of Arcola in November 1796, in another headlong charge involving repeated attempts to cross a bridge, the reckless bravery of Napoleon was over-matched only by Lannes (now a brigadier general), who, alongside him again and this time already wounded, used himself as a human shield for Napoleon, being wounded three more times in the process. Napoleon, from the start to the finish of his fighting career, was unafraid to expose himself to the thickest of the fighting – and, by this example, was able to inspire (indeed, expect) such reckless bravery from his subordinates. And, to inspire the sort of rash courage that he considered a vital soldierly quality, Napoleon showed great loyalty and offered considerable rewards to those who also displayed such courage. Ney (*Le Brave des Braves*), despite Napoleon's repeated irritation and doubt over his competence and even personal loyalty, was repeatedly trusted with the most important of jobs and had rewards and titles heaped upon him. It was no coincidence that those who charged alongside Napoleon at Lodi in 1796 (Lannes, Berthier and Masséna, amongst others) found themselves as marshals as his power grew. For Napoleon, physical courage, in hot blood (and preferably delivered with a bit of style, élan and panache) were the hallmarks of his most trusted leaders.

Wellington also provides history with plenty of examples of bravery, even if, in his case, they were delivered with rather more sang-froid than his Corsican counterpart and his marshals. For reasons of both control and as an inspiration to his soldiers, Wellington was often found in the thick of the fighting when he believed that he could have best effect through his presence. At the Battle of Salamanca in July 1812, having spotted an opportunity to seize the tactical initiative from the French, Wellington opened the battle by riding the length of his army, under almost constant fire from the French, stopping to brief his commanders as he went. Hit repeatedly by musket balls, in the flying tails of his coat and in his horse's saddle, he wrote to his brother that evening saying that he could have survived such a ride only if he had been 'genuinely touched by the finger of God'. At Waterloo, three years later, he endured the fiercest of the fighting from the start of the engagement until the dying light saw him lead the start of the pursuit of the French Army. In the final moments of the battle shell splinters narrowly missed him (but took off the leg of his second in command, Lord Uxbridge). Wellington was also no stranger to moral courage, that very different quality. Modern soldiers like to refer to his famous (and biting) letter to Whitehall in which he chastises his masters in London for bombarding him with petty requests for detail, explaining that he can either concentrate on driving Napoleon's forces from Spain or training up an army of uniformed clerks to answer their pestering missives: 'I construe that perforce it must be one of two alternative duties, as given below. I shall pursue either one with the best of my ability, but I cannot do both.' Bitingly shrewish, perhaps, but for that alone requiring considerable courage to send. To enable him to concentrate his personal efforts on the former (driving the French from Spain) he relied heavily upon the staff skills of the likes of Sir Thomas Graham and Sir William de Lancey.

Importantly, both generals understood the value of information and intelligence. Napoleon needed to run an empire, keep political rivals in check and run his campaigns. For the first two functions he had the thin-faced Joseph Fouché, his spymaster, Minister of Police and ruthless seeker-out of dissent. He was a master of the collection of information and intelligence, especially as it pertained to personal and political loyalties and threats. In the military sense, Napoleon's focus was on strategic decision-making and what we would now call the 'operational level' of war. Although details of troop numbers, types, dispositions, morale, et cetera were important details, his focus was on gathering an understanding of enemy intent on a campaign scale and on the directions of movement and concentrations of forces at that scale. Napoleon's focus was on outmanoeuvring his enemies on a Continental level, then to use a complex reconnaissance screen to identify concentrations of mass. This then allowed him to bring his mini-armies (army corps) to bear – marching to the sound of the guns – at the right place and moment to unhinge enemy armies on a large scale. 'My job is not to win my battles, but to put my people in the right place to win my battles for me.' And behind that tactical and operational machine, Napoleon, who had an inexhaustible eye for detail, understood that he could not hope to stand back and make the big decisions if he was lost in running that detail. For that, he had, and relied heavily upon, Marshal Louis-Alexandre Berthier, his loyal Chief of Staff from 1796 through to 1814.

Berthier had joined the French Royal Army in 1766 at the age of 13 as an engineer. His painstaking concentration on detail was noted from the start of his career. By the 1790s he had earned a reputation not just as a talented and courageous fighting soldier but also, principally, as a meticulous, thoughtful and highly efficient staff officer. His services were sought out by Revolutionary France's new generals. In 1796, when Bonaparte was appointed commander of the Army of Italy, he demanded, and received, Berthier as his Chief of Staff. They stayed together for 18 years, until the abdication in April 1814. As with de Guingand and Montgomery, the relationship between Bonaparte and Berthier was one of contrasts and complementarity in terms of character and personality. Certainly, many of the functions that Berthier delivered could, in a modern world, be delivered by AI and machines: the collection, filtering, analysis and dissemination of data and intelligence; the formulation and dissemination of orders; and collection and maintenance of meticulous records, for example. But Berthier also possessed two (human) qualities that served Napoleon well, and which underpinned his utility and ensured his longevity in post. First, like de Guingand, he was modest and had no ambition to wear the Emperor's laurels. Second, he was patient, tactful and level-headed – the ideal counterbalance for Napoleon's impetuosity, fiery temper and caustic tongue. This arrangement suited Berthier well: 'As he said to a friend who asked him how he could serve a man with such a temper, "remember that one day it will be a fine thing to have been second to Bonaparte". So the two worked admirably together.'[4]

Wellington, throughout his military career, from India to Waterloo, had his own share of political and personal loyalty worries – but they bore little resemblance to the size or scale of Napoleon's concerns in that respect. Wellington's considerable intelligence network, led by the likes of the indefatigable Colonel Colquhoun Grant, concentrated, broadly speaking, on two things: his enemies' campaign intent, and, to misuse his own words, what was on the other side of the tactical hill. Especially in the Peninsular War, one can see his emphasis on understanding where and at what strength the various French army corps, operating throughout the peninsula, were located, and in ensuring that they were not able to combine their strengths to engage and over-match his much smaller force. The operational ebb and flow of the war, as dictated by the campaign movements of Wellington's army, was driven by Wellington's understanding of the locations, interactions and concentrations (or lack of them) of and between the various French corps and their commanding generals and marshals. He was also interested in tactical detail. What was the enemy morale like? Were they well-fed? What tactics were they using? Where were they putting logistic emphasis? What were the organisational troop mixes, where and when? In other words, he was, for sure, interested in campaign-influencing information at the operational level, but, equally, he was interested in the minutiae of military information concerning his enemies – both the commanders that he faced and the detail of their troops. He was also interested in reports of the (often fractious) interpersonal relationships between the various French commanders of the corps that he may, potentially, face. In a world without machines and AI both generals relied heavily upon a slow-moving, slowly analysed, slowly transmitted, human-centric pipeline of information and intelligence to inform their decision-making (but this was data that was also often overlaid by the sort of 'gut feeling' that various sources could offer, that remains alien to machines' capabilities).

As for the two generals' contrasting approaches to the tactical fight, actually their differences were more practical than instinctive. Wellington had been provided with one, small army with which to fight. For much of the Peninsular War his Spanish allies were unreliable and his Portuguese allies not yet trained. His deeply held instincts, like Napoleon's, were in favour of the aggressive use of the offensive. His resources and context led him to favour the husbanding of resources and the preservation of the force. The lines of Torres Vedras were an operational necessity, not a tactical preference. The hill at Bussaco enabled not just the protection of his force, and a covered escape route, but the tool to turn upon and sting his tormentors.

Napoleon, on the other hand, was not constrained by the availability of manpower. The French *Levée en Masse*, and reliable allies like Poland, Bavaria and the wider

---

4   R. P. Dunn-Pattison, *Napoleon's Marshals: Twenty-Six Military Commanders of the First Empire* (Driffield: Leonaur Ltd., 2011), p.19.

Confederation of the Rhine, provided him with an almost inexhaustible supply of manpower. This enabled him to concentrate his talents on campaign manoeuvre and leave the tactical fight to his brave and hard-charging, hard-fighting marshals. This made Napoleonic doctrine and tactics relatively simple: observe the enemy; look for weaknesses; throw mass headlong against those weaknesses; find the tipping points (in time) and launch reserves or freshly arriving corps into those places of best effect at the times of maximum impact. And if that meant taking huge casualties, never mind – they were replaceable.

Wellington relied upon the patience, coolness, steadiness, professionalism and initiative of his subordinates. Napoleon relied upon *élan*, *esprit de corps*, the value (and reward) of courage and persistence, and upon marshals who could obey orders, but use their own initiative, in a mission command sense, when the circumstances demanded it. Both men were professionally competent and had a habit of winning. Both valued a steady and highly professional flow of information and intelligence to inform their decision-making. Both men allowed instinct only to surface as a contributor to intuition. Both men were as good as they were at their metier, however, because they possessed an inbuilt intuitive talent that they had spent many years of study and experience building and nurturing. But their own talents were not enough, alone, to cope with the size and scope of the demands upon them: Wellington needed his Colquhoun Grant and his William de Lancey, and Napoleon needed his Joseph Fouché and his Louis-Alexandre Berthier, and the systems built up around those individuals. Perhaps AI could have delivered to them a faster, better, fuller, more reliable, less exhaustible (in both senses) and more flexible service than their necessarily human systems did. But perhaps that is not the point. Both men needed those individuals and the capabilities that they provided not just to furnish them with decision-enhancing information, but, importantly, to give them the time and the 'headspace' to execute their own particular function – to use their personal intuition to decide what was decisive. To exercise their extraordinary, and human, talent of *coup d'oeil*.

The point is that both commanders understood the value of their own intuition. They were 'great commanders' because they possessed an intuitive ability that others did not. Whether applied, in their very different ways, on the campaign map or the battlefield, it was the 'chicken leg moments', the 'that'll do nicely' insights, that marked their various successes. Whether in the context of campaigns (the breakout from Torres Vedras, the march from Boulogne to Ulm and on to Austerlitz) or of tactical engagements (the right moment to choose to fight at Salamanca, or the seizing of the Pratzen Heights at Austerlitz), it was the intuition of these two great captains that turned military events from stasis and stalemate to tide-turning success.

This chapter has explored the extent to which AI, machines, might be able to go beyond enhancing the performance of staffs and commanders and begin to enter the space of replacing them. It asks: 'How far away are we from being able to replace human commanders and staff officers with machines in the complex business of the command and control of armies?' A brief dip into history has, we hope, offered an insight into two important features of the human aspect of this question that, regardless of the speed and complexity of the talents of AI, regardless of its utility in helping commanders make better decisions (or, at least, better-informed decisions), remain constant. People, not machines, have instincts and use intuition. People, not machines, understand, generate, cultivate and cause emotions in other humans that lead to those human factors such as cooperation and inspiration that are so vital to the successful prosecution of war.

Thus war will likely remain, for as far ahead as we try to see, a business in which how people feel matters, and the ability of leaders to decide, wisely and using their hard-won intuition, what will be decisive is likely to remain a key determinant of outcomes. The bottom line is this: regardless of whatever help a machine might give them, the foolish will still make foolhardy decisions. And a prevaricator will probably prevaricate more and more the more information is available to them (or is about to be available, or potentially available). AI can be a great accelerant but is no replacement for the very human roles of intuition, leadership and persuasion.

So, AI is a support tool, not a replacer. *Coup d'oeil* or *coup d'AI*? A bit of both, frankly; but here is the test: can a great captain prevail if they have superior *coup d'oeil* but inferior AI? Yes (with limits, of course). Can a not-so-great captain prevail when they have little intuitive skill but a wealth of rapidly-(AI)-processed information at their fingertips? Unlikely. In a profession in which the great commanders have had an ability to spot what will be decisive – and then decide – machine-supported information provision and analysis can only ever be a welcome supporting tool. The great will still be great, and the idiots will still make idiotic decisions.

And let us never forget that in Clausewitz's 'at the first and the last, very human business of war' two things would seem to be, for now at least, enduring factors in the conduct of the command and control of warfare. First, relationships matter; the interaction of commanders, their supporting staff, and those who they lead, turn, for the better or the worse, upon how people get on with each other, persuade each other and inspire each other. Second, if Napoleon was right and 'the moral is to the physical as three is to one' then how fighting humans feel about their cause and their commander will continue to matter a great deal – and it is humans, not machines, that will both generate and harbour those feelings. For much of the history of the study of warfare the 'Great Man Theory' of war has had its place. It is now, increasingly and not before time, being replaced by the 'Great Person Theory' of war. It is likely to remain a very long time before that view of warfare is overtaken by the 'Great Machine Theory'.

15

Doubling Fighting Power: The Challenge of Ensuring 'what is thought is fought'

Luke Turrell

'…we think about the future but fight in the past.'
General Sir Roly Walker, Chief of the General Staff.

General Sir Roly Walker's vision to double and then triple the British Army's fighting power by 2030 has prioritised modernisation, readiness and the Army's people. Modernising as the Chief of the General Staff (CGS) wishes to do – fundamentally and at pace so that the British Army can 'destroy a force at least three times its size…' – requires the Army to 'pull the future of fighting power into the present, faster than we thought we could'.[1] CGS also wants the British Army to field fifth-generation land forces capable of enabling the joint force for an 'unfair fight', exploiting artificial intelligence (AI) and autonomous systems to integrate data from all domains and generate precise battlefield impact.[2] This has inevitably led many commentators to focus on the technological path to that goal. Perhaps with corresponding attention to the required industrial capacity and resilience – influenced by the ongoing conflict in Ukraine. General Roly has, however, also focused on the time between the development of advanced technological capability and the production of field manuals to teach the new ways of fighting. At the RUSI Land Warfare conference he said: 'There can therefore be a gap of twenty years between what is thought and what is taught…. with the pace of technological change today, that should be nearer twenty weeks, and twenty minutes for urgent adaptation in combat.'[3]

1   'Chief of the General Staff Keynote Speech', RUSI Land Warfare Conference, Church House, London, 23 July 2024.
2   'Chief of the General Staff Speech', 23 July 2024.
3   'Chief of the General Staff Speech', 23 July 2024.

CGS is keen to stress that achieving the aim of doubling the fighting power of land forces by 2027 and tripling it by 2030 'relies on both thinking and then doing differently'. This is not a case of hoping that predictions about the future character of conflict will enable clairvoyant capability decisions. Sir Lawrence Freedman, in his book, *The Future of War: A History*, was clear that this was the path to military disaster. Nevertheless, the path to achieving CGS' vision for ensuring 'what is thought is taught' appears straightforward. CGS has already outlined that the Land Training System, will provide the ready-made spirals for accelerated force modernisation.[4]

In addition, the British Army has long-established doctrine and doctrine processes that provide 'a shared conceptual basis for thought and action.'[5] Therefore, it would appear the task can be achieved through management and leadership, by increasing the regularity, speed, and robustness of institutional feedback loops to turn tactical lessons and the employment of emerging technology into doctrine, written at the speed of relevance. To achieve this, the economist Felix Martin considers that a human or institutional version of an AI neural network is required. This would create a culture of 'gradient' learning whereby beta versions of doctrine could be generated and, through robust feedback loops, reviewed, refined and improved.[6] However, there are a number of challenges to that simple solution. This chapter will discuss three, but far more qualified and distinguished authors have also identified other barriers to institutional learning by and in the British Army.

Michael Howard, writing in 1984, commented that 'the complacent anti-intellectualism which has long been a predominant tendency of a British army… takes a perverse delight in learning its lessons the hard way'.[7] A sentiment that echoes and perhaps provides more context to the oft-quoted statement from Field Marshal Erwin Rommel that: 'The British write some of the best doctrine in the world; it is fortunate their officers do not read it'. This tendency for anti-intellectualism was also noted by General Sir John Kiszely, writing for the *RUSI Journal* in 2006, on the challenges of adapting for counterinsurgency. He went on to discuss four other factors, the first of which was that learning organisations must have an ability to accommodate internal and external criticism, something strictly hierarchical and proudly insular militaries are particularly resistant to. Secondly, Kiszely noted that historically militaries lacked a central location for learning, rectified, in the case of the UK, by the establishment of the UK Defence Academy, of which Sir John was Director General. Thirdly, General Kiszely noted that change is the necessary conclusion to the learning process but militaries, as inherently conservative organisations, are often wary of structural or cultural change. Experience of Army HQ in recent years may suggest this is now less of a barrier. Kiszely's final factor

---

4   'Chief of the General Staff Speech', 23 July 2024.
5   H. Hoiback, 'What is doctrine?', *Journal of Strategic Studies*, 34:6 (2011), pp.879–900.
6   Rory Stewart, 'The long history of ignorance', *BBC Podcast*, Episode 4, https://www.bbc.co.uk/programmes/m0021cbt
7   Carl von Clausewitz (Peter Paret and Michael Howard, trans. & eds), *On War* (Princeton, NJ: Princeton UP, 1984), p.38.

was that armies tend to diligently train for the wrong character of warfare and conse-quently struggle to adapt to novel forms of warfare.[8]

All chime with anyone who has served in or studied the British Army and indeed lead on to the three factors discussed in this chapter. The first issue is that unlearning and then re-learning is scientifically acknowledged to be psychologically challenging for anyone. The second is that the true potential of radically new technology is rarely, if ever, recognised immediately. And the third issue is the character and disposition of soldiers and officers generally in British and other Western armies, and, critically, their ability to cope with rapid change. Firstly, however, it is worth considering briefly what doctrine is, how it can serve the goal of institutional learning and some of its weaknesses.

Why Bother With Doctrine?

As stated, the purpose of doctrine is to provide a shared conceptual basis for thought and action. Clausewitz recognised that: 'Theory becomes a guide to anyone who wants to learn about war from books. It will light his way, ease his progress, train his judgement, and help him to avoid pitfalls.'[9] However, successful doctrine is more than just publishing insights. Doctrine is what is believed and acted upon by the organisation and the people within it. It provides an institutionally endorsed concept of war that also serves to provide a shared lexicon, a unity and cohesion of thought and deed. It has been argued that new, dynamic and constantly evolving doctrine can alter beliefs and the way an army operates. However, in practice, the opposite can also be true. J. F. C. Fuller was at pains to point out that '...[doctrine] is apt to ossify into a dogma.... and be seized upon by mental emas-culates who... rest assured that their actions, however inept, find justification in a book'.[10] More recently, General Jim Mattis, former Commander of the U.S. Joint Forces and U.S. Central Command, called doctrine 'the last refuge of the unimaginative.'[11]

The challenge then, to support CGS' intent, is to generate a process that captures and then inculcates lessons at the speed of relevance to reform practices and maintain a technological advantage over an adversary. But without, to borrow from the dictionary definition of dogma, producing a set of principles and then presenting them as incon-trovertibly true and unreformable.[12] For doctrine to be successful, it must be recognised for what it is, a snapshot in time, and just as readily replaced with new thinking. Sadly, unlearning and re-learning is not something humans do well.

---

8   John Kiszely, 'Learning about Counterinsurgency' in *RUSI Journal* 151:6 (December 2006), pp.16–21.

9   Clausewitz, *On War*, p.141.

10   J. F. C. Fuller, *The Foundations of the Science of War* (London: Hutchinson & Co., 1925), p.254.

11   Jim Mattis, *Call Sign Chaos* (New York: Ballantine Books, 2019).

12   Dictionary definition – 'Dogma', https://www.oxfordlearnersdictionaries.com/definition/english/dogma#:~:text=%2F%CB%88d%C9%92%C9%A1m%C9%99%2F,expected%20to%20accept%20without%20argument

Unlearning and Re-learning

Confucius points out that loving learning means always being open to changing course.[13] Basil Liddell Hart's truism suggests this is seemingly more difficult for military people – 'the only thing more difficult than getting a new idea into a military mind is getting the old one out'. However, Liddell Hart was perhaps doing a disservice to soldiers and officers by stating it so directly.

In 1995 Roger Schank and Robert Abelson's research argued that humans explain new events by remembering and then adapting existing stories to fit the new circumstances. They argued that understanding new events in a complex world was made manageable by remembering an action or event similar to the new experience, thereby making a potentially unmanageable task achievable.[14] This built on their earlier work on 'scripts'. Scripts are essentially cribs for life, 'a set of expectations about what will happen next in a well-understood situation…. to make mental processing easier, by allowing us to think less'.[15]

Schank and Abelson argued that in normal circumstances, life is simply a process of finding the right, previously experienced script – such as the 'how to make a cup of tea' script or 'how to introduce yourself to someone you haven't met before' script. This is because, frankly, it is easier to use a 'script' than to work out how to respond to a new situation. However, Schank and Abelson acknowledged that humans routinely respond to new and novel experiences. But that they do so 'by seeing new experiences in terms of old experiences'. When we try to learn new concepts and doctrine, we are likely to see any new concept through the lens of the old one. Moreover, the challenge with unlearning and then rapidly re-learning new concepts is that the process of learning the old concepts (often through repetition) increases its availability.[16]

This intersects with the 'illusory truth effect', the tendency to believe false information if it is repeated enough times. This is again, broadly, based on availability. We find information we have heard before more believable than something unfamiliar or new. Fazio et al explained that 'repetition makes statements easier to process (i.e. fluent) relative to new statements, leading people to the (sometimes) false conclusion that they are more truthful'.[17] In essence, the brain mistakes the ease with which it can recall the information as evidence that it is true. And in the same way, the process of learning new doctrine is in a battle with old doctrine for credibility and space.

---

13   Michael S. Roth, *The Student: A Short History* (London: Yale University Press, 2023), p.21.
14   Roger C. Schank and Robert P. Abelson, 'Knowledge and Memory: The Real Story', in Robert S. Wyer, Jr (ed.), *Knowledge and Memory: The Real Story* (Hillsdale, NJ: Lawrence Erlbaum Associates, 1995), pp.1–85.
15   Schank and Abelson, 'Knowledge and Memory'.
16   Amos Tversky and Daniel Kahneman, 'Availability: A heuristic for judging frequency and probability', *Cognitive Psychology*, 5:2 (1973), pp.207–232.
17   Lisa K. Fazio et al, 'Knowledge does not protect against illusory truth', *Journal of Experimental Psychology: General*, 144:5 (2015), pp.993–1002.

True Utility of New Technology is Rarely Recognised Immediately

An example, in the interwar period, of trying to introduce new technology is when the American army recognised the value of the internal combustion engine and introduced mechanisation. However, their doctrine did not recognise the real utility of the technology. They considered the best use of the trucks would be to transport horses to the battlefield. This would prevent them becoming too tired so they could then conduct a traditional cavalry charge. The key lesson here is that, much like Schank and Abelson's research, new technology is understood through the lens of old technology.

This is replicated more recently with the introduction of uncrewed aerial vehicles (UAVs) – or drones to use their more common term – into the British Army. The first drones were used by the Royal Artillery to provide a stand-off capability for observers to acquire targets for prosecution with conventional artillery. This provided the ability to find targets without exposing the observers or fire support teams to greater risk. Of note, artillery observers until the early 2000s were referred to as forward observation officers – the clue being in the name in terms of their location on the battlefield. In the Second World War numerous gallantry awards were awarded to forward observation officers for exposing themselves to extreme threat in order to be able to see and then accurately prosecute targets. One example was Captain David Haddow who was awarded a Military Cross for his actions during Operation Jupiter and the breakout of Allied forces from the D-Day beaches. In a personal account to the author, Captain Haddow described how, from his observation post, he called in and directed artillery fire on a group of German soldiers in the open. When asked how close he was to the Germans, David said 'I could hear them'.

The emergence of UAV technology thus provided a way of seeing 'over the hill' although for many years policy meant that observers were not able to prosecute targets using UAV footage – they had to move into a position to physically see the target. This evolved during the conflicts in Iraq and Afghanistan so that fire support teams could fire artillery at targets observed through a UAV camera. At the same time, armed UAVs were introduced although they were exclusively operated by the Royal Air Force, essentially treated as an uncrewed version of a fast jet and still requiring a highly qualified and experienced pilot. To date, British Army doctrine still considers UAVs an extension of an observer's eyes. The haphazard strapping of grenades to commercially purchased drones by ISIS and other terrorist groups began to shift opinion,[18] before the conflict in Nagorno-Karabakh and the success of Turkish loitering munitions changed the way UAVs were perceived forever.[19] In the current Ukraine conflict, it is widely reported there

18   Flight Lieutenant Peers Lyle, 'Air Power Proliferation: How "Commercial-off-the-shelf" Drones are being used by Violent Extremist Organisations to Influence The Future of Warfare in the Air' in *Air and Space Power Review*, 22:3 (2019), pp.102–121.
19   Michael Kofman and Leonid Nersisyan, 'The Second Nagorno-Karabakh War, Two Weeks In' in *War on the Rocks* (2020), https://warontherocks.com/2020/10/the-second-nagorno-karabakh-war-two-weeks-in/.

are two first-person view (FPV) drones for every kilometre of the 1,609-kilometre front line.[20] Commentators have suggested that FPVs can now replace artillery altogether, a seemingly poetic evolution from their role supporting artillery observers.

The utility of UAVs has been seen to mark the end of artillery, tanks and, frankly soldiers. This appears overblown as artillery and armoured vehicles remain critical capabilities in Ukraine and in conflict globally, but time will ultimately tell. Reality perhaps sits somewhere between new technology changing everything and the words of Admiral William Benson, the U.S. Chief of Naval Operations in 1919, who considered aeroplanes to be 'just a lot of noise'.[21] The clear conclusion therefore is that the true utility of new technology is rarely recognised immediately.

Another factor to consider is the lingering impact of culture over doctrine on militaries. The artillery were the superstars of the French Army at the turn of the last century. Known as the 'Virtuosos', their dash and bravado came from nationalistic pride[22] and their technologically cutting-edge, 75mm 'quick firing' gun deployed in a direct fire position.[23] This also influenced the British Royal Artillery who sought to emulate them, notably on the Mons to Charleroi road on 22 August 1914 when E Battery, Royal Horse Artillery, fired the first British artillery round of the First World War.[24] E Battery sited their guns on a forward slope, just as gunners had done 50 kilometres and 99 years earlier, at the Battle of Waterloo, and, like the French gunners, engaged the Germans in direct fire, sustaining huge casualties. British doctrine at the time, shaped by the Boer War, recognised the value of direct fire to providing close support and reassurance to the infantry. However, the official doctrine was to engage indirectly, from the reverse slope, to protect against counter-battery fire. For all their glamour and panache, the French artillery had been blinded to the evolving character of conflict by their supposed technological superiority. And the culture was infectious. As a result, E Battery neglected their own doctrine of indirect fire to protect against counter-battery fire.[25]

These three examples demonstrate two interconnecting issues. Firstly, that humanity struggles to unlearn old concepts and secondly, they see new technology through the lens of the old and fail to appreciate its true utility. In a similar way that it is difficult to

20   David Hambling, 'Russian Dolls: FPV Drone-Carrying Drones Are Now In Action In Ukraine' in *Forbes Magazine*, 17 September 2024, https://www.forbes.com/sites/davidhambling/2024/09/17/russian-dolls-fpv-drone-carrying-drones-are-now-in-action-in-ukraine/.
21   John T. Correll, 'Billy Mitchell and the Battleships', 21 July 2021 in *Air and Space Forces Magazine*, https://www.airandspaceforces.com/article/billy-mitchell-ostfriesland/.
22   Douglas *Porch, The March to the Marne: The French Army 1871–1914* (Cambridge: Cambridge University Press, 1981), pp.214–216.
23   Christopher Miskimon, 'The French 75 Gun: The Secret Cannon Used for Over Half a Century' in *Warfare History Network* (February 2008).
24   David Lomas, *Mons 1914: The BEF's Tactical Triumph* (London: Osprey, 2014).
25   See Major Luke Turrell, 'Programme THEIA: Transforming the Army for 2021 and Beyond', *Defence Digital*, 17 March 2021, https://defencedigital.blog.gov.uk/2021/03/17/programme-theia-transforming-the-army-for-2021-and-beyond/.

correct people once they are exposed to falsehood and their previously held views linger (the 'continued influence effect'),[26] when CGS asks the British Army to rapidly introduce new technology and subsequent doctrine to ensure 'what is (newly) thought, is taught' – the Army needs to remember its history and recognise that it will not be that easy. Nevertheless, it is therefore reassuring that the narrative of the new 1* Leadership and Education Development Command acknowledges the need for 'an Army that…. learns, but also "unlearns" then "relearns" where necessary, as the context changes'.[27]

Prevalence of Neurodiversity in Military Personnel

A third factor follows research by the U.S. Department of Defense about the prevalence of neurodiversity in the U.S. military.[28] The research suggested the percentage of U.S. solders with attention deficit hyperactivity disorder (ADHD) from 2008 to 2018 was between 1.7 percent and 3.9 percent. However, research published in 2021 suggested that many new recruits did not disclose neurodiversity diagnoses during enlistment and,[29] given ADHD is 'the most common paediatric neurodevelopmental disorder diagnosed in the U.S.',[30] the prevalence could be much higher. A separate study suggested the prevalence of ADHD could be as high as seven percent and constituted one of the three most common psychiatric conditions in non-deployed U.S. Army soldiers.[31] It has also been associated with a higher risk of post-traumatic stress disorder.[32] A study in Korea noted that military personnel had, on average, a higher age of neurodiversity

26   U. K. H. Ecker, S. Lewandowsky, M. Chadwick, 'Can corrections spread misinformation to new audiences? Testing for the elusive familiarity backfire effect' in *Cognitive Research: Principles and Implications*, 5:41 (2020).
27   'Verbal Leadership and Education Development Command brief to Chief of the General Staff', RMAS, Camberley, 11 October 2024.
28   Staff Sergeant. Jarred Woods, 'Serving with ADHD' in *NCO Journal*, 7 February 2022, https://www.armyupress.army.mil/Journals/NCO-Journal/Archives/2022/February/Serving-with-ADHD/#:~:text=By%20the%20numbers&text=The%20rate%20of%20ADHD%20among,served%20alongside%20Soldiers%20with%20ADHD.
29   David Sayers et al., 'Attrition rates and incidence of mental health disorders in an attention deficit/hyperactivity disorder (ADHD) cohort, active component' in *Medical Surveillance Monthly Report*, 28:1 (2021), p.2.
30   'The Prevalence of Attention-Deficit/Hyperactivity Disorder (ADHD) and ADHD Medication Treatment in Active Component Service Members, U.S. Armed Forces, 2014–2018' in *Health.mil*, 1 January 2021, https://health.mil/News/Articles/2021/01/01/Prevalence-of-Att-MSMR-Jan-2021
31   R. C. Kessler et al., 'Thirty-day prevalence of DSM-IV mental disorders among nondeployed soldiers in the U.S. Army: results from the Army Study to Assess Risk and Resilience in Service Members (Army STARRS)' in *JAMA Psychiatry*, 71:5 (2014), pp.504–513.
32   J. R. Howlett et al., 'Attention Deficit Hyperactivity Disorder and Risk of Posttraumatic Stress and Related Disorders: A Prospective Longitudinal Evaluation in U.S. Army Soldiers' in *Journal of Traumatic Stress*, 31:6 (2018), pp.909–918.

diagnosis than non-serving participants, indicating an ability and willingness to mask the symptoms.[33] A Freedom of Information request in November 2022 revealed that more than 1,000 serving British soldiers had a neurodiversity diagnosis[34] and followed the statement in 2021 by the Second Sea Lord Vice Admiral Nick Hine that he had been diagnosed with autism.[35]

The conclusion of the U.S. military research in 2021 was that it had potential recruitment, readiness and health implications, with a suggestion that a more permissive entry standard, to maximise U.S. military recruitment, may be acceptable. However, in the context of CGS' mission to ensure what is 'thought is taught', the imperative to unlearn and re-learn and the challenges of utilising new technology, the prevalence of neurodiverse soldiers and officers is significant. Neurodiverse people can struggle with change because they value stability, predictability, and systematic patterns in their employment.[36] Moreover, 'set routines, times, particular routes and rituals all help…. Trying to keep everything the same reduces some of the terrible fear'.[37] This may mean that the ability to change views radically and dynamically, and alter behavioural processes – required to ensure the British Army can rapidly 'think and then do' differently – could be affected. This is not to suggest that ADHD is entirely negative – research suggests individuals with ADHD are unusually good at divergent thinking tasks or brainstorming new ideas.[38]

Conclusion

As outlined, the challenge of closing the 20-year gap between what is thought and what is taught is far more challenging than simply refining management processes and feedback loops. It requires recognition and engagement with the scientific, educational and cultural factors. It requires cultural recognition that, when trying to update doctrine, the British Army, individually and organisationally, will more than likely try, as identified

33   G. M. Noh et al., 'Social function of adult men with attention-deficit/hyperactivity disorder in the context of military service' in *Neuropsychiatric Disease and Treatment*, 14 (2018), pp.3349–3354.
34   Army Policy and Secretariat to unknown, 30 November 2022, Ref: Army/Sec/FOI2022/12906, https://assets.publishing.service.gov.uk/media/63d2750ae90e071ba1c26872/FOI2022-12906.pdf
35   'Stories from the Spectrum: Vice Admiral Nick Hine', *National Autistic Society*, n.d., https://www.autism.org.uk/advice-and-guidance/stories/stories-from-the-spectrum-nick-hine.
36   M. B. MacLean et al., 'Postmilitary adjustment to civilian life: Potential risks and protective factors', *Physical Therapy*, 94:8 (2014), pp.1186–1195.
37   See P. Howlin, *Autism and Asperger Syndrome: Preparing for Adulthood* (London and New York, Second Edition: Routledge, 2004), p.137.
38   Holly White, 'The creativity of ADHD: More insights on a positive side of a "disorder"' in *Scientific American*, 5 March 2019, https://www.scientificamerican.com/article/the-creativity-of-adhd/.

by Schank and Abelson, a 'script'. General Kiszely noted that: 'Those embarking on an operation can tend to identify the anticipated circumstances in terms of the doctrine perceived to be closest to it, reach for the doctrinal publication concerned, and end up trying to fit the circumstances to the doctrine, rather than the other way round.'[39]

The reasons he attributed to this were anti-intellectualism, intellectual laziness and a lack of imagination, coupled, on occasion, with an unhelpful focus on the value of personal experience. However, as described, there are more instrumental psychological and human reasons. The first stage is therefore to acknowledge their significance and then build solutions. It is also important, in order for the British Army to achieve a doubling and then tripling of fighting power, to acknowledge the skills of the workforce. Vice Admiral Hine, when discussing his autism diagnosis, discussed broadening entry standards to encourage neurodiverse applicants who could 'think differently' and as recognition that it was 'the only way the UK could compete with better funded and technologically superior adversaries'.[40] Equally, to make reasonable adjustments, fundamental change must be communicated in a more manageable way for all members of the Armed Forces with a clear explanation of the unifying purpose – the why[41]. Whether neurodiverse or not, it is critical to ensuring 'what is thought, is taught'.

39   Kiszely, 'Learning about Counterinsurgency'.
40   Larisa Brown, 'Vice Admiral Nick Hine: "To be blunt, autism made me a better naval officer"' in *The Times*, 12 March 2021.
41   Sergeant Major Emmanuel A. Emekaekwue, 'Leading Soldiers with ADHD', *NCO Journal*, 16 July 2021, https://www.armyupress.army.mil/Journals/NCO-Journal/Archives/2021/July/Leading-Soldiers-with-ADHD/

Conclusion: Storm Proofing 101: Don't Wait for the Storm!

Andrew Sharpe

'I am a pessimist because of intelligence, but an optimist because of will.'
Antonio Gramsci, *Prison Notebooks*, December 1929.[1]

The very varied chapters of this book have had one thing in common. At their roots there is an agreement by their authors that the world is an unsafe place and that the defence establishments of the countries in which they live (largely the UK, but wider Europe and the U.S. too) are not properly prepared, physically, conceptually or morally, to meet the challenges that they exist to counter, should latent and developing threats progress to deliver their patent worst. We have offered thoughts, personal and therefore flawed no doubt, on some areas in which positive impact may be had in this respect. The established demands of rearmament are not considered in detail in the pages of this book – we have chosen to hope that they are already understood and know that they have been extensively covered elsewhere. The point of the scope of the issues that have been covered, and their deviation from the rearmament and force generation norms, is that we believe that the breadth and depth of the problem facing defence, and the land environment in particular, is such that a development agenda based upon gradual change and evolution in traditional areas and traditional ways, and a hope that the worst either never happens or is sufficiently distant from us to enable us to take serious risk in resource terms, is simply not a responsible course of action. We have attempted to address this undertaking, as Antonio Gramsci urged from his prison cell, by maintaining a positive belief that this challenge can (and must) be met, but balancing that belief with the application of measured logic to ensure that the size and weight of the task are not wished away or ignored through wilful optimism.

The pragmatic realities of the context in which the developing security threats exist are understood. The distraction of the domestic (and especially economic)

---

1   Antonio Gramsci was the Nobel-Prize-winning Marxist leader of the Italian Communist Party who was imprisoned by Mussolini from 1926 until his death in 1937. In his writings while in prison he argued that ideology alone was not enough, but that a combination of ideology and pragmatic calculated logic was much more likely to produce productive practical outcomes.

consequences of the post-pandemic and global-instability-driven background have led the hard-pressed treasuries of many governments, and especially of democracies, to channel their meagre resources into those areas that are most immediately felt by their populations. Economic wellbeing, health, welfare, housing, government-paid salaries and education are all the real daily concerns of their electorates. Their demands are current and tangible. A failure to address those demands will have immediate and tangible negative outcomes. Those effects will translate rapidly into equally negative results in opinion polls and, ultimately, on tenures of democratically bestowed power. In straightened times it makes all kinds of sense to put resource where it can be most immediately and tangibly felt. The insurance policy that is a nation's strategic defence posture, under these circumstances, will, almost inevitably, see a reduction in resource based on the hope that latent threats remain manageable and distant. Evidence that this predictable distance may not be the case, no matter how strong, will always be unwelcome. Cassandras, Noahs, Galileos, et al, will all likely still go unheeded. But, we argue, they must no longer be ignored. A belief in the pursuit of accepted force development norms, along with hope, we suggest, is not a reasonable strategic approach. But we have not written a book urging the purchase of vast amounts of expensive and advanced equipment or the recruiting of huge numbers of people. The argument for those things has been made, variously, elsewhere. Instead, in a context in which the pace and breadth of technological change is unprecedented, and human relations with and use of machines is rapidly changing the character of war, we have sought to suggest ways in which we might think about (and in) warfare differently, and how we might think about organising ourselves differently (both of which, surely, can be achieved with little expense in these straightened times). And we believe that intellectual and practical application in this respect is both necessary and urgent.

A couple of days before Christmas 2024, and therefore a couple of weeks after the sudden fall of President Assad of Syria, quite by chance, I bumped into a (very) senior UK Defence official who was conducting some last-minute Christmas shopping. After exchanging seasonal greetings, we, rather less seasonally, fell to discussing recent events. The official's views of events in Syria, and their strategic consequences more widely, were interesting. The narrative went something like: the events were a surprise, or rather, the speed of the collapse was a surprise. The events themselves were interesting in their own right, but the knock-on effects were much more interesting. Iran, and Iran's relative malign influence over Middle Eastern (and, by extension, global) events had been dramatically reduced. Importantly though, and this was the main point, Russia had been shown to be 'even weaker' than we thought, and was, therefore, less of a threat than we had supposed. The conversation cast around more widely (Syrian instability and a likely further period of considerable internal strife; Turkey's involvement and interests (and, by extension, NATO's); Israel's opportunist conduct; and so on), but, tellingly, returned several times to those first two points: Iran and, more significantly, Russia were less of a threat than we had thought. It seemed to me, either deliberately or subliminally, that a message was being passed, within a context:

times are hard, we have a painful strategic review in progress that we know won't (or possibly can't) deliver Defence the resource it needs, but be reassured that the threat is less than we thought – or at least less immediate and proximate – so we will be able to manage what is coming (both externally driven and domestically imposed). Don't worry!

I left the conversation feeling not reassured, but, instead, deeply uncomfortable.

In matters of defence and security, weakness is relative. In matters of deterrence, perceptions of weakness are important. Pondering 'Russia is much weaker than we thought' I wondered: 'compared to who? The UK?'. In numbers alone, for example, Russia lends an obvious truth to the old maxim that 'quantity has a quality all of its own' that we (even if supported by our allies, especially if the Russians were supported by their actual and potential allies) could not hope to match in human terms. Perceptions of threat proximity, whether realistic or convenient, did not, to my mind, make our need to think hard about ways that we can make our capabilities better and stronger any less real or less pressing. It was thus not just our differing interpretations of the implications of recent events that troubled me. More profoundly concerning was a feeling that I was being encouraged not to expend energy on thinking too deeply about the scale, shape, proximity or urgency of the problem and therefore about the range of alternative possible solutions to it. 'Steady as she goes', I felt, was not a responsible command. I believe that the scale of the problems that are facing us, patently, is such that the broader and more imaginative thought that we can apply to it, the more likely we are to get ahead of those problems.

Russia may be a wounded bear, but wounded animals, and especially those that find themselves cornered, are more likely to lash out than those that are not. The perceived threat of encirclement which, rightly or wrongly, remains a key tenet of Russia's strategic outlook, has proven an immoveable constant throughout this century. A view on the chances of conflict 'by mistake' joining the 'fear, honour and interest' calculus of which we spoke in the opening chapter, surely, had grown as a result of a glance through the lens of the recent events, not reduced. Despite this, we have not argued that the arrival of the storm is inevitable. This book has not been about that context: it has hoped that that context is recognised, and therefore we have sought to contribute to the thinking that will be needed to make our militaries better prepared to prevail within it.

The areas of interest that are visited in the chapters of this book, therefore, offer two contrasting imperatives. The first is a need for strategic long-termism. We must acknowledge the root-and-branch rethink that has become a fundamental requirement and accept that, while maintaining and developing those capabilities that we still have, we should begin to move the defence super-tanker into an altogether different physical, conceptual and moral space. This will require not just getting some long-discarded or forgotten very old ideas back into people's minds, but getting some new ideas in, against a backdrop of deep and visceral experience in a way of war and warfare that might have little to do with what we might face next. As I have observed elsewhere, the British Army, like many of its allied armies, as a result of its significant experiences (and essentially positive and laudable conduct in the most demanding of circumstances) over the last 25 years, has become less of a war-machine and more of a COIN-operated machine.[2] This necessary change of mind-set and direction is therefore a big ask, and an even bigger undertaking. The second is the need, rather paradoxically, for a renewed understanding of short-termism, especially in the area of force development and procurement. It is plainly apparent that the pace of change, especially technological change, is now such that cumbersome, cautious and red-tape-tangled procurement structures (connected to a neglected and too-often-abused defence industry) simply will not meet the requirement to match the steepness of the military evolution curve with that of the global development and technology curve. The UK Chief of the General Staff's recent exhortation to his Army to 'double and then triple its lethality and fighting power' over a three and then six-year period can only be realistic if it is released from the chains of procurement practices that had their conception in the mid-twentieth century. Without agility, both in thought and in action, this may prove to be an impossible goal.

This book has been an attempt to contribute to the task of changing, developing, improving and readying our armed forces, and especially our armies, to be better able to face the oncoming storm of challenges. Army force development traditionally blends the threats, competitors, likely contexts and circumstances with the advance of technological possibilities and the realistic freedoms and constraints of policies and resources to shape the development of an army in an accepted and tried-and-trusted process. Contextual research along with novel thinking is developed into concepts, which then drive capability acquisition and improvements, alongside developments in doctrine, tactics and procedures. This book, understanding that this force development work is in earnest progress in the hands of the most qualified, motivated and competent of men and women, seeks to add to that discussion by offering some extra thought in this arena; thought on how we may be able to add effect multipliers to this traditional thinking. We have suggested a renewed and open-minded examination of: how armies might structure; how soldiers, and especially commanders and those practising generalship, might think, and how machines may or may not be able to help with that; and we have considered how people feel (and machines do not) and what that might mean for both the changing character and the unchanging nature of war. None of these thoughts pose as clever solutions to the pacing threats and challenges that face our militaries. We have sought, instead, to widen that urgent discussion and offer food for thought, and, perhaps, an exhortation or two.

In summary, as Gramsci urged in the quote at the start of this closing chapter, we are not pessimists abandoning hope, nor fantasists offering unrealistic or unachievable solutions or proposals. The contributors to this book are, largely, optimistic realists. If we apply intellect and logic to the problems that we face, we may find some of the practical

---

2   Which is to say, an army both practised in, and fixated upon, counterinsurgency operations, rather than one focused upon, and trained in, delivering high-end war fighting, at scale, as its core purpose.

solutions. If we apply a positive approach to how we address both the challenges that face us and the possible solutions to them, then we are much more likely to deliver an advantageous counter to them. If, on the other hand, we allow ourselves to slip into an opposite world, in which we apply optimism to our logic and pessimistic fatalism to our approach to our challenges we are highly likely to face forthcoming defence and security challenges unprepared. A change of attitudes is the least expensive (but perhaps hardest to achieve) of the solutions to our potential problems.

Selected Bibliography

Anon., *General Orders: Spain and Portugal: April 27th to December 28th, 1809, Vol. I* (London: 1811)

Anon., *Minutes of Evidence Taken Before the Royal Commission on the War in South Africa, Volume II, CD.1791* (London: HMSO, 1903)

Bacevich, A. J., *The Pentomic Era: The U.S. Army Between Korea and Vietnam* (Washington, DC: National Defense University Press, 1986)

Bailey, Jonathan, Iron, Richard and Strachan, Hew (eds), *British Generals in Blair's Wars* (Farnham: Ashgate Publishing Ltd., 2013)

Barclay, C. N., *The First Commonwealth Division: The Story of British Commonwealth Land Forces in Korea, 1950–1953* (Aldershot: Gale and Polden Limited, 1954)

Batten, Simon, *Futile Exercise? The British Army's Preparations for War 1902–1914* (Solihull: Helion & Co., 2018)

Baynes, John, *Morale: A Study of Men and Courage* (London: Cassell, 1967)

Bean, Tim, Flint, Edward, Kitchen, James E. and Latawksi, Paul (eds), *Orchestrating Warfighting: A History of the British Army's Corps and Divisions at War since 1914* (London: Routledge, 2024)

Becke, A. F., *History of the Great War. Order of Battle of Divisions, Part 2A The Regular British Divisions* (London: HMSO, 1936)

Beckett, Ian F. W., *The British Army: A New Short History* (Oxford: Oxford University Press, 2023)

Beech, Jim, *Haig's Intelligence* (Cambridge: Cambridge University Press, 2013)

Biddle, Stephen, *Military Power Explaining Victory and Defeat in Modern Battle* (Princeton: Princeton University Press, 2004)

Bihan, Benoist and Lopez, Jean, *Conduire la guerre, entretiens sur l'art opératif* (Paris: Perrin, 2023)

Bijker, W. E., Hughes, T. P., and Pinch, T. (eds), *The Social Construction of Technological Systems: New Directions in the Sociology and History of Technology* (Cambridge, MA: The MIT Press, 2012)

Blackett, P. M. S., *Studies of War: Nuclear and Conventional* (London: Oliver and Boyd, 1962)

Blanken, L., *Rational Empires: Institutional Incentives and Imperial Expansion* (Chicago: University of Chicago Press, 2012)

Boguslawski, Albrecht von (Lumley Graham, trans.), *Tactical Deductions from the War of 1870–71* (London: Henry S. King & Co and Creswell's, 1872)

Bourne, John and Sheffield, Gary, *Douglas Haig: War Diaries and Letters 1914–1918* (London: Aurum, 2006)

Bradley, Omar, *A Soldier's Story* (New York: Henry Holt and Company, 1951)

Bristow, Adrian, *A Serious Disappointment: The Battle of Aubers Ridge 1915 and the Munitions Scandal* (Barnsley: Pen and Sword, 1995)

Bronk, Justin Bronk and Watling, *Jack, Mass Precision Strike: Designing UAV Complexes for Land Forces* (London: RUSI, 2024)

Brooks, Rob, *Artificial Intimacy: Virtual Friends, Digital Lovers, Algorithmic Matchmakers* (New York: Columbia University Press, 2021)

Brose, C., *The Kill Chain: Defending America in the Future of High-Tech Warfare* (New York: Hachette Books, 2020)

Carew, Tim, *Korea: The Commonwealth at War* (London: Cassell, 1967)

Chandler, David, *The Campaigns of Napoleon* (London: George Allen & Unwin, 1967)

Clark, Richard M., and Mitchell, William L., *Deception: Counterdeception and Counterintelligence* (Washington DC: CQ Press, 2018)

Clarke, Alan, *The Donkeys* (London: Mayflower, 1964)

Clausewitz, Carl von, (Michael Howard and Peter Paret, trans.), *On War* (Princeton: Princeton University Press, 1984)

Coser, Lewis A., *Functions of Social Conflict* (New York: Simon and Schuster, 1964)

Creveld, Martin van, *Fighting Power: German and U.S. Army Performance, 1939–45* (Westport, CN: Greenwood Publishing, 1982)

Crosbie, Thomas, *Military Politics: New Perspectives* (New York: Berghahn Books, 2023)

David, Mike, *Planet of the Slums* (London: Verso, 2006)

Dirou, Armel, *La guérilla en 1870, résistance et terreur* (Paris, 2e édition: L'Artilleur-Giovanangeli, 2021)

Doughty, Robert, *The Seeds of Disaster: The Development of French Military Doctrine 1919–39* (Hamden, CT: Archon Books, 1985)

Du Picq, Ardant (Roger Spiller, trans. & ed.), *Battle Studies* (Lawrence, KA: Kansas University Press, 2017)

Dunlop, John K., *The Development of the British Army 1899–1914* (London: Methuen, 1938)

Dunn-Pattison, R.P., *Napoleon's Marshals: Twenty-Six Military Commanders of the First Empire* (Driffield: Leonaur Ltd., 2011)

Edmonds, J. E., *Military Operations, France and Belgium, 14 volumes* (London: HMSO, 1923–1949)

Eich E., et al, *Cognition and Emotion* (New York: Oxford University Press, 2000)

Foch, Ferdinand, *Éloge de Napoléon* (Paris: Berger-Levrault, 1921)

Fox, Aimée, *Learning to Fight: Military Innovation and Change in the British Army 1914–1918* (Cambridge: Cambridge University Press, 2016)

Freedman, Lawrence, *The Evolution of Nuclear Strategy* (New York, Third Edition; Palgrave MacMillan, 2003)

Freedman, Lawrence, *Command: The Politics of Military Operations from Korea to Ukraine* (London: Allen Lane, 2022)

French, David, Army, *Empire, and Cold War: The British Army and Military Policy, 1945–1971* (Oxford: Oxford University Press, 2012)

Fremont-Barnes, Gregory (ed.), *Armies of the Napoleonic Wars* (Barnsley, South Yorkshire: Pen and Sword Military, 2011)

Fridman, Ofer, *Russian Hybrid Warfare Resurgence and Politicisation* (Oxford: Oxford University Press, 2018)

Fuller, J. F. C., *The Foundations of the Science of War* (London: Hutchinson & Co, 1925)

Fuller, J. F. C., *Generalship. Its Diseases and Their Cure. A Study of the Personal Factor in Command* (Harrisburg, U.S.A.: Military Service Publishing Co., 1936)

Gould-Davies, Nigel (ed.), Strategic Survey 2022: The Annual Assessment of Geopolitics (London: International Institute for Strategic Studies, 2022)

Harris, J. P., *Douglas Haig and the First World War* (Cambridge: Cambridge University Press, 2008)

Hastings, Max, *Armageddon, The Battle for Germany, 1944–1945* (New York: Alfred A. Knopf, 2004)

Hawking, Stephen, *A Brief History of Time. From the Big Bang to Black Holes* (London: Bantam Dell Ltd, 1998)

Heuser, Beatrice, *The Evolution of Strategy: Thinking War from Antiquity to the Present* (Cambridge: Cambridge University Press, 2010)

Holdstock, Douglas and Barnaby, Frank (eds), *The British Nuclear Weapons Programme 1952–2002* (London: Frank Cass, 2003)

Holmes, Richard, *Firing Line* (London: Penguin, 1986)

Holmes, Richard, *Riding the Retreat: Mons to the Marne Revisited* (London: Pimlico, 2007)

Howard, Michael, *Studies in War and Peace* (London: Temple Smith, 1970)

Howard, Michael, *The Causes of Wars and other essays* (London: Temple Smith, 1983)

Howard, Michael, *War and the Liberal Conscience* (New Brunswick, NJ.; Rutgers University Press, 1978)

Howlin, P., *Autism and Asperger Syndrome: Preparing for Adulthood* (London and New York, Second Edition: Routledge, 2004)

Hubin, Guy, *Perspectives tactiques* (Paris: ISC-Economica, 2009)

Janowitz, Morris (ed.), *The New Military: Changing Patterns of Organization* (New York: Russell Sage Foundation, 1964)

Johnson, David E., *Fast Tanks and Heavy Bombers: Innovation in the U.S. Army, 1917–1945* (Ithaca, NY: Cornell University Press, 1998)

Jones, Spencer, *From Boer War to World War: Tactical Reform in the British Army 1902–1914* (Norman: University of Oklahoma Press, 2013)

Jones, Spencer (ed.), *Stemming the Tide: Officers and Leadership in the British Expeditionary Force 1914* (Solihull: Helion & Co., 2013)

Jones, Spencer, *The Great Retreat of 1914: From Mons to the Marne* (London: Sharpe Books, 2014)

Jones, Spencer (ed.), *Courage without Glory: The British Army on the Western Front 1915* (Solihull, Helion & Co., 2015)

Jones, Spencer (ed.), *The Darkest Year: The British Army on the Western Front 1917* (Solihull: Helion & Co., 2022)

Junger, Sebastian, *War* (London: Fourth Estate, 2010)

Kahneman, Daniel, *Thinking, Fast and Slow* (London: Penguin, 2011) / (New York: Farrar, Strauss, and Giroux, 2013)

Khong, Yuen Foong, *Analogies at War: Korea, Munich, Dien Bien Phu, and the Vietnam Decisions of 1965* (Princeton: Princeton University Press, 1992)

Kim, W. Chan and Mauborgne, Renee, *Blue Ocean Strategy: How to Create Uncontested Market Space and Make the Competition Irrelevant* (Boston, MA: Harvard Business Review Press, 2014)

Kimmel, Michael S., Hearn, Jeff, and Connell, Raewyn (eds), *Handbook of Studies on Men and Masculinities* (Thousand Oaks, California: Sage Publications, 2005)

King, Anthony, *The Combat Soldier: Infantry Tactics and Cohesion in the Twentieth and Twenty-First Centuries* (Oxford: Oxford University Press, 2013)

King, Anthony, *Command: The Twenty-First-Century General* (London: Cambridge University Press, 2019)

Kiras, James D. and Kitzen, Martijn (eds), *Into the Void: Special Operations Beyond the Global War on Terror* (New York: Oxford University Press, 2024)

Kiszely, John, *General Hastings 'Pug' Ismay: Soldier, Statesman, Diplomat, A New Biography* (London: Hurst Publishers, 2024)

Latiff, Robert H., *Future War Preparing for the New Global Battlefield* (New York, Alfred A. Knopf, 2017)

Leggett, D., *Shaping the Royal Navy: Technology, Authority, and Naval Architecture, c.1830–1906* (Manchester: Manchester University Press, 2016)

Linn, Brian M., *Elvis's Army: Cold War GIs and the Atomic Battlefield* (Cambridge, MA: Harvard University Press, 2016)

Lloyd George, David, *War Memoirs, Volume I* (London: Ivor Nicholson and Warts, 1936)

Lociccro, Michael, *A Moonlight Massacre: The Night Operation on the Passchendaele Ridge, 2 December 1917* (Solihull: Helion & Co., 2014)

Lomas, David, *Mons 1914: The BEF's Tactical Triumph* (London: Osprey, 2014)

Luce, RD. and Raiffa, H., *Games and Decisions: An Introduction and Critical Survey* (New York: Wiley & Sons, 1957)

Mallinson, Allan, *The Making of the British Army: From the English Civil War to the War on Terror* (London: Transworld Publishers, 2011)

Mansoor, P. R. and Murray, W. (eds), *The Culture of Military Organizations* (New York: Cambridge University Press, 2019)

Marble, Sanders, *British Artillery on the Western Front in the First World War* (Farnham: Ashgate, 2013)

Marshall, S. L. A., *Men Against Fire: The Problem of Battle Command* (Norman, OK: Oxford University Press, 1947)

Mattis, Jim, *Call Sign Chaos* (New York: Ballantine Books, 2019)

McInnes, Colin and Sheffield, G. D. (eds), *Warfare in the Twentieth Century: Theory and Practice* (London: Unwin and Hyman, 1988)

McIntyre, Lee, *Post-Truth* (Cambridge, MA: Massachusetts Institute of Technology Press, 2018)

McManners, Hugh, *The Scars of War* (London: Harper Collins, 1993)

McNeill, W. H., *The Pursuit of Power: Technology, Armed Force, and Society since AD 1100* (Chicago: University of Chicago Press, 1982)

Miksche, F. O., *Atomic Weapons and Armies* (London: Faber, 1955)

Moody, Simon, *Imagining Nuclear War in the British Army, 1945–1989* (Oxford: Oxford University Press, 2020)

Morrow, J. D., *Order Within Anarchy: The Laws of War as an International Institution* (New York: Cambridge University Press, 2014)

Moskos, Charles, *The American Enlisted Man: The Rank and File in Today's Military* (New York: Russell Sage Foundation, 1964)

Murray, Horatius, *'A Very Fine Commander': The Memoirs of General Sir Horatius Murray* (Barnsley: Pen and Sword, 2010)

Osinga, Frans, *Science, Strategy and War: The Strategic Theory of John Boyd* (Abingdon: Routledge, 2007)

Payne, Kenneth, *I, Warbot: The Dawn of Artificially Intelligent Conflict* (Oxford: Oxford University Press, 2021)

Porch, Douglas, *The March to the Marne: The French Army 1871–1914* (Cambridge: Cambridge University Press, 1981)

Prior, Robin and Wilson, Trevor, *Command on the Western Front: The Military Career of Sir Henry Rawlinson 1914–1918* (Barnsley: Leo Cooper, 1994)

Raugh, Harold E. Jr (ed.), *The British Army 1815–1914* (Aldershot: Ashgate, 2006)

Ridley, Nicholas, *Far from Suitable? Haig, Gough and Passchendaele: A Reappraisal* (Solihull: Helion & Co., 2024)

Riley, Jonathon, *Napoleon as a General: Command from the Battlefield to Grand Strategy* (London and New York: Continuum Books, 2007)

Roth, Michael S., *The Student: A Short History* (London: Yale University Press, 2023)

Samuels, Martin, *Command or Control? Command, Training and Tactics in the British and German Armies, 1888–1918* (London: Routledge, 1996)

Sheffield, Gary, *Forgotten Victory* (London: Abacus, 2001)

Sheffield, Gary, *The Chief: Douglas Haig and the British Army* (London: Aurum, 2011)

Simkins, Peter, *From the Somme to Victory* (Barnsley: Pen & Sword, 2014)

Simmel, George, *Conflict and The Web of Group Affiliations* (New York: Simon and Schuster, 2010)

Simpkin, Richard, *Race to the Swift: Thoughts on Twenty-First Century Warfare* (London: Brassey's Defence Publishers, 1988)

Smith, Edward, *Effects Based Operations: Applying Network Warfare in Peace, Crisis and War* (Washington, DC: Command and Control Research Program, 2003)

Smith, Rupert, *The Utility of Force* (London: Penguin, 2005)

Sokolski, H. D. (ed.), *Getting MAD: Nuclear Mutual Assured Destruction, Its Origins and Practice* (Carlisle Barracks, PA: Strategic Studies Institute, 2004)

Spiers, Edward M., *Haldane: An Army Reformer* (Edinburgh: Edinburgh University Press, 1980)

St Aubyn, Giles, *The Royal George 1819–1904: The Life of H.R.H. Prince George Duke of Cambridge* (London: Constable, 1963)

Strachan, Hew, *Wellington's Legacy: The Reform of the British Army, 1830–54* (Manchester: Manchester University Press, 1984)

Strachan, Hew, *The Direction of War* (Cambridge: Cambridge University Press, 2014)

Svechin, Aleksandr A., *Strategy* (London: East View, 1993)

Terraine, John, *White Heat: The New Warfare 1914–18* (London: Sedgwick & Jackson, 1982)

Tetlock, Philip and Gardener, Dan, *Super-forecasting: The Art and Science of Prediction* (London: Random House, 2015)

Travers, Tim, *The Killing Ground* (London: Unwin & Allen, 1987)

Trevor, Jonathon, *Re:Align: A Leadership Blueprint for Overcoming Disruption and Improving Performance* (London: Bloomsbury, 2022)

Triandafillov, Vladimir, *The Nature of the Operations of Modern Armies* (London: Jacob W. Kipp, 1994)

Tzu, Sun (James Clavell, ed.), *The Art of War* (New York: Barnes & Noble, 1983)

Verner, Willoughby, *The Military Life of H.R.H. George, Duke of Cambridge* (London: John Murray, 1905)

Warden, John, *The Air Campaign: Planning for Combat* (Washington, DC: National Defense University Press, 1988)

Watling, Jack, *The Arms of the Future: Technology and Close Combat in the Twenty-First Century* (London: Bloomsbury Press, 2024)

Watts, Barry D., *Clausewitzian Friction and Future War* (Washington DC: Institute for National Strategic Studies, National Defense University, 2004)

Whaley, Barton, *Stratagem: Deception and Surprise in War* (Cambridge, MA: Center for International Studies, Massachusetts Institute of Technology, 1969)

Wilson, H. W., *Administrative Planning* (London: War Office, 1952)

Wilson, R. D., *Cordon and Search: With 6th Airborne Division in Palestine* (Aldershot: Gale and Polden Limited, 1949)

Wyer, Robert S. Jr (ed.), *Knowledge and Memory: The Real Story* (Hillsdale, NJ: Lawrence Erlbaum Associates, 1995)